China's Offshore Investments

China's Offshore Investments

A Network Approach

Dexin Yang

Professor of Economics, Director, Centre for International Investment Studies, Shandong University of Finance, PR China

Edward Elgar

Cheltenham, UK • Northampton, MA, USA

Published by
Edward Elgar Publishing Limited
Glensanda House
Montpellier Parade
Cheltenham
Glos GL50 1UA
UK

Edward Elgar Publishing, Inc.
136 West Street
Suite 202
Northampton
Massachusetts 01060
USA

A catalogue record for this book
is available from the British Library

Library of Congress Cataloguing in Publication Data
Yang, Dexin, 1960-
    China's offshore investments : a network approach / Dexin Yang.
        p. cm.
    Includes bibliographical references and index.
    1. Investments, Foreign—China. 2. China—Commercial policy. 3.
China—Economic policy. I. Title.

HG5782.Y353 2006
332.67'351—dc22   2005044779

ISBN 1 84542 504 9

Printed and bound in Great Britain by MPG Books Ltd, Bodmin, Cornwall

Contents

Figures

Tables

Abbreviations

Baosteel	Baoshan Steel and Iron Corporation
Chalco	Aluminium Corporation of China
CITIC	China International Trust and Investment Corporation
CNOOC	China National Offshore Oil Corporation
CNPC	China National Petroleum Corporation
CSIESR	China State Institute of Economic System Reform
CSPC	China State Planning Committee
ETDZ	economic and technological development zone
FDI	foreign direct investment
FDI affiliates	overseas affiliates established by firms through FDI, such as wholly owned subsidiaries, joint ventures, etc.
GDP	gross national product
GNI	gross national income
IDP	investment development path
IIE	Institute of Industrial Economics under the Chinese Academy of Social Sciences
IMD	International Institute for Management Development
IMF	International Monetary Fund
ITD	Industrial and Transportation Department of the National Bureau of Statistics (China)
L&MFs	large- and medium-sized firms
M&A	merger and acquisition
MNE	multinational enterprise
MOFCOM	Ministry of Commerce (of China)
MOFTEC	Ministry of Foreign Trade and Economic Cooperation (of China), predecessor of MOFCOM
Multinationals	multinational enterprises
NBS	National Bureau of Statistics (of China)
NOI	net outward investment
OECD	Organisation for Economic Co-operation and Development
PRC	People's Republic of China
R&D	research and development
RMB	'Money of the People', the Chinese name of the Chinese currency
SAFE	State Administration of Foreign Exchange (of China)
SAIC	Shanghai Automotive Industry Corporation
SEZs	Special Economic Zones

Shougang	Capital Steel and Iron Corporation
Sinopec	China Petrochemical Corporation
Sinochem	Sinochem Corporation, formerly named China National Chemicals Import and Export Corporation
SOEs	state-owned enterprises
TNC	transnational corporation
TVEs	township and village enterprises
TWFDI	Third World FDI
TWMNE	Third World multinational enterprise
UNCTAD	United Nations Conference on Trade and Development
UNCTC	United Nations Centre of Transnational Corporations
WTO	World Trade Organisation

Acknowledgements

This book would not have been possible without many individuals' valuable advice, stimulation and encouragement, which simply cannot be forgotten.

First, I am greatly indebted to Professor Bhajan Grewal and Professor Peter Sheehan for their generous advice, encouragement and support. My research has benefited substantially from discussions with them. Professor Grewal's detailed comments on previous drafts and Professor Sheehan's methodological and analytical advice are especially appreciated.

I am very grateful to Professor John H. Dunning for his commendation on the draft and support in publishing this book. His intelligence, insights, stamina and kind-heartedness are impressive.

I thank Enjiang Cheng, Fiona Sun, Margarita Kumnick, Prabodh Malhotra and Tri-Dung Lam for their support, help and encouragement.

I appreciate the financial support received from Victoria University and the Centre for Strategic Economic Studies for undertaking the research. I have benefited from the assistance of the staff in the Centre.

My thanks also go to the anonymous referee from Edward Elgar Publishing Limited for valuable comments on the draft for publication.

I thank my editors, especially Alexandra Minton, for their work, kindness and patience.

Last but not least, without the love, patience and strong support of my family, this book would never have come into being. I wish to express my deepest love and thanks to my mother, my wife Yujuan and my children Xiaohan and Tangwei. For the sake of my academic career, my wife and children have had to put up with disruptions in their lives.

Any remaining errors are my own responsibility.

Dexin Yang
Shandong University of Finance

Preface

It is quite extraordinary that since the present phase of Chinese economic reforms came on stream, how much scholarly attention has been paid to the extent, pattern, determinants and impact of inward foreign direct investment (FDI) in China. But it is no less noteworthy that, within only a single generation of embracing the market economy, Chinese firms are now becoming important outward direct investors; something which took the United States and Japan a century or more to achieve. In 2004, the People's Republic of China recorded an outward foreign direct investment stock of US$38.8 billion (UNCTAD, 2005), nine times greater than that of 1990. Though still *relatively* less important to the home economy than its counterparts Hong Kong, Singapore and Taiwan, China is now ranked sixth as a Third World outward direct investor, behind the three Asian economies just identified plus Brazil and Korea.

As yet, there have been few detailed scholarly studies appraising the significance and role of China's outbound MNE (Multinational Enterprise) activity. That of Dr Dexin Yang's is one of these, and the author is to be commended, not only for collecting and interpreting a considerable amount of data on the growth and geographical distribution of Chinese foreign direct investment, but for deploying his considerable intellectual skills in setting these data within a rigorous theoretical framework, and relating them to the particular challenges of the world's largest transition and developing economy.

Perhaps the most novel, and I believe wholly fitting, approach taken by Dr Yang in his monograph is to apply a business network model explaining the motives for, and the benefits likely to be derived from, outbound MNE activity. In so doing, he distinguishes between the rationale for, and the implications of, asset *exploiting* and asset *augmenting* outbound investment, both for Chinese firms and the Chinese economy. He then goes on to explain how the latter objective may also be sometimes achieved by a variety of non-equity modalities, each of which is designed to promote the access to new or additional created assets, learning experiences and markets, through networking with foreign firms. Sometimes these networks comprise competitors, which may or may not be located in close proximity to each other; sometimes suppliers and sub-contractors; sometimes customers; sometimes government agencies; sometimes particular interest groups; and sometimes, indeed more frequently than not, a combination of two or more of these.

Looking at the history of outward foreign investment, and the pattern of the investment development path and industrial restructuring which has been suggested by Rajneesh Narula and myself (Dunning and Narula, 2004) and

Terutomo Ozawa (Ozawa 2005), it is clear that, until quite recently, most initial cross border forays by home country MNEs were designated either to exploit a specific competitive advantage, or to gain access to natural resources. Rarely were they intended to seek out new knowledge or capabilities; and even less to take advantage of the learning experiences and relational advantages of being part of a network of complementary activities.

Globalisation and the knowledge-based economy has changed all this. The 1990s, in particular, saw a spate of across border acquisitions and mergers involving firms located in advanced industrial economies. Today, in the early 21st Century, an increasingly competitive international environment, coupled with the need to exploit scale and scope economies, to jointly promote and fund costly and complex research and development, and to market (successful) innovations in the shortest possible time, is prompting even more asset augmenting FDI, as well as a range of strategic alliances designed to tap into the innovatory and organisational capabilities, institutions and marketing expertise of the participating private and public organisations. Chinese firms, in particular, in their desire to become global competitive players, need to draw upon, and interact with, their more technically advanced and experienced counterparts in the industrialised economies. At the same time the *Guangxi* philosophy and Confucian ethic of Chinese managers and workers make them natural and excellent networkers; that indeed is one of their unique ownership specific advantages which help them compete with foreign firms. Another is a good supply of finance capital provided both by domestic and corporate savings, and loans from Chinese banks.

Dr Yang explores all of these, and many other related issues in this fascinating and well researched study. In several places in the volume he underlines the need for policy makers to take a developmental and dynamic approach to the understanding and examination into the future of China's offshore investments. He emphasises – and rightly so – the critical need to upgrade the domestic institutional structure and promote more effectively a variety of micro-management policies. He also acknowledges the importance of inbound direct investment in helping to restructure Chinese manufacturing and service industries, and to stimulate the entrepreneurship and knowledge creating capabilities of indigenous firms. I particularly applaud his emphasis on the value of an integrated approach to evaluating the costs and benefits of inward and outward MNE activity; and of how both the Chinese national and regional governments can, and should, provide the physical and human infrastructure necessary both to attract the right kind of foreign MNE activity, and to help their own firms better augment their global competitive advantages through outbound direct investment and alliance formation with foreign firms.

I feel certain there will be many monographs on Chinese offshore investments in the next decades or more. In particular, I foresee that, just as the last fifteen years or so has led to a huge increase of inbound foreign direct investment (in 2004 China recorded the third largest inflow of any major country (after the US and the UK) and its stock (at US$245 billion) was no less than twelve times that of 1990), so the next decade (or more) will witness a substantial burgeoning of both asset seeking and asset exploiting Chinese owned outbound investment. After all, in 2004, as a proportion of its GDP, the outward foreign investment stock of China was only 2.4 per cent. This compared with an average of 13.4 per cent for all Asian developing countries, and 24.0 per cent for all countries. China indeed, has a huge way to go.

I believe Dr Yang has produced an original and impressive monograph. His efforts are to be particularly praiseworthy bearing in mind the quite modest array of statistics at his disposal, in particular the paucity of the published data on the industrial composition of outbound Chinese foreign direct investment. But Dr Yang has indeed cut a stylish and well fitting coat from the cloth provided him; and has most excellently applied a variety of international business related theoretical insights to analysing and evaluating one of the most significant evolving events of the globalising economy of the first decade of the 21st Century. This book deserves to be widely read and carefully studied by IB scholars, by business practitioners, and by government advisory policy makers.

John H. Dunning

REFERENCES

Dunning, J. H. and R. Narula (2004), *Multinationals and Industrial Competitiveness*, Cheltenham, UK and Northampton, MA, US: Edward Elgar.

Ozawa, T. (2005), *Institutions, Industrial Upgrading and Economic Performance of Japan*, Cheltenham, UK and Northampton, MA, US: Edward Elgar.

UNCTAD (2005), *World Investment Report: Transnational Corporations and the Internationalisation of R&D*, New York and Geneva: UN.

1. Introduction

This book presents an interpretation of China's outward direct investment in the last quarter of a century. The research is motivated by the phenomenon that, compared with foreign investment in China, direct investment from China has so far attracted relatively little attention from researchers. It is hoped that this research can make a small contribution to the body of knowledge on foreign direct investment (FDI), especially FDI from developing countries in their desire to catch up with developed countries in the current era of globalisation and FDI from transitional economies embracing market economic systems.

1.1. PATTERN OF CHINA'S OUTWARD FDI AND THEORETICAL ISSUES

1.1.1. Growth and distribution of China's outward FDI

It is well known that China has absorbed a huge amount of FDI since the implementation of the open-door policy in the late 1970s. By 2003, the total number of the foreign capital invested projects approved by the Chinese government was 465 277, total contractual foreign investment was US$943.13 billion[1], and realised foreign investment was US$501.47 billion (MOFCOM, 2004, p.87). Considering that in the three decades before the economic reform, FDI in China was essentially zero as a result of its policy of economic autarky, the surge in FDI in China is indeed impressive. While China only ranked as the fifth largest host country in the developing country group in the early 1980s, it has been the largest host country for inward FDI in the developing world since 1992 and the largest host country in the world after the United States since 1993. Huge inflows of FDI have penetrated almost all industries and regions and are playing an ever-growing role in the Chinese economy.

It is not well known, however, that China's direct investment abroad has also been proceeding rapidly. According to the Ministry of Commerce of the People's Republic of China (MOFCOM), by the end of 2003, the number of Chinese foreign affiliates was 7470, covering almost all countries in the world (MOFCOM, 2004, p.760). Average annual FDI outflows increased substantially from US$150 million in 1980-85 to more than US$711 million in 1986-90. This figure increased further to more than US$2.66 billion during the next five-year interval (1991-95), nearly quadrupling the FDI outflow of the 1986-90 period.

Average annual FDI outflows remained above US$2.6 billion in the following eight years (1996-2003) (SAFE, 1999; UNCTAD, 1994-2004). For a developing country with a very short history of foreign direct investment, the development of China's outward FDI is also remarkable.

The rapid expansion of FDI outflows makes China one of the main sources among developing economies. Since 1985, China has been among the top five of those economies and it ranks as the third largest source country in terms of outward FDI stock in recent years (UNCTAD, 2004). Six of the top 50 multinational enterprises based in developing economies, ranked by foreign assets in 1997, were from China (UNCTAD, 1999, pp.86-7).

Another distinctive feature of China's outward FDI is its high geographical concentration in a few developed countries. While China's outward FDI reaches more than 152 countries/regions, until 2001, more than 29 per cent of Chinese government approved outward direct investment went to the United States, Canada and Australia, each accounting for 12.5, 8.8 and 7.9 per cent of total outflows, respectively. These three countries, plus Hong Kong, Peru, Thailand, Mexico, Zambia, Russia, Cambodia, South Africa and Brazil, accounted for about 67 per cent of China's outward FDI, leaving the remaining 143 countries/regions accounting for less than 33 per cent of China's outward FDI (MOFTEC, 1993-2002).

1.1.2. Theoretical issues raised by China's outward FDI

The rapid growth of China's outward FDI calls for an explanation of the underlying rationale. However, the mainstream theory of FDI has difficulties providing ready answers to the main issues involved in such a pattern of FDI from a developing country.

1.1.2.1. Ownership advantages for the Chinese investors

The mainstream theory of FDI claims that the possession of proprietary advantages of some kind is a critical factor in explaining a firm's direct investment overseas. These proprietary advantages are derived from the ownership of intangible resources, such as technology, managerial skill and organisational capabilities,[2] which can be easily transferred from one country to another within a firm but are very difficult to transfer between firms due to the imperfection of the market for such resources. In response, a firm would prefer to undertake foreign direct investment to internalise (the market for) such resources to avoid transaction costs (the internalisation model) or to improve its market power (the market power model) (Graham and Krugman, 1991). It follows that the main actors in foreign direct investment are large firms with abundant proprietary advantages. However, it is hard to find evidence for this claim from China's outward FDI, especially when considering the fact that China's outward FDI has developed countries as its principal destination.

Chinese firms can be classified into four groups, that is, state-owned enterprises, collective-owned enterprises, individual-owned enterprises and enterprises of other types of ownership (NBS, 2000, pp.462-3). Before economic reforms, state-owned enterprises (SOEs), though dominating in non-agricultural sectors, did not have suitable opportunities to grow due to the rigid central planning system of the past. They still did not have favourable conditions for growth after the start of economic reforms due to their inability to adapt to the intense competition in a market economy as well as government discrimination policy in favour of foreign capital-invested firms. The other three types of enterprises only had the opportunity to emerge and develop after the introduction of market economic mechanisms about two decades ago and, therefore, most of them have not had enough time to develop into big enterprises. As a result, the average size of Chinese firms is relatively small. For example, in 1996, General Motors of the United States realised sales of US$5.26 billion, which was equal to the sum of the sales of the 342 largest Chinese firms or 32 times that of Daqing Oil Company, the largest firm in China in terms of sales. The total sales of the world's three largest firms, General Motors, Ford and Shell, exceeded the total sales of all 23,927 large- and medium-sized firms (L&MFs) in China (CSIESR *et al.*, 1999, pp.111-2). In addition, most Chinese firms operate in a single industry and the variety of their products is correspondingly limited.

Chinese firms as a whole are also inferior in management in comparison with their counterparts from developed and most newly industrialised countries. The management competitiveness of firms in China ranked 30th out of 46 sample countries in 1998. The major host countries for China's outward FDI – the United States, Canada and Australia – were ranked first, eleventh and seventeenth, respectively, much higher than China (IMD, 1998). One of the main reasons for the relatively poor management competitiveness of Chinese firms is that China is still in the process of introducing macro and microeconomic institutions and practices appropriate for a market economy. Consequently, it will take more time for Chinese firms to fully embrace and internalise these institutions and practices in their operations.

Furthermore, compared with their counterparts from developed and newly industrialised countries, Chinese firms are weak in research and development (R&D) activities. Though total employment in R&D activities in China is very large, less than 30 per cent of R&D workers are employed by firms. In 1998, less than one-third of China's large- and medium-sized firms had their own specialised R&D institutions. Even among those firms with R&D institutions, 37 per cent did not have relevant inputs (NBS, 1998). This contrasts sharply with developed and newly industrialised countries where more than half of R&D employees nationally work in firms. In the United States, for example, R&D employees in firms accounted for nearly 80 per cent of the national total in 1998 (IMD, 1998).

1.1.2.2. Timing of China's outward FDI
The investment development path (IDP) developed by Dunning (1988) claims that the outward and inward FDI position of a country is systematically related

to its economic development, relative to the rest of the world. Since its relative ownership, location and internalisation advantages change over time as its economy develops, a country tends to go through five main stages of FDI development. In sequence they are: (1) the non-existence of both inward and outward FDI; (2) the emergence and expansion of inward FDI and negligible outward FDI; (3) the expansion of outward FDI and slowing growth of inward FDI; (4) outward FDI stock exceeding inward FDI stock; and (5) net outward FDI stock (that is, gross outward FDI stock less gross inward FDI stock) fluctuating around the zero level (Dunning and Narula, 1996, ch.1). This implies that a country will not engage in large-scale outward FDI until its inward FDI has developed enormously.

However, China's outward FDI shows different features. Contrary to the IDP pattern, the emergence and development of outward and inward direct investment flows coincide with each other. The period of 1982-2004 witnessed steady growth of both inward and outward FDI. In addition, compared with the huge inward direct investment, China's outward FDI remained relatively small, but its absolute value was by no means negligible. Up to the end of 2004, the total FDI outflows amounted to about US$ 37 billion (MOFCOM, 2004). This is a substantial amount for a developing country with a very short history of foreign direct investment. These features suggest that China's outward FDI has skipped the first and part of the second stage of the investment-development path and has now entered the early period of the third stage. Therefore the process of the development of China's outward FDI is difficult to explain using the IDP paradigm.

1.1.2.3. Geographical distribution of China's outward FDI

China's outward FDI is heavily concentrated in the United States, Canada and Australia. Developing countries were not its major destination in the first two decades. This fact seems to deny the decisive role of proximity in economic development and geography between home and host countries for the choice of destination of FDI, as the mainstream theory of FDI suggests.

Given the importance of ownership advantage in the mainstream theory of FDI, the choice of location of FDI is largely a function of the possession of ownership advantages. For example, Hymer (1960) suggests that national firms enjoy the general advantage of better information about their country: its economy, language, law, politics and so forth. Since foreign firms do not possess that knowledge, they will incur additional transaction costs in operations conducted within that country. Accordingly, a firm must have sufficient firm-specific advantages (ownership advantages) to offset the comparative disadvantage of being foreign if it is to compete successfully in the host country. By the same token, if a firm chooses to invest in countries with closer cultural, economic or physical ties to the home country, it will need fewer ownership advantages to tackle barriers to international operation, as the 'short' distance implies fewer barriers. Therefore, firms tend to enter markets that are closer to the home country, not only in terms of physical distance but also in terms of differences in economic development, language, culture and political system. Thus, firms are predicted to start their internationalisation by moving first into markets they can most easily cope with and entering more distant countries only at a later stage (Benito and Gripsrud, 1995). As firms from developing countries are normally characterised as small in size, weak in technological innovation and less experienced in international operation, their outward FDI in the early stages generally targets other developing countries as its main destination. This implies that the pattern of FDI by developing countries displays heavy regional concentration (UNCTC, 1983). The tremendous differences in the level of economic development and economic structure between China and developed countries have militated against large-scale entry of Chinese firms' direct investment into developed countries and some developing countries. On the one hand, as indicated above, Chinese firms do not possess clear technological and managerial advantages over their counterparts in developed countries. On the other hand, Chinese firms cannot obtain substantial labour cost savings in their outward FDI either, as labour costs are much lower in China than in most other countries, including developing countries. In the 1995-1999 period, the yearly labour cost per worker in manufacturing in China was US$729, only about 2.5 per cent of that in the United States, 2.6 per cent of that in Canada and 2.8 per cent of that in Australia (World Bank, 2000). If labour cost saving were the major concern in foreign direct investment, Chinese firms would be much better off operating at home.

1.2. RESEARCH ON FDI FROM DEVELOPING COUNTRIES

Foreign direct investment from developing countries or Third World FDI (TWFDI) can be traced back to about a century ago (Katz and Kosacoff, 1983). However, the share of TWFDI was infinitesimal before the 1970s. The real surge, encompassing many more countries and continents, has taken place in the last three decades. The 1990s witnessed a big jump in FDI from developing countries: its share in world total FDI outflow reached about 15 per cent, approximately three times that during the 1980s (UNCTAD, 1994-2000). As FDI from developing countries is concentrated geographically in terms of sourcing – several East Asian countries plus a few Latin American countries accounting for the major share – the growth of FDI from developing countries is impressive. In addition, as the process of economic catch-up and FDI development goes on, multinational enterprises headquartered in developing countries have been increasing in number, size, complexity of organisation and transnationality. Among the 50 top multinational enterprises from developing countries in 1998, there were 29 with foreign assets above US$1 billion and two ranked 43rd and 73rd respectively in the world's top 100 multinationals (UNCTAD, 1998, pp. 36-8, 48-9).

The development of TWFDI to a large extent accompanies the industrialisation and catch-up of relevant countries. Or more accurately, outward FDI is an integrated part of industrialisation and catch-up by the relevant countries. For a developing country, while inward FDI plays an important role in improving its international competitiveness through its effects on technological change, structural upgrade, market competition and the expansion of foreign trade and business links, engagement in outward FDI is essential and inevitable for the further improvement of the country's international competitiveness (Lall, 1998; Dunning and Narula, 1996).

The academic community has paid attention to FDI from developing countries since the late 1970s. It is acknowledged that Lecraw's 1977 paper, 'Direct Investment by Firms from Less Developed Countries', signified the start of FDI from developing countries as a subject of research (Dunning et al., 1997). In this paper, Lecraw presented his findings about the characteristics of firms established by FDI from developing countries based on a questionnaire-based study. Thereafter, the interest from economists and business researchers has yielded many publications on the subject. Many interesting observations and assertions have been made about the causes, nature and operational mode of the invested firms, as well as explanations of developing countries' FDI. Representative theoretical publications in this literature include Lecraw (1977), Lall (1983a), Wells (1983), Riemens (1989), Tolentino (1993), Dunning et al. (1997) and Yeung (1998).

Notwithstanding the above theoretical contributions, the existing literature on FDI from developing countries consists mainly of empirical studies, focusing on specific cases of certain countries, business operations of certain types of firms or specific functional issues of some firms. There is a lack of a theoretical framework that can shed light on FDI from developing countries in general. Rather, the analyses apply mainstream FDI theory to the study of FDI from developing countries. Wells' (1983) work is an example. He studies multinationals of developing countries in the framework of Dunning's eclectic paradigm of ownership, location and internalisation advantages (OLI), holding that FDI from developing countries are realised by combining the particular advantages available to developing countries' multinationals. These advantages are the same as those of developed countries' multinationals in nature but different in form or source. According to Wells (1983), while the ownership advantages for FDI from developed countries derive from frontier technologies and sophisticated management and marketing, those for investors from developing countries derive from technologies and management which suit the market and production conditions of other developing countries. These advantages include small-scale, labour-intensive and flexible processes and low R&D and management expenditure associated with mature manufacturing as well as fewer levels of management. Also stressing ownership advantages, Lall (1983b) and Tolentino (1993) attribute these to the ability of developing countries to adapt foreign technologies to local production and markets.

It is generally acknowledged in the literature that FDI from a developing country is most likely to be directed at its neighbouring developing countries. This pattern is attributed to the claim that FDI is based on firm-specific advantages to overcome disadvantages faced by subsidiaries in the host country and firms from developing countries are relatively weak in international competitiveness. Therefore FDI from developing countries should choose in its early stages countries with economic, cultural and geographical proximity as a destination in order to bypass or to reduce the disadvantages. Only after having gained international experience through overseas operations and consolidated firm-specific advantages can firms invest on a relatively large scale in more developed countries that are distant geographically (see, for example, Dunning and Narula, 1996; Riemens, 1989; Tolentino, 1993).

The phenomenon of using the mainstream theory to interpret FDI from developing countries has also attracted some criticism. Yeung argues that such attempts to explain FDI from developing countries result in under-research and misleading treatment of this subject:

> When these theories, based on the experience of American and British transnationals, are applied to emerging TNCs from the developing world, as manifested in the 'Third World Multinationals' literature, the problem of Western-centric interpretation arises. Whereas TNCs from developed countries are given the arbitrary status of 'mainstream', 'Third World multinationals' are regarded as 'deviants' and 'unconventional'. The deviations of 'Third World multinationals' are explained away by established economic theories of international production. Genuine developments of TNCs from developing countries are subsumed under the overarching explanatory power of these theories. The net result of this academic exercise is the production and perpetuation of misleading stereotypes. For example, 'Third World multinationals' are often seen as very small in their assets and sales, labour-intensive in their operations, low in technological capabilities and restricted in geographical coverage. (Yeung, 1998, p.3)

This view may appear oversimplified, but it is not baseless. The dominant FDI theories were advanced from the 1960s to the 1980s. They were to a large extent based on the observations of FDI from the United States and Britain after World War II. The internationally super-strong position of both source economies and their investing firms at that time has inevitably influenced the hypotheses and arguments of these theories. As indicated earlier, FDI has mainly been characterised as being motivated by a firm's desire to exploit its existing proprietary advantages abroad or as part of the firm's strategy in a game of imperfect international competition (Graham and Krugman, 1991). This implies that the focus of the mainstream theory of FDI is the supply side of FDI. Correspondingly, ownership advantage is implicitly or explicitly assigned crucial importance in FDI. In comparison, the demand side of FDI, basically asset-seeking FDI, has not attracted sufficient attention in the literature (Wesson, 1999). As a result, 'the theory of FDI has its own dramatic tension between existing theory and apparent fact' (Ethier, 1994, p.105). For example, the largest part of FDI is between developed countries rather than from developed countries to developing countries; and FDI is increasingly two-way and intra-industry, irrespective of the home country, for example, Germany is both home and host to a large amount of FDI in the chemical and auto industries, as is the United States (Ethier, 1994; Graham, 1997). Explaining FDI from a developing country, such as China, to developed countries remains a challenge for the mainstream theory of FDI.

1.3. METHODOLOGY AND STRUCTURE OF BOOK

The difficulties in providing a convincing explanation of the pattern of China's outward FDI by using the mainstream theory call for a different approach. For this purpose, a network model of FDI is developed in this book by formalising network ideas from business analysis for application to economic analysis of FDI.

In this model, FDI is defined as a means of choosing the most appropriate form of economic organisation by using an ownership-based hierarchy and involving international markets and firms. It leads to the expansion of the investing firm's boundary into the host country and the formation of a node there. This node can be used for further networking.[3] As a form of economic organisation, the rationale for FDI lies in economic organisation in the global market economy.

Economic organisation involves issues of both how and where to organise economic activity. With regard to the first issue, this book argues that the organisation of economic activity in a market economy has two possible methods (namely, price and hierarchy) and three alternative institutions (namely, the market, the network and the firm) to use these methods of organisation. While the market uses the price system to organise transactions between firms and the firm organises internal activities via hierarchy, the network organises activities across the market and the firm by using a blend of price and hierarchy. For a market-based transaction, firms are faceless entities engaged in 'sharp in' and 'sharp out' transactions; and the boundaries between 'in' and 'out' at the beginning and 'in' and 'out' at the end, are clear (MacNeil, 1974, p.750). In contrast, for organising economic activity via the network, a certain kind of interlocked relationship is formed between the firms due to the overlap of economic and governance boundaries between the firms. This overlapping of boundaries is a result of the partial market transaction and the partial internal organisation for the economic activity concerned. This leads to the formation of external networks around a firm that becomes the hub firm in a particular network. As a consequence, the organisation of networking activities reshapes the boundaries of all the firms that are part of a network.

The second issue of where to organise economic activity is related to the heterogeneity of the market and the industrial logic of interconnected activities and resources. For various reasons, the market is not universal and homogeneous, but consists of different markets at different locations for different factors and products and economic activity can take place in different regions, including at home and abroad. In addition, a firm is not deemed to be a single-plant production unit with all its activities based in a single location. In principle, it is natural that, in a market economy, entrepreneurs are free to displace market transactions by increasing the scope of allocations made administratively within their firms and the most profitable pattern of enterprise organisation should ultimately prevail. Where more profitable results can be obtained from placing plants under wholly or partly common administrative control, multi-plant enterprises will dominate and single-plant firms will merge or go out of business.

As economic activity can be organised via the market, through networking or within the firm and the organisation can take place either at home or abroad, a firm has six possible choices for the organisation of an activity. The final choice is made essentially on the basis of total cost-benefit comparisons. Multinational enterprises are outcomes of such choices of economic organisation.

A multinational enterprise (MNE), the main subject of FDI and a consequence of such investment, is a firm which controls and manages production establishments – plants – located in at least two countries (Caves, 1996, p.1). It involves not only the dimension of the boundary between the administrative allocation of resources within the firm and the market allocation of resources between firms, but also the dimension of the international setting of the boundary between the firm and the market as well as the dimension of the form of hierarchy. From this perspective of economic organisation, wholly owned overseas subsidiaries are the international expansion of the parent firm's boundary based on hierarchy. Joint ventures are similarly the international expansion of the parent firm's boundary based on a mixture of price and hierarchy.

Within the framework of the network model of FDI, the main body of the book interprets China's outward direct investment during the last two decades. Ideally, the network model would be applied to the decision-making calculation at the firm-level. But such application requires firm-level data on FDI. In China, such data do not exist, except for a few sample studies.

China's outward FDI has a very short history and statistics have not kept pace. Comprehensive data on industrial composition and overseas subsidiaries' operations are not available. The main sources are China's two government institutions, the State Administration of Foreign Exchange (SAFE) and the Ministry of Commerce (MOFCOM, of which the predecessor is the Ministry of Foreign Trade and Economic Cooperation – MOFTEC). The SAFE data represent actual flows of capital, including equity capital and reinvested earnings and UNCTAD uses this source of data. Unfortunately, this source only provides figures at the national aggregate level. MOFCOM is the Chinese government institution responsible for the administration of outward FDI. It provides data on the amount of investment, the number of investment projects as well as Chinese investors' share in total investment of the invested projects, all of which go down to destination country level. However, its data are based upon approval figures for initial investments rather than actual outflows and it does not screen all outward FDI (also see UNCTAD, 1995, p. 56).

Given these limitations, the approach in this book had to be adapted to the available information. Accordingly, the analysis is carried out along the lines of the environment-response principle in business operations, with the focus on the relationship between changes in macro environment and FDI from China. Also, due to the unavailability of detailed data on the operations of overseas subsidiaries of Chinese firms, the method of approach is essentially descriptive and the interpretation is mainly based on qualitative analysis rather than econometric analysis.

Although the unavailability of detailed statistical data on the operation of China's FDI subsidiaries has ruled out the possibility of more specific testing with formal econometric analysis, we take some survey data and case study materials as supplement to test our arguments. Among these are Zhang and Bulcke's (1996a) survey data, Li's (2000) survey data and Tseng's (1994) and Tseng and Mak's (1996) case study materials.

1.4. BRIEF SUMMARY OF BOOK

The book consists of four parts. The main contents of each part are summarised below.

1.4.1. Part I (Chapters 2-4)

Chapter 2 documents the pattern of China's outward FDI. China's outward FDI has exhibited two conspicuous characteristics, rapid expansion in a relatively short period and high geographical concentration in a few developed countries, namely, the United States, Canada and Australia. These characteristics are not readily compatible with the prediction of the existing mainstream theories of FDI.

Chapter 3 reviews previously developed theories of foreign direct investment, as a backdrop to the pursuit of a plausible explanation for the pattern of China's outward FDI. It shows that though research on foreign direct investment has so far made significant progress in interpreting the determinants and basic features of FDI, due to the empirical evidence on which the theoretical foundation of FDI is based, the existing theories of FDI are dominated by supply-side focused theories. Correspondingly, ownership advantage is implicitly or explicitly assigned crucial importance in FDI. In comparison, the demand side of FDI, basically asset-seeking FDI, has not attracted sufficient attention in the literature. This is one of the main reasons why the conventional theories of FDI are inefficient in explaining the changing pattern of FDI, especially FDI from developing countries and cross-investment flows between developed countries in the same industries. In the meantime, literature on FDI from developing countries consists mainly of empirical studies within the framework of the mainstream theory of FDI. Investors from developing countries have been characterised as very small in terms of assets and sales, labour-intensive in operations, low in technological capabilities and restricted in geographical coverage. Accordingly, it is claimed that FDI from a developing country is directed at neighbouring developing countries. Only after having gained international experience through overseas operations and consolidated firm-specific advantages can firms invest on a relatively large scale in more developed countries that are located geographically, culturally and economically at a greater distance.

Chapter 4 analyses the pattern of China's outward FDI in the framework of conventional theory of FDI, with the focus on the aspects of ownership advantages, timing and geographical distribution of Chinese FDI. The analysis shows that the generally acknowledged pattern of FDI from developing countries is not found in China's outward direct investment. Rather, China's outward FDI exhibits two conspicuous characteristics, rapid expansion in a relatively short time and high geographical concentration in the United States, Canada and Australia. A further examination of China's outward FDI reveals that Chinese firms do not possess a clear competitive advantage, especially when considering the fact that China's overseas direct investment takes developed countries as its principal destinations. Therefore, China's outward FDI is not readily explained by the insights gained from existing theories of FDI from developing countries. The difficulties in providing a convincing explanation of the pattern of China's outward FDI by using mainstream theory call for a different approach.

1.4.2. Part II (Chapters 5-6)

Chapter 5 provides a brief survey of network research in business organisation, as a background for searching for an explanation of the underlying rationale for China's outward FDI. The survey is confined to issues regarding the basic nature of network relationships and their relevance to foreign direct investment.

Chapter 6 develops a network model of FDI by formalising network ideas from business analysis for application to economic analysis of FDI. This model sheds light not only on economic organisation in the market and within the firm, but also on economic organisation lying between the classic dichotomy of the market and the firm. As a result, the decision to undertake FDI can be captured in a more comprehensively integrated framework. In such a framework, both the supply side and demand side of FDI can be stressed. Dunning had indicated several years ago (1993b, p.92) that 'network analysis would seem to have a lot more to offer than it has so far been able to demonstrate, but it needs to be integrated with work now being done by industrial organisational economists'. The establishment of the network model of FDI is an attempt in this direction.

1.4.3. Part III (Chapters 7-9)

Chapter 7 develops an explanation for the growth of China's outward FDI from the perspective of governance configuration in economic organisation. The results show that there is a positive relationship between the growth of the nation's outward FDI and economic reform. Such a relationship reflects the intrinsic dynamics of the Chinese firms engaging in networking for various networking benefits. Specifically, the emergence and development of China's FDI reflect a change in firms' networking behaviour as China began to be transformed from a centrally planned economy towards a market economy. The arranged networking typical of the previous traditional planning system is replaced by semi-autonomous networking during the system transition. Due to the existence of a two-track system during the transition, engaging in outbound direct investment enabled the relevant firms not only to obtain normal international networking benefits but also to exploit the two tracks. Hence, the growth of outward direct investment was extraordinarily rapid when the benefit from exploiting the two tracks was thick. Growth retreated to a more normal rate when such benefits were lessened due to the maturing of marketisation.

Chapter 8 analyses the technological configuration of the rationale for China's outward FDI. As the transition of the economic system is nearing completion, rationales of technological configuration in economic organisation are becoming more important to China's investors. Resource seeking, transaction enforcing and position improving objectives are crucial to the development of the Chinese economy and are relevant to firms as well. FDI aimed at these is not only a normal response to the opportunities and the constraints raised by economic development, but is also a quite beneficial response.

Chapter 9 interprets the geographical distribution of China's outward FDI. This analysis shows that the high geographical concentration of China's outward FDI reflects the motives of Chinese firms investing abroad as well as the conditions in target countries for meeting investors' needs. In general, investments in resource seeking are concentrated in a few natural resource-rich countries and technologically advanced countries. Investments in market transaction enforcing and position improving are distributed in countries with relatively large markets for the products of investing firms. In particular, overseas manufacturing investments mainly go to developing countries to serve local markets. Target countries' domestic transaction efficiencies for goods and labour and their existing linkages with China further shape the direction of China's FDI flows.

1.4.4. Part IV (Chapter 10)

This chapter synthesises the results of the analysis in Part III and provides a complete picture of the interpretation of China's outward direct investment. The main findings are as follows. FDI as a form of economic organisation in market economies depends upon the functioning of market mechanisms. The planned and closed economic system in China before the late 1970s ruled out opportunities for China's enterprises to carry out outward FDI. With the introduction of the market mechanism into China's economy, firms began to organise economic activity by using price and hierarchy, and correspondingly, to decide whether the organisation was carried out in the market, through the network or within the firm, and whether the organisation was undertaken at home or abroad. The importance of networking would motivate some Chinese firms to undertake FDI. As economic reform in China is characterised by gradual transition and a two-track system, the development of market elements and the autonomy of firms has proceeded gradually. As a result, the expansion of China's outward FDI is affected by the process of firm-related reforms. As a form of economic organisation, China's FDI is naturally attracted to activities which have abundant network benefits. These activities are mainly aimed at overseas technology and natural resource seeking as well as at market exploring. The geographical distribution of China's outward FDI reflects the geographical distribution of various network benefits and the related cost-saving effects.

NOTES

1. Billion is used in the US meaning of a thousand million throughout the book.
2. There is no unanimous view on what encompasses intangible assets or resources. Grant (1991, p.119) categorises intangible resources into four subclasses: human resources, technological resources, reputation and organisational assets. Hall (1993) classifies intangible resources into two categories: intangible assets and competencies. Intangible assets include 'having' capabilities, which typically are regulatory (for example, patents) or positional (for example, reputation). Competencies (intangible skills) are related to 'doing' capabilities, which include functional capability (for example, know-how) and cultural or organisational capability (for example, routines). Intangible skills are typically people dependent, while intangible assets are considered as people independent.
3. The defining characteristic of FDI is the cross-border reallocation of resources in the form of a more integrated package deal and the conferral of control over the investment project to the foreign investor. Though there are many definitions of FDI in the literature, all conventional definitions stress ownership-based control of the investment project by an investor. For example, the United Nations (UNTACD, 1996, p.219) defines FDI based on OECD (1992) and IMF (1993): 'Foreign direct investment is defined as an investment involving a long-term relationship and reflecting a lasting interest and control of a resident entity in one economy (foreign direct investor or parent enterprise) in an enterprise resident in an economy other than that of the foreign direct investor (FDI enterprise or affiliate enterprise or foreign affiliate). Foreign direct investment implies that the investor exerts a significant degree of influence on the management of the enterprise resident in the other economy'. Theoretically, foreign direct investors include individuals and public institutions as well as firms. FDI by individual and public institution investors is normally not separately stressed in conventional analysis, as it is very limited in volume and importance. My investigation adheres to that tradition. However, in the light of my specific model and explanation of China's outward FDI, I have introduced network ideas into that definition.

PART I

China's Outward FDI and Theoretical Issues

INTRODUCTION

China's outward FDI started in the early days of the nation's economic reform and opening up. After a quarter of a century of rapid development, Chinese FDI has so far amounted to a volume that is huge for a developing country with a very short history of FDI. As a result, China is now one of the main source countries of FDI within the developing country group. In the current era of accelerating globalisation and knowledge-based economy, to understand the rationale underlying FDI from China, a developing country that is catching up, is of theoretical importance for bettering our knowledge of the changing pattern of FDI as well as of policy importance for other developing countries also in the process of catching up.

Nevertheless, the pattern of China's outward FDI is not readily explainable by conventional theories of FDI. In addition to the timing of its emergence, which seems premature judged by the propositions of the conventional theories, the pace of development and the geographical distribution of Chinese outbound investment are also not readily compatible with the predictions of a mainstream theory. It is generally acknowledged in the literature that FDI from a developing country is most likely to be directed initially at its neighbouring developing countries and to grow gradually in volume and distance. However, this is not the case with China's outward FDI, which developed rapidly after the first few years and is concentrated heavily in a few developed countries, that is, the United States, Canada and Australia.

In such a situation, it is worth bringing to light the essential features of both China's outward FDI and the previous developed theories of FDI regarding the determination of FDI and its spatial distribution, so as to present a backdrop for our pursuit of a plausible explanation of the pattern of China's outward FDI.

2. Emergence and Development of China's Outward FDI

This chapter describes the pattern of China's outward FDI, which on the whole has exhibited two distinct characteristics, that is, rapid expansion in a relatively small amount of time and high geographical concentration in a few developed countries, namely, the United States, Canada and Australia. These characteristics appear to make China's outward FDI different from the generally acknowledged pattern that FDI from a developing country is most likely to expand gradually in volume and to target neighbouring developing countries as the main destinations in its early stages of development.

2.1. DEVELOPMENT OF CHINA'S OUTWARD FDI

China's outward direct investment emerged in the early period of economic reforms. It began on a small scale, with an annual outflow of less than US$40 million in the first few years. However, as the economic reforms proceeded, Chinese enterprises invested abroad on a large scale and the volume of direct investment expanded rapidly. According to the Ministry of Commerce of the People's Republic of China, by the end of 2003, the number of Chinese foreign affiliates was 7470, covering almost all countries in the world (MOFCOM, 2004, p.760). Average annual FDI outflows increased substantially from US$150 million in 1980-85 to more than US$711 million in 1986-90. This figure increased further to more than US$2.66 billion during the next five-year interval (1991-5), nearly quadrupling the FDI outflow of the 1986-90 period (SAFE, 1999; UNCTAD, 1994-2004) (Figure 2.1).

China's outward FDI has mainly experienced three stages in its development detailed below.

Stage 1 (1979-84): Emergence. In November 1979, the Beijing Friendship Commercial Service Company set up a joint venture in Tokyo with a Japanese firm, which signified the start of China's overseas direct investment. Investors during this period were basically trade enterprises, which might be grouped into two types: one being specialised foreign trade corporations with import and export licences, and the other economic and technological corporations affiliated to provincial or city governments. Encouraged by the open-door policy, these firms sought to enter into overseas business by taking advantage of their higher autonomy in operation granted by central and local governments and their existing international business links. As the economic reforms were at an early stage and negative views of multinational enterprises were influential at home, China's overseas direct investment during this period was quite small, in both volume and number of projects. For example, the annual FDI outflow in 1982 and 1983 was US$44 million and US$93 million respectively, and even in 1984 this figure was only US$134 million (SAFE, 1999).

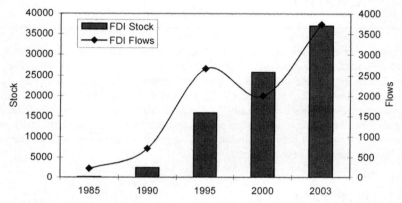

Note: Outflows are annual average figures for 1980-5, 1986-90, 1991-5, 1996-2000, and 2001-2003, respectively.

Sources: SAFE (1999); UNCTAD (2002, 2004).

Figure 2.1 China's outward FDI (US$ million)

Stage 2 (1985-91): Early Boom. In 1985, the Ministry of Foreign Economy and Trade passed a resolution: 'Any economic entity can apply for setting up overseas joint ventures if it has the relevant financial resources, a certain level of technology and business speciality, and joint partners'. In response, a group of large enterprises and conglomerates began to undertake foreign direct investment. Soon after that, the State Council formally gave approval to the China National Chemicals Import & Export Corporation (Sinochem) to experiment with overseas business (IIE, 1998, p.127). During this period, not only trading enterprises engaged in international business, but manufacturing enterprises such as Shougang (the Capital Steel and Iron Corporation) also began to join the ranks of overseas direct investment. As a result, annual FDI outflows jumped from US$134 million in 1984 to US$629 million in 1985 and further mounted to US$850 million in 1988 (SAFE, 1999). However, this boom was severely affected as the Chinese government backtracked towards re-tightening central control and suspended the approval of trade-type overseas enterprises in 1989 after the Tian'anmen Square incident.

Stage 3 (1992-present): Steady Development. In the early 1990s, the Chinese government clearly set out that the aim of the economic reforms was to establish a market economic system and formulated the strategy of 'utilising two kinds of resources and developing two markets'.[1] Many local governments and enterprises acknowledged the strategic importance of overseas business for accelerating economic development. As a result, China's overseas direct investment began to expand at an unprecedented rate. Annual FDI outflows jumped to US$4,000 million in 1992 from US$913 million in the previous year and further to US$4,400 million in 1993. Though this figure fell to US$2,000 million in 1994, average annual FDI outflows remained at a level above US$2.6 billion in the following eight years (1996-2003) (SAFE, 1999; UNCTAD, 1994-2004).

The rapid expansion of FDI outflows makes China one of the main sources of FDI among developing economies. During 1985-98, it was among the top five of those economies in terms of annual FDI outflows. As a result, its outward FDI stock mounted to US$27.6 billion in 2001, close to that of South Africa (US$29 billion) (UNCTAD, 2002, pp.307-17). Six of the top 50 multinational enterprises based in developing economies, ranked by foreign assets in 1997, were from China (UNCTAD, 1999, pp.86-7). Considering the fact that there was basically no outward FDI before the economic reform, the development of China's outward FDI is indeed remarkable.

2.2. DESTINATION OF CHINA'S OUTWARD FDI

There are two general types of data on FDI. One is the financial data from balance of payments accounting, which record inward and outward flows of FDI and the resulting stock. The other source is data on the operations of FDI affiliates and their parents, including their sales, production, employment, assets and expenditures on R&D. In discussing the differences in source and feature of these two types of data, Lipsey (2001) indicates that the financial data are the only data on FDI that cover virtually all countries, but they contain no information on the economic activity of FDI affiliates and their parents. In contrast, data on FDI operations can reveal more detailed information, but their comprehensiveness depends on how the home country carries out the survey.

In China, the financial data are provided by SAFE and the operations data by MOFCOM. UNCTAD uses SAFE data. Though UNCTAD and SAFE provide data on the growth of China's FDI outflows at the aggregate level over the years from the late 1970s, they do not provide data on the distribution of FDI for different countries. Fortunately, the Ministry of Commerce (MOFCOM), the Chinese government institution responsible for the administration of outward FDI, has recorded every single investment project approved by or registered with the government, including investment from Chinese investors and destination country. It is the only detailed data source available so far from Chinese authorities and we will trace the geographical distribution of China's outward FDI based on data from this source.

MOFCOM data show that China's outward direct investment covers as many as 152 countries (economies). However, its distribution is quite uneven among different regions and individual countries. A further breakdown of geographical distribution shows that China's outward FDI is concentrated in a handful of countries.

2.2.1. Distribution among different regions

In term of flows, Asia and North America are the two major recipients of FDI from China. They accounted for 59.8 and 13.6 per cent respectively of China's outward FDI for the period 1979-2002. They are followed by Africa, Latin America and the Oceania-Pacific region, each accounting for 8.8, 7.0 and 6.0 per cent, respectively. European countries as a whole only received 4.9 per cent of China's outward FDI, the lowest share among all the regions.

In terms of the number of FDI projects, Asia is the biggest host region, accounting for about 54.5 per cent of China's outward FDI between 1979 and 2002. It is followed by Europe, North America and Africa, each accounting for 15.3, 12.2 and 8.3 per cent, respectively, for the same period (Table 2.1).

The regional distribution of China's outward FDI has been changing over time (Table 2.1 and Figure 2.3). North America attracted a large share of Chinese investment in the early years. Up to 1990, more than 33 per cent of China's outward FDI went to North America. This figure jumped to 86 per cent in 1991. However, Chinese investment in North America fell to a lower level in most of the following years. In the meantime, investment in Africa kept increasing in terms of FDI projects. Up to 1990, only 99 investment projects, involving a total investment of about US$50 million, went to Africa. In the following eight-year interval, 196 Chinese FDI projects went to Africa, involving a total investment of US$294 million. Over the whole of period 1979-2002, Asia was a region that attracted relatively constant interest from Chinese investors, with 3672 Chinese FDI projects involving a total investment of US$5482.3 million. In most years of the 1990s, more than 30 per cent of Chinese investment flows went to Asia. China's FDI in Asia is heavily concentrated in Hong Kong, which accounted for 55.1 and 74.3 per cent of China's FDI projects and flows respectively in that region (MOFCOM, 2003).

2.2.2. Distribution among three groups of countries

The distribution of China's outward FDI among the three groups of countries, developed, developing and Central and East European, is very uneven. Until 2002, Central and East European countries received less than 3 per cent, leaving the remaining 97 per cent of investment flows to be distributed to developed and developing countries (Table 2.1). During the entire 1979-2002 period, China carried out 643 investment projects involving a total investment flow of US$274.4 million in Central and East European countries, but most of the investment was carried out in the early 1990s and the early 2000s (MOFCOM).

Table 2.1 Distribution of China's government approved outward FDI (%)*

		1979-90	1991-5	1996-2000	2001-2	1979-2002
1. Among different regions						
Asia	Flows	19.4	22.5	31.4	64.4	59.8
	Projects	41.9	37.5	45.7	45.2	54.5
Africa	Flows	4.9	8.3	28.8	7.9	8.8
	Projects	12.4	8.9	22.1	13.4	8.3
Europe	Flows	5.7	11.1	3.8	5.9	4.9
	Projects	12.7	24.4	11.9	13.4	15.3
L. America	Flows	5.1	3.9	22.1	4.5	7.0
	Projects	5.9	7.0	6.9	10.3	5.2
N. America	Flows	33.2	45.1	9.1	5.2	13.6
	Projects	18.5	14.5	8.3	9.9	12.2
O&Pacific	Flows	31.7	9.1	3.1	4.3	6.0
	Projects	8.6	7.5	4.0	4.3	4.7
2. Among different types of countries						
DC	Flows	67.0	56.5	15.3	20.5	22.7
	Projects	38.0	28.8	20.1	25.8	26.3
LDC	Flows	30.3	34.5	80.1	76.4	74.4
	Projects	57.7	50.8	70.5	65.8	64.7
C&E Europe	Flows	2.7	9.0	3.0	3.3	2.9
	Projects	4.4	20.3	9.1	7.6	9.2

Note: * Due to rounding, the sum for a particular year may not equal 100.

Source: MOFTEC, various issues.

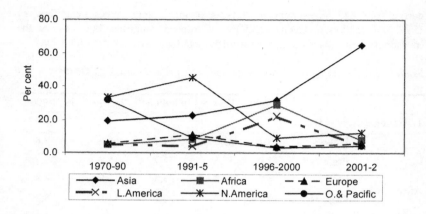

Source: MOFTEC, various issues.

Figure 2.2 Geographical distribution of China's FDI outflows

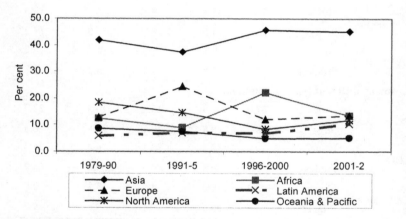

Source: MOFTEC, various issues.

Figure 2.3 Geographical distribution of China's outward FDI projects

While for the whole period between 1979 and 2002, the developed country
group and developing country group received about 23 per cent and 74 per cent
of China's outward FDI flows respectively, several distributional features are
worth noting. First, the average size of China's FDI projects in developed
countries was larger than that in developing countries before 2001. This feature
was reflected in the shares of FDI flows and projects received by these two

groups of countries. During the 1979-2001 period, the distributional shares of China's FDI flows to developed and developing countries were 35 per cent and 60 per cent respectively, involving 29 and 60 per cent of China's outward FDI projects respectively. This implies that the average size of China's outward FDI projects in developed countries (that is, 35/29) was about 1.2 times that in developing countries (that is, 60/60). This difference was even larger in the earlier stage of this period, with the average size of projects in developed countries being double that in developing countries between 1979 and 1998.

Secondly, China's FDI flows were concentrated heavily in developed countries before 1991. More specifically, between 1979 and 1991, more than 72 per cent of China's FDI outflows went to developed countries, while developing countries only received 24 per cent. The share of FDI in developed countries was especially high in 1991, reaching 88 per cent, while that in developing countries was only 6 per cent (Table 2.1 and Figure 2.4). This feature is contrary to the generally claimed pattern that FDI from developing countries should have other developing countries as its main destination, especially at an early stage.

Thirdly, China's investment in developing countries kept rising and a growing share of investment went to this group of countries after 1992. In 1991, the developing country group only received 6 per cent of China's outward FDI flow. However, this group accounted for 42 per cent of China's outward FDI flow in 1992. This figure rose further to 59, 76 and 68 per cent in the following three years, respectively. The share of China's outward FDI flow to developing countries was even higher in the 1996-2000 period, reaching 83 per cent (Table 2.1 and Figure 2.4). The number of China's FDI projects to developing countries also rose along with the rising share of FDI flows. Developing countries accounted for more than 50 and 70 per cent of China's outward FDI projects during the periods of 1991-5 and 1996-2000, respectively.

2.2.3. Distribution among individual countries

The distribution of China's outward FDI among different countries is much more uneven than that among different regions or different groups of countries.

In Asia, Hong Kong and the ASEAN countries are the main destinations of China's outward direct investment. Up to 2002, these two regions absorbed US$4074 million and US$716 million respectively, each accounting for 74 and 13 per cent of Chinese government approved direct investment in Asia. In ASEAN, Thailand and Cambodia are the largest recipients. They absorbed US$214 million and US$125 million respectively of direct investment during the 1979-2002 period. They were followed by Vietnam, Myanmar and Indonesia, each absorbing US$85 million, US$66 million and US$65 million, respectively. Laos received the smallest share (MOFTEC, 2003). It is worth noting, however, that the trend for the annual number of China's FDI projects to ASEAN is going down.

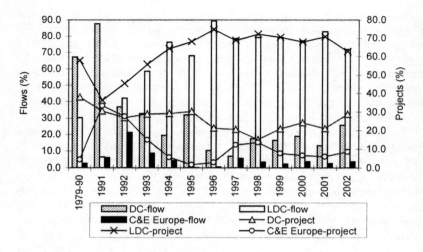

Source: MOFTEC, various issues.

Figure 2.4 Distribution of China's outward FDI among the three groups

In Africa, North Africa received only a very small share of China's FDI, the majority went to central and southern African countries. Among them, Zambia, South Africa, Mali and Nigeria are the major destinations; until 2002, each received US$134 million, US$119 million, US$58 million and US$44 million respectively. The other major recipients in Africa are Tanzania, Zimbabwe, Democratic Republic of Congo, Kenya, Mauritius, Ghana, Madagascar, Gabon and Côte D'Ivoire.

In Latin America, Peru is the biggest recipient. Up to 2002, it received about US$200 million of Chinese government approved investment. It was followed by Mexico, Brazil and Chile; each received US$167 million, US$120 million and US$25 million respectively during the 1979-2002 period.

On the whole, West Asia, Central Asia and East Europe (except for Russia) are the regions that attracted least interest from Chinese investors. For example, twelve West Asian countries (Cyprus, Iran, Israel, Jordan, Kuwait, Oman, Qatar, Saudi Arabia, Syria, Turkey, United Arab of Emirates, Yemen) together only received US$147 million of Chinese investment in the 1979-2002 period. Similarly, six Central Asian countries, Georgia, Kazakhstan, Kyrgyzstan, Tadzhikistan, Turkmenistan and Uzbekistan, together received only US$106 million of Chinese investment until 2002. Until 2002, China invested US$274 million in Central and East Europe, of which 75 per cent went to Russia.

Overall, China's FDI outflows are highly concentrated in a few developed countries, namely, the United States, Canada and Australia. Up to 2001, about 30 per cent of Chinese government approved FDI went to these three countries, each accounting for 13, 9 and 8 per cent, respectively. These three countries, plus Hong Kong, Peru, Thailand, Mexico, Zambia, Russia, Cambodia, South Africa and Brazil, accounted for about 67 per cent of China's outward FDI, leaving the remaining 143 countries (regions) accounting for 33 per cent of China's outward FDI (Figure 2.5).

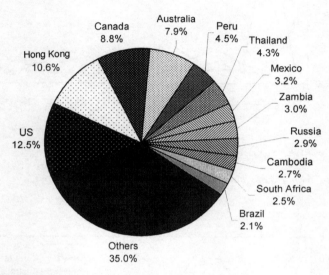

Source: MOFTEC, various issues.

Figure 2.5 Main destinations of China's outward FDI (1979-2001)

It is worth noting that the share of China's FDI in the United States, Canada and Australia was even larger in the early stages. During the 1979-90 period, these three countries received 25 per cent of China's government approved outward FDI projects, involving more than 63 per cent of China's FDI outflows (Figure 2.6 and 2.7). Australia was the largest recipient at that time, accounting for 30 per cent of China's FDI outflows. In 1991, Canada alone absorbed 84 per cent of China's FDI outflows (Figure 2.6).

China's Offshore Investments

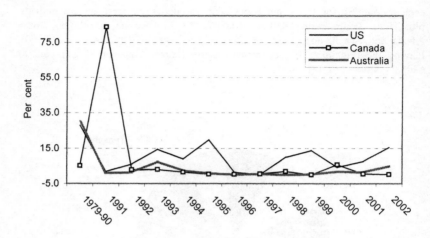

Source: MOFTEC, various issues.

Figure 2.6 Shares of China's government approved FDI outflows

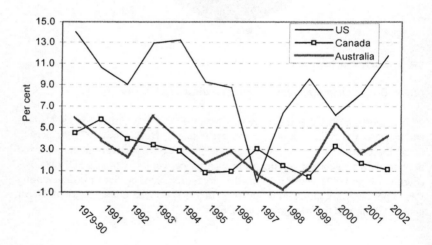

Source: MOFTEC, various issues.

Figure 2.7 Shares of China's government approved FDI projects

2.3. CONCLUDING REMARKS

China's outward FDI began to emerge shortly after the beginning of the economic reforms of the late 1970s. It expanded rapidly afterwards. From 1982 to 2003, total FDI outflows climbed to US$39 billion (UNCTAD, 2004). This is a substantial amount for a developing country with a very short history of foreign direct investment. While covering almost all the countries in the world, China's outward FDI is heavily concentrated in the United States, Canada and Australia. The share of investment in these countries was even larger in the early stages of FDI growth. These features seem to differentiate China's outward FDI from the acknowledged pattern according to which FDI from a developing country is expected to be directed initially at its neighbouring developing countries, expanding gradually in volume and distance. There is a need, therefore, for an explanation of the underlying rationale for China's outward FDI.

NOTE

1. The two kinds of resources refer to domestic resources and overseas resources; and the two markets refer to the domestic market and the international market.

APPENDIX

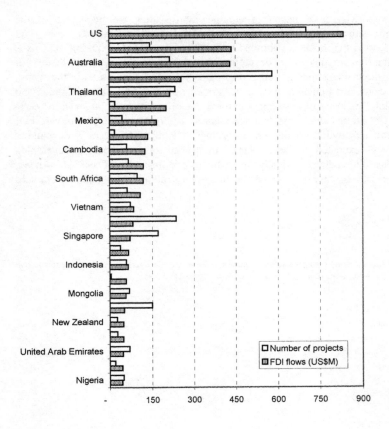

Source: MOFTEC, various issues.

Figure 2.8 Twenty-five largest recipients of China's outward FDI

3. Theories of Foreign Direct Investment

This chapter reviews previously developed theories of foreign direct investment, to provide a backdrop to the pursuit of a plausible explanation for the pattern of China's outward FDI. The survey focuses on the main strands of FDI theory and states the main arguments about some important issues.

3.1. THEORIES OF FOREIGN DIRECT INVESTMENT

3.1.1. Research on foreign direct investment

Foreign direct investment is the major mode by which investors, normally firms, extend their span of control of business activities internationally via acquisition or establishment of overseas enterprises.[1] It differs from international portfolio investment by involving the international transfer of a package of factors in addition to financial capital and by conferring a significant degree of influence over the foreign enterprises of the investing firms.

Foreign direct investment has a long history. In the seventeenth century, firms headquartered in London and Amsterdam began to acquire productive assets abroad. The Hudson Bay Company was engaged both in marketing abroad and in the acquisition of raw materials for the English market, while the Dutch East India Company marketed and sourced in what is now Indonesia.[2] However, FDI played only a relatively minor role in the international economy until the first rapid expansion during the period between the late 19th century and the early 20th century, which was soon destroyed by the two world wars and the 1930s Depression. The situation changed tremendously after World War II when FDI from developed countries expanded rapidly: from the late 1950s until 1967 a boom in FDI occurred which was fuelled largely by the international expansion of the activities of US-based manufacturing and petroleum firms (Graham, 1997, p.100). This boom led to the steady development of FDI afterwards.

Rapid expansion of FDI and related activities by multinational enterprises from the 1950s onwards fundamentally altered the pattern of the world economy, giving rise to new realities that remained inexplicable within established theories. To deal with this change, two new broad approaches have been developed. One is the macroeconomic approach by mainstream economists who attempt to adapt the neoclassical theory of international trade. This approach to FDI is basically developed within the framework of the Heckscher-Ohlin trade model. The perspective of this approach starts out from differences in factor endowments between countries and emphasises the influence of factors external to the multinational enterprise. These range from the size and growth of relevant countries to government policies like tariffs, domestic taxes and labour laws. The other is the microeconomic approach that is grounded in the theory of the firm. This approach to FDI is basically developed within the framework of imperfect competition. It addresses the basic question of why firms undertake investment abroad to produce the same goods as they produce at home. Though views of different economists within this approach vary, the basic point is that 'firms investing abroad represent a distinctive kind of enterprise' (Blomström and Kokko, 1997). It is worth noting that these two broad approaches in their later development have borrowed concepts and ideas from each other and from other disciplines rather than remaining totally independent of each other. The line of demarcation between FDI theories based on the trade theory approach and on the firm-oriented approach is not clear cut.

It is generally acknowledged in academia that Hymer's doctoral dissertation, 'The International Operations of National Firms: A Study of Direct Foreign Investment' (Hymer, 1960), is a path-breaking work that marks the beginning of the study of FDI as a separate field.[3] Before then, FDI was grouped with portfolio investment or firm investment in general; no special attention was given to explaining the relative importance of either of these two types of foreign investment or of the distinction between investment at home and abroad.[4] Since then, the literature on FDI has grown in volume and sophistication. Roughly speaking, this growth has taken place in three major waves. The first wave (before the early 1970s) created the foundation of the field and set the framework for the analysis; the second wave (mid-1970s to 1980s) elaborated, extended and tested the basic ideas; and the third wave (1990s onwards) focuses on the changing patterns of FDI.

In the last decade or so, research on FDI has been spurred on by developments in the practice of FDI and multinational enterprises as well as relevant economic theories and approaches. On the one hand, the acceleration of economic globalisation and the knowledge-based economy and the more rapid growth of some economies have been changing market scopes and competition in the world. As a result, MNEs are inclined to take a global perspective. In adopting global strategies, MNEs from different countries penetrate each other's market. As services and technology play an increasingly important role, international economic activity is organised in innovative ways and motivations are becoming increasingly complex. At the same time, FDI from developing countries expands. These have called for further efforts from economists and business researchers. On the other hand, progress has been made in economic analysis during the past decades. For example, the new trade theory has been advanced by incorporating market imperfection into traditional general equilibrium trade models. Such progress supplies economists and business researchers with new approaches or an improved theoretical basis for the analysis of FDI.

3.2. MACROECONOMIC THEORIES OF FDI

Macroeconomic theories of FDI approach FDI in a framework essentially derived from neoclassical economics, based on the critical assumptions of profit maximisation and a perfectly competitive market. They offer an explanation of FDI flows when certain aspects of market imperfections are recognised.

3.2.1. Factor-endowments approach

Factor-endowment approach can be traced back to an analysis by Mundell (1957) which shows how a prohibitive tariff would induce capital movement from a capital-abundant country as a substitute for trade in goods. This capital movement causes the equilibrium production point in the capital-receiving country to shift in such a direction that the capital-intensive industry (that is, that country's comparatively disadvantaged industry) expands while the less capital-intensive industry (that is, that country's comparatively advantaged industry) contracts. This pattern of output change is predicted in the well-known Rybczynski theorem (1955). Exactly the opposite phenomenon is observed in the capital-investing country. As a consequence, the basis for trade, that is, the existing pattern of comparative advantage between the two countries, is progressively eroded by the capital movement.

Mundell's argument implies that the same equilibrium in terms of commodity prices, factor prices and welfare can be achieved by trade in goods or by FDI. It follows that FDI is attributable to the imposition of prohibitive barriers to trade. This is obviously inconsistent with empirical observation: the last decades have witnessed both an enormous growth of FDI and a reduction in trade barriers manifested in the rapid progress towards regionalisation and globalisation. The weakness of Mundell's argument is that he shows FDI in the context of a two-by-two Heckscher-Ohlin model with zero trade costs in both goods and factors as well as identical technologies in the two countries. Cheng *et al.* (1999) show that it is transaction efficiencies rather than endowments that play a critical role in determining the trade pattern between two countries. With increasing improvement in transaction efficiencies, the general equilibrium jumps from autarky to partial international division of labour and further to complete division of labour between two countries along with increasing improvement in transaction efficiencies. There are two preconditions for a capital-abundant country to export capital-intensive goods. One is that the transaction efficiencies in both the exporting and importing countries are sufficiently high. Another is that the exporting country has no comparative technological disadvantage in producing the capital-intensive goods or even if it has, the country's technological disadvantage is dominated by its comparative endowment advantage. Their claims imply that it is transaction conditions that determine the emergence of FDI between relevant countries.

Also focusing on the relationship between FDI (or factor movement) and trade, Kojima (1978) advances a different theorem to explain Japan's foreign investment in manufacturing. According to Kojima, there are two types of FDI, namely anti-trade-oriented FDI and trade-oriented complementary FDI. If outward FDI occurs in the industry with internationally comparative or monopolistic advantage, this FDI is trade substituting, which means it will result in the contraction of exports of this industry's goods as the production moved abroad by the FDI will reduce the foreign country's imports of these goods. The basic conjecture is that comparatively advantaged industries should serve foreign markets by exports rather than by FDI. Conversely, however, if outward FDI does take place in the industry where the home country has been losing its international competitive advantage, FDI will contract the home production of this industry further. Factors thus released can contribute to the expansion of industries with ever-growing internationally comparative advantage. For the host country, the first type of FDI may contribute little to or even worsen the national economy if the invested industry is the disadvantaged one. However, as the host economy is less developed than the home economy, it is likely to possess comparative advantage in the less capital-intensive industry. With inward FDI, the host country's production frontier expands in such a direction that that country's comparatively advantageous industry expands while the capital-intensive industry, that is, that country's comparatively disadvantaged industry, contracts. The result is an enhancement of the basis for trade. So FDI may promote free trade and mutual prosperity if it facilitates relocation of production corresponding to the international shift of comparative advantages.

In contrast to Mundell, Kojima has included in the context of analysis the technological comparative advantages in the formation of FDI. However, he still ignores the critical role of transaction efficiencies in FDI and trade. Therefore, his theorem cannot predict whether the investing country (Japan) would still invest in countries where transaction efficiencies are too low to sustain inward FDI. It also fails to explain the rationale for cross-investment between developed countries within the same industries and for investment from developing countries into developed countries.

In the framework of the new trade theory, Markusen (Markusen *et al.*, 1996; Markusen, 1997) advances a 'knowledge-capital model' which interprets motivations for horizontal and vertical investment and foreign affiliates' pattern of production for local markets versus production for exports as functions of country characteristics such as market size, size differences and relative endowments differences. This model sets out from three assumptions: (1) services of knowledge-based and knowledge-generating activities, such as R&D, can be geographically separated from production and supplied to production facilities at low cost; (2) these knowledge-intensive activities are skilled-labour intensive relative to production; and (3) knowledge-based services have a (partial) joint-input characteristic: they can be supplied to additional production facilities at low cost. The first two characteristics give rise to vertical multinational investment and the last one gives rise to horizontal investment. This model suggests that the volume of FDI from a source country to a host country is a function of the sum of their economic size, their similarity in size, the relative abundance of skilled labour in the source country and the interaction between economic size and relative endowment differences.

This model has captured more phenomena than Mundell's and Kojima's theorems do by integrating imperfect competition into the analysis. However, it fails to identify the economic meanings of national economic size in determining FDI and trade. In the meantime, it does not pay enough attention to the importance of transaction efficiency in determining FDI: it does not recognise the differences in transaction efficiencies for different goods and factors within and between countries, even though it does include a variable called 'trade costs'. In addition, the assumption of international immobility of all factors is consistent neither with the conventional definitions about factors, goods and FDI, nor with economic reality. As a result of these weaknesses, this model contradicts some empirical observations. For example, the United States has a huge amount of oil-extracting investment in some oil-rich countries in the Middle East. However, that fact in no way implies that the United States and these countries are 'somewhat similar in size' as claimed by the model: 'vertical multinationals dominate when the countries are sufficiently dissimilar in relative endowments but somewhat similar in size' (Markusen *et al.*, 1996, p.28).

3.2.2. Product cycle and FDI

The investigation into the relationship between product life cycle and outward investment was started by Vernon (1966).[5] This approach relates FDI and technology transfer by MNEs to the diffusion of innovations.

According to Vernon, FDI normally takes place in the course of the process of technology diffusion. Most inventions and innovations, the model assumes, are labour saving. Process innovations substitute capital for labour or reduce the input requirements of labour relative to capital. Product inventions and innovations such as household durable goods substitute capital for labour in the production of utility within the household. The value of such inventions and innovations is therefore greatest in countries where wages and, therefore, the value of people's time, are highest relative to the use cost of capital. So inventions and innovations tend to be concentrated in high-income countries. Demand and supply forces tie in the early stages of production closely to the high-income geographical market. Buying power supports a strong take-up rate of the invention or innovation, while the ready supply of scientists, engineers and high-skilled workers facilitates improvements of the product as well as the process. High uncertainty, low price elasticities of demand, small market size and low levels of competition are likely to prevail. Therefore, production as well as consumption of the invention or innovation sticks to the high-income market. As the invented or innovated process or product progresses towards maturity, a growing number of imitators compete for the high profits of the new industry (or new product). In the meantime, large-scale production becomes technically feasible, reducing the real cost of production. This leads to exporting the product to other developed countries to meet demand from local high-income consumers for the product. When competition becomes more intense and the process or product becomes more standardised, the shift of production to low-cost production locations overseas, normally first to other developed countries and later to developing countries, is both necessary and feasible.

Obviously, product cycle theory focuses on a special case of FDI, that is, the FDI motivated by exploiting respective differentials in product and related process technology between countries. Therefore it cannot explain other types of FDI.

3.2.3. Dynamic position of foreign direct investment

Some economists attempt to explain the dynamics of a country's inward and outward FDI in terms of stages of economic development. This approach can be traced back to ideas about the relationships between foreign investment, the balance of trade and economic growth that stretched from Cairnes through Taussig and on to Lewis. They hold that there is likely to be a sequence whereby nations move from being immature debtors (with net borrowing and an import trade balance) to mature debtors (with net debt repayment and an export trade balance), to immature creditors (with net lending and an export trade balance), and finally to mature creditors (receiving net debt repayment and running an import trade balance). Gordon quotes Taussig's classic account about how the process was supposed to have been played out in the United States in the nineteenth century:

> The loan being made (in our assumed case) by British to Americans ... an excess of exports develops in Great Britain. ... In the United States an excess of imports gradually appears. ... The people of Great Britain send merchandise to the United States, and add to the tangible equipment of the Americans, or to their consumable goods, giving up for the time being some of their own possessions and adding to those of the Americans. (Taussig, 1927, quoted from Gordon, 1961, p.37)

In a similar way, the *investment development path* (IDP)[6] was advanced by Dunning (Kumar and McLeod, 1981; Dunning, 1986) as an analytical framework to interpret the relationship between economic development and the FDI position of a country. This framework has been revised and extended in several papers and books (Narula, 1996).

The IDP theorem is empirically based on observation of the historical FDI evidence of some developing and developed countries and theoretically on Dunning's eclectic theory. The FDI position of a country 'will rest on the extent and pattern of the competitive or ownership specific (O) advantages of the indigenous firms of the countries concerned, relative to those of firms of other countries; the competitiveness of the location-bound resources and capabilities of that country, relative to those of other countries (the L specific advantages of that country); and the extent to which indigenous and foreign firms choose to utilise their O specific advantages jointly with the location-bound endowments of home or foreign countries through internalising the cross-border market for those advantages, rather than by some other organisational route' (Dunning and Narula, 1996, p.1).

The IDP paradigm suggests that as a country develops, its international direct investment position tends to go through five main stages of development. The first stage is characterised by very low income levels (that is, GDP per capita) and little or no FDI inflows. Neither domestic market nor resources (in particular, the created assets[7]) offer opportunity for corporate profits, nor do indigenous firms possess the necessary competitive advantages to undertake outward investment. As income and domestic demand rise, and local resource capabilities improve through education and training and by provision of more infrastructure, the country moves to the second stage, at which inward FDI of import substitution or resource-based activities occurs. Outward FDI emerges in this stage but remains restrained by the fact that indigenous enterprises have not generated sufficient ownership advantages of their own to overcome the barriers to foreign production. At the third stage, the country has the ability to undertake outward FDI on a relatively large scale, provided the government chooses to participate in the international specialisation of trade and production instead of promoting economic self-sufficiency. At the same time, the rate of growth of inward direct investment gradually decreases. When the country moves to the fourth stage, it becomes a net outward investor 'because the real costs of indigenous immobile resources become less favourable than those offered by other countries and/or because their comparative advantages become increasingly concentrated in the production of intermediate products such as management and organisational skills, advanced technology, information, etc, which are easily transferable abroad' (Dunning, 1986). However, there is a possibility that the country moves further to the fifth stage, in which a re-convergence of outward and inward investment flows emerges due to the growth of intra-industry rationalised FDI. The intra-industry rationalised FDI itself is based primarily not on factor endowments but rather on the advantages of internalising international markets.

According to Dunning, the speed and direction of a country's investment development path depends on the structure of its indigenous resource endowments, including cultural endowments; its interaction with the rest of the world economy; its trading position; the extent of its ethnic communities abroad; the size of the local market; its economic system; the role played by government policy and the nature of the markets for the kind of transactions its own companies wish to engage in with foreign entities.

With a similar approach, Ozawa (1992) advanced a paradigm of FDI as a means to facilitate structural upgrading along the process of economic development. His model stresses economic structural change and upgrading, and is based on the recognition of the basic structural characteristics of the world economy: (1) inter-economy divergences in supply and demand conditions; (2) firms as creators and traders of intangible assets; (3) a hierarchy of economies; (4) natural (stage-compatible) sequencing of structural upgrading and development; and (5) a strong trend away from inward-looking towards outward-looking trade and investment policy. In a world economy with such characteristics, the economic development in a country is likely to experience different stages, which are specified by Porter (1990) as (i) factor-driven; (ii) investment-driven; (iii) innovation-driven; and (iv) wealth-driven. At different stages the economy has different structures and different comparative advantages and disadvantages. The favourable pattern (nature and direction) of FDI, both inward and outward, at a particular stage is that it is compatible with the use and improvement of the comparative advantages at this stage, and the pattern of FDI should change *pari passu* with the structural transformation of the economy. Dynamically, when the economy moves from the stage of factor-driven to investment-driven and further to innovation-driven, inward FDI should change from that of factor-seeking to market-seeking and further to market/technology-seeking; while outward FDI should change from trade-supporting and resource-seeking to low-cost-labour-seeking and further to market/technology-seeking and surplus-recycling.

3.3. MICROECONOMIC THEORIES OF FDI

Many approaches to the theory of FDI are built on the various approaches to the theory of the firm, which was developed to explain why firms expand beyond the size of the small and relatively anonymous units contemplated in the textbook models of perfectly competitive industries. Hymer's 1960 doctoral thesis, 'The International Operations of National Firms: A Study of Direct Foreign Investment', is a pioneering work in this direction. By using Bain's concepts of market power, Hymer argues that firms go abroad to exploit their power more fully, and their market power explains why the investing firms can survive in competition with local host-country firms (Hymer, 1960). In other words, in order to operate multinationally, a firm must possess some sort of advantage over local competitors in the host country, as foreign operations often bear more transaction costs than local firms mainly because of being 'foreign'. The specific advantages identified by Hymer are (1) economies of scale that can be realised by integrating operations owned by a single firm across more than one market and (2) 'marketing skills'. Most authors now would include as ownership advantages other intangible assets such as proprietary products and process technologies, the ability to create new technologies, organisational and managerial skills other than marketing, and intellectual property not technological in nature.

The research based on the firm during the 1970s and 1980s divided quickly into two broad streams: one stressing transaction cost, and the other focusing on market power.

3.3.1. Transaction cost approach

This approach uses concepts from institutional economics, such as Coase's and Williamson's transaction cost, to explain why FDI takes place, why MNEs exist, and how they are structured. Buckley and Casson (1976) apply transaction-cost analysis explicitly to the MNE. MNEs exist, they argue, because the transaction cost of doing business through an 'internalised' network of wholly owned subsidiaries is in many cases lower than that of arm's length relationships (Buckley and Casson, 1976). Their argument is based on the observation that modern production is a process involving the participation or input of various units, with each specialising in a different aspect of economic activity, such as manufacturing, marketing, research and development, human resources development, procurement, and management of financial assets. These units are interdependent, and the process forms a value-added chain by a flow of tangible intermediate products including materials, components and semi-finished goods and of intangible and knowledge-based intermediate goods such as patents, engineering expertise, management and marketing skills, and quality control. Market imperfections due to information asymmetries and asset specificity make it difficult and inefficient to use the market to organise transactions of intermediate products. The cost-saving efficiency of exchange and transaction through a hierarchy urges firms to bypass the market and create an internal market that brings the related intermediate product markets and production under common ownership and control. The MNE is therefore the result of the process of internationalisation of markets across national boundaries.

This explanation of FDI and multinationals is supported by the indirect pricing theory of the firm. By stressing the pricing of factors and goods, Cheung (1983) argues that the firm, rather than replacing the market with a non-market institution, replaces the market for intermediate goods with the market for labour that is hired to produce the intermediate goods. By formalising and developing Cheung's idea, Yang and Ng (1995) show that a firm is a structure of residual rights between trade partners such that one party (the employer) has the authority to allocate the labour of the other party (the employee) and claims the residual of the contracts between the two parties that specify payment for the labour of the employees. The institution of the firm can be used to include in the division of labour the activities involving intangible outputs and effort inputs, for which pricing efficiency is prohibitively low. By doing so, the direct pricing and marketing of these activities can be avoided, and therefore transaction costs are reduced and the division of labour is promoted. Nevertheless, theoretical developments in this direction have to make a special effort to stress the

differences in transaction efficiencies for goods and factors within and between
countries. By failing to do so, Buckley and Casson's theory of FDI cannot
explain why a firm would invest abroad to save transaction costs rather than
doing so at home.

Noting the importance of host country characteristics in determining FDI and
multinational activities, Dunning (1977) advances a trinity paradigm of
ownership, location and internalisation advantages (OLI). This paradigm
represents a bridge between the industrial organisation/firm approach and more
traditional trade economics. While also seeing internalisation as the key to the
MNE, Dunning argues that internalisation considerations alone cannot tell us
why an MNE goes to country A instead of country B. Hence, there must be
something that makes country A more favourable than country B for the MNE's
operation. He designates the favourable conditions which a country possesses as
'location advantage'. His 'eclectic approach', introduced roughly at the same
time as Buckley and Casson's internalisation model, explains how MNEs use
internalisation to exploit the advantages of locating production abroad (Dunning,
1977). As to the transaction costs which lead to internalisation, Dunning (1994a)
specifies seven categories: (1) search and negotiation costs; (2) costs of broken
contracts; (3) cost associated with buyers' uncertainty about the nature or value
of inputs; (4) costs associated with lack of futures markets; (5) costs associated
with government intervention in markets; (6) costs associated with conditions of
sale; and (7) costs associated with moral hazard and adverse selection.

3.3.2. Industrial organisation approach

Caves' (1971) article on multinationals has become the classic statement on how
to marry industrial organisation (IO) economics and the study of FDI and
MNEs. He agrees with Hymer that firms need a firm-specific advantage to
compete successfully with local host country firms, because the latter benefits in
various ways from being at home. But he goes further in defining the various
sources of such advantage and provides conceptual links between IO
economists' treatment of market power at home and abroad. He stresses product
differentiation and argues that the market power of MNEs allows them to
differentiate products in the market and secure a time stream of cash flows.

Some scholars take the IO approach further by introducing ideas from risk
and game theories. Graham (1978) develops a model of strategic interaction
between MNEs, where firms follow each other abroad or reciprocate each
other's moves. He hypothesises that when a large firm in MNE-prone industries
finds its domestic market invaded by a new subsidiary of a foreign MNE, it is
likely to retaliate by invading the foreign MNE's home turf. Its proprietary
assets can aid its subsidiary to earn a nominal profit once its strategic value is
counted. The strategic value arises if the subsidiary on the invader's turf
establishes both a means of retaliation and a hostage that can be staked out in
any subsequent understanding between the two parents. So both following each
other abroad and reciprocating each other's moves result from the drive to

reduce uncertainty in an interdependent world. Another risk-reducing strategy, argues Kogut (1983), is sequential investment in foreign locations, which could be regarded as options that the MNE would exercise later, depending on exogenous trends.

3.3.3. Learning option and signal effects

Peng (1995) argues that given the sequential nature of FDI, MNEs' investment behaviour can be interpreted in terms of the incremental approach prescribed by option theory. When an investor enters the option market, he is entitled to make an optional choice in the future. If the market situation becomes favourable, the investor will exercise his option to make a big deal. And if the market situation becomes worse, he can forfeit his right and bear only a relatively small loss. This principle can be used in FDI. Typically, a small amount of FDI is initially made in a host country. As the MNE gradually gains market knowledge and operating experience, more investments may be drawn into that country. In terms of the mode of entry, FDI may be used initially to acquire a minor equity in a foreign agent, later to establish a joint venture with a foreign partner, and eventually to set up a wholly owned subsidiary abroad. Viewed through such an 'option lens', FDI can be conceptualised as an option to maintain access to technology and innovation in host countries, thus permitting the MNE wider strategic choices for future growth.

The firm-oriented theory of FDI focuses on replacement of the market by internalising transactions via foreign direct investment. However, the firm still relies on the market in its business operations. This raises questions about the rationality of the market and therefore the theory of FDI. Liu (1997) seeks to explain FDI by drawing on signal theory. He argues that a firm's possession of superior know-how gives it the incentive and capability to become a multinational enterprise. FDI not only enables the firm to bypass the market and its asymmetric information, but also to convey information to less-informed outsiders and tell them something about the quality of the firm's intangible assets. As a result, the firm's FDI action becomes a market signal which influences the perceptions of market participants. This signalling effect may give the firm an additional incentive to pursue the path of multinationalisation.

3.4. INTERPRETATION OF FDI FROM DEVELOPING COUNTRIES

3.4.1. Research on FDI from developing countries

Although foreign direct investment from developing countries (so-called Third World FDI – TWFDI) can be traced back to about a century ago (Katz and Kosacoff, 1983, p.139), it has only become a common phenomenon during the last three decades. The 1990s witnessed a big jump in TWFDI: its share in the world total FDI outflow rose to about 15 per cent (UNCTAD, 1994-9), approximately three times that of the 1980s.[8] Given that TWFDI is geographically concentrated in terms of its sources – several East Asian countries plus a few Latin American countries accounting for the major proportion of TWFDI – its growth is all the more impressive. In addition, as the process of economic catch-up and FDI development goes on, multinational enterprises headquartered in developing countries have been increasing in number, size, complexity of organisation and transnationality. Among the 50 top multinational enterprises from developing countries in 1998, there were 29 with foreign assets above US$1 billion, and two ranked 43rd and 73rd respectively in the world's top 100 multinationals (UNCTAD, 1998, pp. 36-8, 48-9).

The expansion and the increasing importance of TWFDI have caught academic attention since the late 1970s. As noted above, Lecraw's 1977 paper, 'Direct Investment by Firms from Less Developed Countries', signified the start of TWFDI as a subject of considerable research (Dunning *et al.*, 1997). Based on a survey covering 200 local and foreign-invested firms (including 20 TWFDI established firms) in Thailand, Lecraw (1977) characterises TWFDI as involving labour-intensive technologies for small-scale production of mature and undifferentiated goods. Investors prefer a minority interest in joint ventures with local partners, and family and ethnic links with local groups play an important role in business. Compared with FDI from developed countries, TWFDI affiliates have higher autonomy and retain a larger proportion of earnings for further development.

Thereafter, interest from economists and business researchers grew, leading to a boom in research into TWFDI between the late 1970s and 1980s. This boom offered a theoretical justification for the specific characteristics of FDI and international operations of firms from developing countries. Representative theoretical publications during this period include Lall (1983a, 1983b), Wells (1983) and Riemens (1989). Research in the 1990s further contributed to the body of knowledge on TWFDI. Seminal contributions in this period include Ferrantino (1992), Tolentino (1993), Dunning *et al.* (1997) and Yeung (1998).

In spite of this progress, the number of studies on TWFDI is relatively small compared to that on FDI from developed countries (Pananond, 1998/9). The existing literature on TWFDI consists mainly of empirical studies within the framework of conventional theories of FDI. These often involve comparing FDI (and MNEs) from developing countries with that from developed countries, focusing on specific cases of certain countries, business operations of certain types of firms or specific functional issues of some firms. TWFDI which is investigated in this research consists mainly of FDI flows to other developing countries.

Nevertheless, questions have been raised about the appropriateness of comparisons between TWFDI and FDI from developed countries. Riemens pointed out, for example, that 'much of what can be said about the nature and consequences of FDI by developing countries rests on the possibility of a meaningful comparison between their MNEs and those of industrial countries. ... (But) by and large, one of the most obvious characteristics of present 3WMNEs[9] is their relatively small size, both in terms of actual FDI and of the size of the parent company'. As little research has been devoted to small-sized developed countries' MNEs that are comparable to Third World MNEs, MNEs of developing countries are usually compared to so-called typical transnational corporations like Unilever, General Motors or IBM. This leads to more confusion than enlightenment (Riemens, 1989, pp.26-30).

3.4.2. Interpretation of FDI from developing countries

3.4.2.1. Ownership advantages for TWFDI

Setting out from the conventional framework for FDI, many analysts try to probe the nature and source of comparative advantages supporting TWFDI in an alien market. It is said that such advantages are no less important for TWFDI than for FDI from developed countries, as TWFDI affiliates often have to compete not only with local companies, but also with other, usually much larger, multinationals from developed countries. Though MNEs from developing countries tend (for the time being) to bear more resemblance to local firms in outlook, size and product lines, these firms are widely believed to hold distinct competitive advantages *vis-à-vis* all their rivals (Riemens, 1989, p.30). These advantages are basically ownership advantages in the sense that they belong to the investing firms in relation to their foreign rivals. However, they may not all be generated within the investing firms, rather they may be derived from external country-specific factors such as the possession of ethnic-specific knowledge or cheaper labour cost.

One of the most frequently quoted advantages for TWFDI is technology adaptation and basic design capability. Empirical evidence shows that most MNEs from developing countries engage in very active technical efforts to assimilate and adapt imported technologies to particular domestic needs and raw materials. For example, Hong Kong firms are considered to be stronger on product improvements for meeting changing demand in developed countries, and they also undertake steps to reduce (rather than increase) labour intensity (Chen, 1983). Indian and Argentinian firms tend to be particularly strong on production engineering and basic design capacity (Lall, 1983a, 1983b; Katz and Kosacoff, 1983). As many developing countries are similar in technological base, factor structure and industrialisation goals as well as market size (small), TWFDI affiliates of a certain type even have advantages over those of MNEs from developed countries. The sources of these advantages include: (1) less use of special-purpose equipment, which enables them to use local low-level inputs even substitutes; (2) mature and more universal products which better match the lower standards of machinery and equipment in local downstream firms; (3) low specialisation of TWFDI affiliates, which can reduce economic scale to the extent of local small market; and (4) the flexibility stemming from lower specialisation and higher universality of machinery and equipment, which facilitates firms greatly to change their products when business environment and market conditions have changed (Wells, 1983).

Small scale of operation is another advantage for investors from developing countries. It is often argued that the smallness of their home market for manufactures gives MNEs in TWFDI an edge over Western MNEs when similar circumstances in other developing countries call for a smaller scale of production. Wells terms this process 'de-scaling' and suggests that it is a type of technology unfamiliar to, and disfavoured by, Western MNEs, but at the same time, it still embodies an amount of know-how not readily available to local firms (Wells, 1983).

Lower management costs and higher autonomous subsidiaries are another source of comparative advantages for TWFDI. Most FDI firms from developing countries are small in size in comparison with those from developed countries. Management levels are thus reduced and flexibility increased. This feature brings about management cost-saving effects for TWFDI affiliates as well as higher autonomy to their overseas subsidiaries (Wells, 1983).

Ethnic-specific knowledge is also an advantage for TWFDI. When a country has large ethnic communities abroad, the possession of intimate knowledge of the local market in terms of tastes and opportunities, and access to channels of distribution, enables firms from the country to save significant costs involved in the collection of such information. Similarly, knowledge of special manufacturing processes and products with an ethnic character gives its possessors monopolistic advantages over competitors (Wells, 1983). In reality, this advantage is most likely to relate TWFDI to developed countries. The reason is that most 'ethnic' products are relatively simple to manufacture, and therefore generally produced by local entrepreneurs belonging to the community in question in developing countries. However, developed countries are more open to external funding and to managing such lines of production, and their markets represent much stronger buying power. It seems that satisfaction of 'ethnic' demand provides a foothold for some TWFDI, especially if they are able to capture some non-ethnic markets as well. But the scope of such markets appears to be limited (Riemens, 1989, p.38).

3.4.2.2. Timing of TWFDI

It is generally acknowledged in the literature that the emergence and development of FDI from a developing country are to a large extent determined by the level of technology accumulation and economic development in the country.

Tolentino (1993) argues that FDI is a choice for firms from developing countries to exploit proprietary advantages which are based on their imitated and innovated technology. She reaches this view by combining Vernon's (1966) product-cycle model and Lall's (1983b) theory of localised technological change. According to Tolentino (1993, ch.4), the competitive advantages of firms from developing countries are predicated on their ability to: (1) imitate and adapt foreign technology in accordance with developing countries' markets and production conditions; (2) innovate on essentially different lines from those of more advanced countries, that is, innovations that are based on lower levels of research, size, technological experience and skills; and (3) achieve improvements by modernising older techniques, including foreign outdated technology. Though the imitated and innovated technology embodied in machinery is easily codified, the methods used in exploiting machinery and firms' accumulated experience as a result of learning by doing and learning by using are not codifiable. In effect, the imitated and innovated technology is largely implicit in the skills and experience of employees and is therefore not easily codified or embodied in patents, blueprints or trademarks. This drives developing countries' firms with imitated and innovated technology to internalise these advantages via outward FDI.

This view implies that the emergence and development of FDI from developing countries correspond to the generating of imitated and innovated technology in these countries. More generally, as Tolentino (1993, ch.4) indicates, the world FDI pattern can be viewed as a pecking order of different countries in which a particular country's position is determined by its ability to produce a particular product and the internationalisation of firms from developing countries as a stage in the product life cycle.

Dunning reaches a similar conclusion, but from a different theoretical framework. Within the framework of his investment development path (IDP) theorem, Dunning views the development of FDI from a country as a process, attributable to the country's economic development. Whether or not a developing country can start its outward FDI depends on whether its firms have generated sufficient ownership advantages to overcome the initial barriers to foreign production. The expansion of FDI afterwards is determined by the further accumulation of ownership advantages (Dunning, 1988).

Dunning, *et al.* (1997) further point out that so far, TWFDI has progressed into its second wave and research on TWFDI in the late 1970s to early 1980s is mainly a description of TWFDI in the first wave. While the first wave consists mainly of some Asian and Latin American countries, for example, India, the Philippines, Argentina, Mexico and Colombia, the second wave consists mainly of newly industrialising economies in East Asia such as Taiwan, South Korea, Hong Kong, China, Singapore and Malaysia. According to Dunning *et al.* (1997), the second wave represents part of a continuum and can best be characterised as an intermediate stage in the evolution of MNE activity between the first wave of Third World MNEs and conventional MNEs. Specifically, the second wave of TWFDI has distinct features in destination, motivation, industrial areas and ownership advantages. These features reflect the structural upgrade in the home economy in response to economic globalisation and the improvement of investors' ownership advantages along with the structural upgrading. A holistic and integrated government policy towards industry development in the home economy is important for the transition from the first wave to the second wave in the country's outward foreign investment.

3.4.2.3. Geographical distribution of TWFDI

Given the importance of ownership advantages in FDI, it follows that FDI from developing countries is likely to be directed at countries with geographical, economic, cultural and ethnical proximity, for such investment enables investing firms to lessen the disadvantages in FDI, to take advantage of cultural and ethnic knowledge, and to facilitate communications between subsidiaries and their parents. When investing firms, through this kind of investment, have gained international business experience, better skills and more access to improved technologies and international networks, they are more likely to extend their area of operation to regions with larger geographical, cultural or ethnical distance (Ferrantino, 1992).

Earlier research shows that, as a reflection of this strategy, FDI from developing countries is characterised by a heavy regional concentration. Firms from Hong Kong, Taiwan, South Korea and India prefer to invest in the neighbouring countries of Indonesia, Malaysia, Thailand and the Philippines. Similarly, the bulk of Argentinian firms' direct investment went to Brazil, Peru and Uruguay. Most of Brazilian firms' foreign direct investment also went to Latin American countries (UNCTC, 1983).

3.5. CONCLUDING REMARKS

The above brief survey has presented an outline of existing research on foreign direct investment. In order to capture the development of FDI theories, this survey focuses on the origin of different approaches. While research on foreign direct investment has so far made much progress in interpreting the determinants and basic features of FDI, due to the empirical evidence on which the theoretical foundation of FDI is based, existing theories of FDI are dominated by supply-side focused theories. Correspondingly, ownership advantage is implicitly or explicitly assigned crucial importance to FDI. In comparison, the demand side of FDI, basically asset-seeking FDI, has not attracted sufficient attention in the literature. This is one of the main reasons that the conventional theories of FDI are inefficient at explaining the changing pattern of FDI, especially FDI from developing countries and cross-investment flows between developed countries in the same industries.

FDI from developing countries has been studied so far mainly within the framework of conventional theories of FDI, and is characterised as being motivated crucially by a firm's desire to exploit its existing proprietary advantages abroad. These advantages are the same as those of developed countries' multinationals in nature but different in form or source. They can be easily transferred from country to country within a firm, but with difficulty between firms. While the proprietary advantages from developed countries are embodied in frontier technologies and sophisticated management and marketing, those for investors from developing countries are derived from localising imported technologies by imitation and adaptation. These technologies are labour-intensive and suitable for small production with low quality inputs. Due to the similarity between developing countries in market size, industry structure and the level of technology, a firm which uses this kind of technology has competitive advantages over its counterparts from developed countries if it operates in other developing countries. Accordingly, FDI from a developing country should be directed towards other developing countries, especially neighbouring ones at earlier stages of economic development. As the expansion of proprietary advantages is a process based on technological improvement, FDI from a developing country can only expand gradually.

NOTES

1. For the official definition of FDI see United Nations (UNCTAD, 1996, p.219) based on OECD (1992) and IMF (1993): 'Foreign direct investment is defined as an investment involving a long-term relationship and reflecting a lasting interest and control of a resident entity in one economy (foreign direct investor or parent enterprise) in an enterprise resident in an economy other than that of the foreign direct investor (FDI enterprise or affiliate enterprise or foreign affiliate). Foreign direct investment implies that the investor exerts a significant degree of influence on the management of the enterprise resident in the other economy.' Theoretically, foreign direct investors include individuals and public institutions as well as firms. FDI by individuals and public institutions is normally not separately stressed in conventional analysis, as it is very limited in volume and importance. The present investigation adheres to that tradition.
2. Mira Wilkins even traces the antecedents of FDI back to 2500 BC when Sumerian merchants found in their foreign commerce that they needed men stationed abroad to receive, store and sell their goods (Wilkins, 1970, p.1).
3. However, Buckley (1997, p.219) holds that Dunning's 1958 work on foreign investment in British manufacturing industry is a milestone in the development of the subject. In this respect Hymer was fortunate in being able to draw on this work.
4. Up to that time, three main approaches to the phenomenon of FDI seemed to dominate the literature: (1) different interest rates. Ohlin (1933) holds that international capital movements occur in response to the different interest rates prevailing in those countries. Interest rates vary according to the differences in factor endowment ratios of labour and capital. As capital moves from low-interest to high-interest countries, equilibrium is achieved. (2) exchange risk premium. Aliber (1970) argues that there are risk premiums in the international equity markets designed to cover uncertainty about the exchange risk on shares bought in weak-currency countries. These premiums do not apply to foreign-owned (therefore hard-currency country) subsidiaries that operate in soft-currency countries. (3) internally financed growth. Kindleberger's (1973) early explanation holds that foreign direct investment results from both the expansion of a firm's market and its use of internally generated funds. When firms attempt to maximise their sales' growth rates, they have to set up plants wherever large markets exist. As internally generated funds are cheaper than externally raised funds, they should be used for expansion.
5. Vernon's product life cycle theorem uses a microeconomic concept – the product cycle – to explain a macroeconomic phenomenon: the foreign activity of US multinationals. It lies between or integrates the micro and macro analysis and therefore is not strictly within either of the two approaches.
6. The investment development path (IDP) was originally called the investment development cycle (Dunning, 1986).
7. According to Dunning (1994b; Dunning and Narula, 1997), resources can be grouped into two categories: (i) natural assets consisting of the 'fruits of the earth' and the stock of unskilled

labour; and (ii) created assets which are those derived from the upgrading of natural assets. The latter assets may be tangible or intangible, and include capital and technology as well as those pertaining to skilled labour, such as technological, managerial and organisational expertise.

8. There are big discrepancies among data on TWFDI from different sources as well as in some cases different periods of the same source. Dunning *et al* (1997) gave an example, 'Dunning (1993) and Narula (1996) utilised estimates based on the US Department of Commerce which that total outward FDI stock from developing countries in 1980 was $15.3 billion, while UNCTAD (1994) and Tolentino (1993) place the figure at a fifth of that level, or $3.4 billion. Even more curiously, discrepancies exist in publications by the same source; for example, the estimate for 1980 published in UNCTAD (1995) gives the same stock figure at $6.1 billion, twice that of UNCTAD (1994), one year previously.' In this research we use UNCTAD's data as the main source for TWFDI. Even though this source is quite conservative, its data on TWFDI still suggest strong trends in the expansion of TWFDI.

9. Multinational enterprises from developing countries.

4. Theoretical Issues Raised by China's Outward Investment

The above review shows that FDI from developing countries is characterised in the literature as being motivated by a firm's desire to exploit its existing proprietary advantages based on imitated and innovated technology. It follows, therefore, that given the importance of these advantages and the similarities between developing countries in market size, industry structure and level of technology, FDI from a developing country should normally be directed at other developing countries, especially those in close proximity and at lower stages of economic development. As the expansion of proprietary advantages is a process of technological accumulation, FDI from a developing country should only expand gradually. However, these patterns of TWFDI are hardly reflected in China's outward FDI, especially when we consider the fact that China's outward FDI targets a few developed countries as its major destinations.

4.1. OWNERSHIP ADVANTAGES

According to mainstream theory, the possession of proprietary advantages of some kind is a critical factor underlying a firm's overseas direct investment. This holds irrespective of whether the investment is said to be motivated by the firm's desire to exploit these advantages overseas to avoid transaction costs or as part of the firm's strategy in a game of imperfect international competition. These proprietary advantages are derived from the ownership of intangible resources,[1] generally, technology, management skills and organisational capabilities, which can be easily transferred from country to country within a firm, but with difficulty between firms. However, this pattern is not found in China's outward investment.

First, the average size of Chinese firms is relatively small. In 1996, General Motors of the United States realised sales of US$5.26 billion, which was equal to the sum of that of the 342 largest Chinese firms, or 32 times that of the Daqing Oil Company, the largest firm in China in terms of sales. The total sales of the world's largest three firms in terms of sales, General Motors, Ford and Shell, exceeded the total sales of all 23 927 large- and medium-sized firms in China. In 1996, the American industrial enterprise Exxon realised a profit of US$7.51 billion, which was about 57.4 per cent of the total profit made by the 23 927 L&MFs in China. In the same year, Baosteel, the largest industrial firm in China in terms of assets, held US$9 billion of total assets, which was only about 2.9 per cent of that of General Electricity from the United States (CSIESR *et al.*, 1999, pp.111-2). The gap in size between Chinese firms and world firms is summarised in Table 4.1. In addition, most Chinese firms are operating in a single industry, and the variety of their products is correspondingly limited.

Table 4.1 Comparisons between Chinese and the world's largest firms

	Sales	Profit	Assets
World no. 1: China's no. 1	32:1	–	34:1
World no. 1: all China's L&MFs (23 927)	41.6:100	57.4:100	42:100
World no. 1 equals China's	342 largest together	–	342 largest together
World largest three: all China's L&MFs (23 927)	109.7:100	211.5:100	112.2:100

Source: CSIESR *et al.* (1999), p.111.

Secondly, compared with their counterparts from developed and newly industrialised countries, Chinese firms are weak in research and development (R&D) activities. Though total employment in R&D activities in China is large, less than 30 per cent of R&D workers are employed by firms. In 1998, only 32.2 per cent of China's L&MFs had their own specialised R&D institutions. Even among those firms which have R&D institutions, 37 per cent did not have all the relevant inputs (NBS, 1998). This contrasts sharply with situations in developed and newly industrialised countries where more than half of national R&D employees work in firms. In the United States, R&D employees in firms accounted for as much as 79.4 per cent of the national total in 1998 (Table 4.3).

As knowledge goods are non-rivalrous and non-excludable in nature, and are difficult to trade externally due to the high imperfection of the market for such goods, the low-input and understaffed R&D activities in Chinese firms inevitably hinder the innovation and invention process in firms. In fact, many Chinese firms badly need technological transformation. For example, the original value of micro-electronic-controlled manufacturing assets was only about 6 per cent of the total original value of all manufacturing assets in large- and medium-sized firms (IIE, 1999, p.69). In 1980, productivity in manufacturing in China was 6.3 per cent of that in the United States. In 1992 this figure was 6.2 per cent (Ren, 1998). 'In the past ten years, the gap in productivity between China and other leading countries including the United States, Japan and South Korea, remains unchanged. In other words, there are no trends for catch-up (for China)' (Ren, 1998).

Table 4.2 Number of employees in R&D activities in firms

Country	(a) Total number of employees in R&D (thousand)	(b) Number of employees in R&D in firms (thousand)	b/a (%)
US	962.7	764.5	79.4
Japan	948.1	573.7	60.5
Germany	470.2	285.0	60.6
France	318.4	162.0	50.9
UK	279.0	148.0	53.1
South Korea	152.2	96.9	63.7
Russia	990.7	671.1	67.7
China	1667.7	477.0	28.6

Source: IMD (1998).

Besides productivity, other indicators also show the unsatisfactory technological conditions in Chinese firms. Generally used indicators for such purposes are the rate of intermediate consumption and commercial energy consumption in production, as well as product quality. In 1996, the rate of intermediate consumption in industry in China was 74.5 per cent, about 23.6 and 16.9 percentage points higher than the United States and Japan respectively in 1993 (NBS, 1997). This implies that there are large gaps between China and many other countries in the technological level of products and the potential for value addition in industry. On the other hand, though the efficiency of energy consumption in industries in China, measured in terms of tons of standard coal/per 100 *yuan* of value-added, had greatly improved from 20.54 in 1980 to 3.89 in 1995, China is still among the countries with lowest efficiency in energy consumption (CSIESR *et al.*, 1999, p.101). In 1995, the energy consumed in the production of 1 US$ of GDP was 49 179 kilojoules, 13.5 times that of Japan, 8.8 times that of Germany, 4 times that of the United States, and 1.6 times that of India (IMD, 1998).

Conditions in product quality in China are also unsatisfactory. In most years between 1988 and 1997, the rate of qualified sample products was around 75 per cent, some years even below 70 per cent. Only in 1991 and 1997 did this rate reach 80 per cent. In the meantime, there were differences between the rate of qualified products and the rate of qualified marketing goods, which implies that many poor quality products have flowed into markets by avoiding quality examinations or through abnormal channels. The situation was most serious for machinery and electricity products, construction materials and textile and footwear products (Table 4.3).

Table 4.3 Quality of products and marketing goods (1997)

	(a) Rate of qualified batch products	(b) Rate of qualified batch marketing goods	(b) – (a)
Products for agriculture	79	71	-8
Processed food and beverage	74	73	-1
Household electricities	81	71	-10
Light industry products	82	70	-12
Textile and footwear products	88	66	-22
Chemical products	88	69	-19
Construction materials	87	62	-25
Machinery and electricity products	88	60	-28
Metallurgy and metal products	76	61	-15
Others	80	65	-15
Total	80	69	-11

Source: NBS (1998).

Thirdly, Chinese firms as a whole are inferior in management in comparison with their counterparts from developed and most newly industrialised countries. According to the International Institute for Management Development, the management competitiveness of firms in China was ranked 30th out of 46 sample countries in 1998 (IMD, 1998). The major host economies for China's outward FDI – the United States, Canada, Australia and Hong Kong – were ranked first, 11th, 17th and fourth respectively, much higher than China (Table 4.4).

Chinese firms are especially weak in the aspects of productivity, corporate performance and management efficiency. China is ranked lowest in overall productivity and labour productivity among all sample countries, including both developing countries and developed ones. For corporate performance, Chinese firms are poor in respect of advertising expenditure and price/quality ratio. In 1995, per capita advertising expenditure in the United States and Japan was US$619.44 and US$460.78 respectively, while in China it was only US$1.81 (CSIESR *et al.*, 1999, p.154). Chinese firms also lack competent senior managers and a good marketing culture.

Table 4.4 Management competitiveness of selected economies (1998)

	Management	Productivity	Labour costs	Corporate performance	Management efficiency	Corporate culture
China	30	42	1	31	29	20
US	1	6	39	1	3	1
Canada	11	16	34	10	12	11
Australia	17	10	27	18	23	15
Russia	46	46	31	46	46	45
Thailand	41	38	8	40	35	39
South Africa	38	37	14	29	41	32
New Zealand	9	25	25	11	14	7
Malaysia	22	30	10	24	17	19
Singapore	2	17	21	5	5	3
Japan	24	20	43	2	33	22
Taiwan	7	23	19	19	7	8
Hong Kong	4	18	24	9	1	10
South Korea	34	27	16	43	42	25
India	32	28	2	41	25	44

Source: IMD (1998).

Table 4.5 International comparison balance sheet of Chinese firms' management

Assets		Liabilities	
Index	Ranking	Index	Ranking
Yearly wages in service professions	1	Overall productivity (PPP)	45
Overall productivity (PPP) growth	2	Labour productivity (PPP)	45
Remuneration of management	2	Agricultural productivity (PPP)	44
Compensation levels	5	Productivity in industry (PPP)	44
Worker motivation	7	Productivity in services (PPP)	44
Entrepreneurship	9	Advertising expenditure	43
Managers' social responsibility	12	Price/quality ratio	42
Corporate boards	14	Competent senior managers	40
		Marketing culture	36

Source: Source: IMD (1998).

One of the main reasons for the relatively poor management competitiveness of Chinese firms is that so far, China has still been in the process of introducing the macro and microeconomic systems and practices of a market economy, therefore firms have taken time to enrich their experience in operating in a market economy while the operation environment has been taking shape.

4.2. TIMING OF CHINA'S FDI

According to Dunning's investment development path (IDP) paradigm (Dunning and Narula, 1997), the emergence and development of outward direct investment of a country is related to its economic development, or more specifically, to its inward direct investment position. Before the emergence of its outward FDI, a country needs to experience a period in which even inward direct investment does not exist. Even if it has started outward direct investment, the country will still have to experience another stage in which inward FDI starts to rise but outward FDI remains low or negligible. Only when the country has entered the third stage, can the rate of growth of its outward direct investment increase while inward direct investment gradually decreases.

China's foreign direct investment position exhibits some conspicuous characteristics. First, the emergence and development of outward and inward direct investment flows coincide. The period of 1982-2003 witnessed the steady growth of outward and inward FDI. Secondly, compared with the huge inward direct investment during the following decade, China's outward FDI remained relatively small, but its absolute value is by no means negligible. From 1982 to 2003, total FDI outflows amounted to US$39 billion (UNCTAD, 2004). This is a substantial amount for a developing country with a very short history of foreign direct investment. Thirdly, due to the two features described above, it is likely that China's outward direct investment has skipped the first stage and part of the second stage of the investment-development path and has now entered the early period of the third stage.

Why has China's outward direct investment skipped the earlier stages of IDP? Is the rapid expansion of China's outward FDI attributable to factors special to the case of China?

Theoretically, Dunning's IDP model is based on his trinity of OLI theorem (1979): the net outward investment (NOI) of a country is attributable to its relative endowments of ownership, location and internalisation advantages. Over time the endowment of these advantages changes, causing adjustment in the NOI position. During the first stage of IDP, no cross-border direct investment occurs since domestic firms have no ownership advantage in undertaking outward direct investment nor are the country's L specific advantages sufficient to attract inward foreign direct investment. The reason for the increasing inward direct investment and negligible outward direct investment during the second stage of IDP lies in the fact that economic development has created sufficient L advantages to attract foreign investment, but at the same time local firms still lack sufficient ownership advantages to undertake outbound investment. With the aid of inward direct investment, over time a country will gain in advantages of created assets while deteriorating in comparative advantages in labour-intensive activities. This will motivate firms of the country as well as exerting pressure to invest abroad, so as to exploit their increasing ownership advantage and to avoid disadvantages in production at home. Therefore in the third stage 'outward direct investment will be directed more to countries at lower stages in their IDP' (Dunning and Narula, 1996, p.4).

Since Chinese firms, as the analysis in Section 4.1 indicates, do not possess sufficient ownership advantages to invest abroad on a large scale, especially in developed countries, the timing of the emergence and development of China's outward FDI is not compatible with the prediction of the IDP paradigm.

4.3. GEOGRAPHICAL DISTRIBUTION OF CHINA'S FDI

It is interesting to note that China's outward FDI is heavily concentrated in the United States, Canada and Australia. Developing countries are not the major destination. This fact seems to deny the decisive role of proximity in economic development and geography between home and host countries in the choice of destination of FDI, as the mainstream theory of FDI suggests.

Given the importance of ownership advantage in the mainstream theory of FDI, the choice of location of FDI is largely a function of the possession of ownership advantages. For example, Hymer (1960) states that national firms enjoy the general advantage of better information about their country: its economy, language, law, politics and so forth. Accordingly, a firm must have sufficient firm-specific advantages (ownership advantages) to offset the comparative disadvantage of being foreign if it is to compete successfully in the host country. On the other hand, if a firm chooses to invest in countries with less cultural, economic or physical distances from the home country, it will need fewer ownership advantages to tackle barriers to international operation, as the 'short' distance implies fewer barriers. Therefore, firms tend to enter markets at an increasing distance from the home country, not only in terms of physical distance but also in terms of differences in economic development, language, culture, political system, etc. Thus, firms are predicted to start their internationalisation by moving into markets they can most easily cope with, entering more distant countries only at a later stage (Benito and Gripsrud, 1995). As firms from developing countries are normally characterised as small in size, weak in technological innovation and less experienced in international operations, their overseas direct investment in the early stages generally targets other developing countries as its main destinations. This implies that the pattern of FDI from developing countries displays heavy regional concentration (UNCTC, 1983).

Generally speaking, developing countries are characterised by the primary production of subsistence (mainly agriculture) and low levels of income per person. By comparison, in developed countries the lion's share of GDP comes

from the services sector while agriculture only accounts for a very small share of
GDP. On this criterion, China is a typical developing country. For example, in
1980, the value added in agriculture accounted for 30 per cent of GDP while
services accounted for only 21 per cent. In the United States, in contrast, these
respective shares were 3 per cent and 64 per cent, respectively. Nearly two
decades later, in 1998, agriculture still accounted for 18 per cent of GDP and
services for 33 per cent in China. In the same year in the United States services
accounted for 72 per cent of its GDP and the share of agriculture had dropped to
2 per cent (Table 4.6). It is worth noting that the average share of the services
sector in the GDP of low-income countries was 38 per cent in 1998, some 5 per
cent higher than that of China. In the meantime, in 1998, per capita GNP in
China was US$750, less than 3 per cent of developed countries (World Bank,
2000).

Table 4.6 Main economic indicators for China and selected countries

	GNP per capita (US$)	Labour cost per worker in manufacturing (US$ per year)		Composition of GDP (%)					
				Agriculture		Industry		Services	
	1998	1980-4	1995-9	1980	1998	1980	1998	1980	1998
US	29 240	19 103	28 907	3	2	33	26	64	72
Australia	20 640	14 749	26 087	5	3	36	26	58	71
Canada	19 170	17 710	28 424	4	3*	38	33*	58	64*
Brazil	4 630	10 080	14 134	11	8	44	29	45	63
Mexico	3 840	3 772	7 607	8	5	31	27	61	68
South Africa	3 310	6 261	8 475	6	4	48	32	46	64
Peru	2 440	2 988	-	10	7	42	37	48	56
Russia	2 260	2 524	1 528	17*	7	48*	35	35*	57
Thailand	2 160	2 305	2 705	23	11	29	41	48	48
China	750	472	729	30	18	49	49	21	33
Indonesia	640	898	1 008	24	20	42	45	34	35

Note: * 1990's figure.

Source: World Bank (2000), tables 1.1, 2.6, and 4.2.

The tremendous differences in the level of economic development and
economic structure between China and the developed countries have militated
against the large-scale entry of Chinese firms' direct investment into developed
countries and some developing countries. On the one hand, as we have indicated
above, Chinese firms do not possess clear technological and managerial
advantages over their counterparts in developed countries. On the other hand,
Chinese firms cannot obtain substantial labour cost savings in their outward
direct investment either, as labour costs are much lower in China than in most

other countries, including developing countries. Countries in Table 4.6 are the main host countries for China's outward direct investment. Labour costs in all these countries are higher than in China. In the 1995-9 period, the yearly labour cost per worker in manufacturing in China was US$729, only about 2.5 per cent of that in the United States, 2.6 per cent of that in Canada and 2.8 per cent of that in Australia. If labour cost saving were the major concern in foreign direct investment, Chinese firms would be much better off operating at home!

Not only is economic proximity barely reflected in the location choice for China's outward direct investment, but geographical and cultural proximity seems to play a very limited role as well. As an East Asian country, China shares a similar cultural tradition with several countries within the region. If Chinese firms invest in this region or other neighbouring countries, they can benefit from geographical closeness as well as easy communication with local Chinese businessmen who are familiar with local markets. However, China for a long time only committed very limited investment to its neighbouring countries. Up to 1998, China's government approved investment in the ten contiguous and nearest developing countries (Laos, Myanmar, Vietnam, India, Bangladesh, Nepal, Pakistan, Mongolia, North Korea and South Korea) was US$45.89 million, only about 11.44 per cent of that in the United States (MOFTEC, 1992-9). Except for Thailand and Cambodia, China's investment in other ASEAN countries is also very limited. For example, up to 1998, China's government approved investment in Indonesia, Malaysia, Singapore and the Philippines was US$30.33 million, US$31.6 million, US$28.74 million and US$10.83 million, respectively (MOFTEC, 1992-9).

4.4. CONCLUDING REMARKS

The above analysis shows that the generally acknowledged pattern of FDI from developing countries is not found in China's outward direct investment. Rather, China's outward FDI exhibits two conspicuous characteristics, rapid expansion in a relatively short time, and high geographical concentration in the United States, Canada and Australia. A further examination of China's outward FDI reveals that Chinese firms do not possess a clear competitive advantage, especially when considering the fact that China's overseas direct investment targets developed countries as its major destinations. Therefore, China's outward FDI is not readily explained by the insights gained from existing theories of FDI from developing countries. The difficulties in providing a convincing explanation of the pattern of China's outward FDI by using a mainstream theory call for a different approach.

NOTE

1. In this analysis we take the most commonly used conception, as there is no consensus of views over what encompasses intangible assets or resources. Grant (1991, p.119) categorised intangible resources into four subclasses: human resources, technological resources, reputation and organisational assets. Hall classifies intangible resources into two categories: intangible assets and competencies. Intangible assets include 'having' capabilities, which are typically regulatory (for example, patents) or positional (for example, reputation). Competencies (intangible skills) are related to 'doing' capabilities, which include functional capability (for example, know-how) and cultural or organisational capability (for example, routines). Intangible skills are typically people dependent, while intangible assets are considered as people independent (Hall, 1993).

PART II

A Network Model and its Application to FDI

INTRODUCTION

The difficulties in providing a convincing explanation of the pattern of China's outward FDI by mainstream theories of FDI call for a different approach. Given the fact that mainstream theories of FDI in general are supply-side focused and 'few sharp tests have been devised to distinguish' demand-side FDI (Caves, 1998), as the documentation and analysis in the previous part show, a possible approach should be able to cover both demand-side and supply-side FDI in the framework of analysis. The network model is such an approach.

Long-term relationships between firms as suppliers and customers are crucial to business operations. To establish, enhance and change these relationships so as to maintain good relationships with other firms are among the highest priorities on the management agenda. Also important are long-term relationships between firms drawing on similar sources of information, technology, capital equipment, labour suppliers and materials, or facing similar problems of distribution and marketing. This is frequently the case amongst firms competing in the same product or input markets. Such relationships lead to the formation of networks among firms in the market.

Though the phenomenon of networks has long been attracting attention from business analysts, resulting in sophisticated literature on networks, networks are not an integrated part of mainstream economic theories of business or business investment. In mainstream economic theory, economic organisation is basically investigated under two sets of conceptions, namely, price and hierarchy, and the market and the firm; transactions between the market and the firm, two alternative forms of organisation, are ignored.

This part develops a network model of FDI by formalising network ideas from business analysis for application to economic analysis. This model sheds light not only on economic organisation in the market and within the firm, but also on economic organisation lying between the classic dichotomy of the market and the firm. As a result, the choice of whether to undertake FDI can be captured in a more comprehensively integrated framework. In such a framework, both the supply side and demand side of FDI can be stressed.

5. Networks and Foreign Direct Investment: An Overview

This chapter provides a brief survey of network research in business organisation, as a background to the search for an explanation of the underlying rationale for China's outward FDI. The survey is confined to issues regarding the basic nature of network relationships and their relevance to foreign direct investment.

5.1. NATURE OF BUSINESS NETWORKS

5.1.1. Networks as relationships

Long-term relationships between firms as suppliers and customers are crucial to business operations. Establishing, enhancing and changing these relationships so as to maintain good relationships with other firms are among the top priorities of the agenda of management. This phenomenon has long attracted academic attention from business analysts. A number of early studies in industrial marketing and purchasing have already demonstrated the existence and importance of these relationships (for example, Blois, 1972; Ford, 1978; Guillet de Monthoux, 1975; Håkansson and Östberg, 1975; Levitt, 1983; Wind, 1970). Webster emphasised that 'for strategic purposes, the central focus of industrial marketing should not be on products or on markets, broadly defined, but on buyer-seller relationships' (Webster, 1979). This stresses that relationships are important to the functioning of industrial markets and to the marketing strategy of industrial firms.

Parallel to long-term supplier-customer relationships, there are long-term relationships between firms drawing on similar sources of information, technology, capital equipment, labour suppliers and materials, or facing similar problems of distribution and marketing. This is frequently the case amongst firms competing in the same product or input markets. This kind of relationship is no less important for business operations than long-term supplier-customer relationships. In imperfect markets, firms of the same trade compete with each other for markets or resources and such competition is featured as a kind of hierarchy due to the capacity differences among relevant firms, and there are opportunities for cooperation between these firms to pool resources, share facilities, exchange information, etc. The importance of such cooperation is increasing as technological developments are accelerating and as product life cycles are shortening.

These two kinds of relationships intertwine to form the industrial system and the networks. To understand the concept of the network, we refer to the following definition:

> A network is a model or metaphor which describes a number, usually a large number, of entities, which are connected. In the case of industrial as opposed to, say, social, communication or electrical networks, the entities are actors involved in the economic process which converts resources to finished goods and services for consumption by end users whether they be individuals or organisations. Thus the links between actors are usually defined in terms of economic exchanges which are themselves conducted within the framework of an enduring exchange relationship. The existences of such relationships are the raison d'être for industrial network. They provide the stability, and hence structure, which makes the network metaphor particularly apposite. (Axelsson and Easton, 1992, p.xiv)

According to Johanson and Mattsson (1988; 1992), an industrial system is composed of firms engaged in the production, distribution and use of goods and services. It consists of two levels and two basic sets of interconnections. One of these levels is an institutional set consisting of industrial networks which are defined as interconnected exchange relationships. This set is perceived as a governance structure, through which exchange in the system of production and consumption is coordinated. The other level is constructed on a technological set – the production system – which exhibits an industrial logic of interconnected activities and resources.

5.1.2. Structure of networks

Networks involve three sets of interrelated elements or dimensions, that is, actors, activities and resources. According to Håkansson and Johanson's (1992) model, a business network is composed of three networks, that is, the network of actors, the network of activities and the network of resources. Actors are defined as those who perform activities and/or control resources. In an industrial network, there are actors at several organisational levels. Actors at lower levels can be part of actors at higher levels. Håkansson and Johanson (1992, pp.28-30) have described five characteristics of actors:

1. They perform and control activities. They determine which activities to perform, how these activities are to be performed and which resources are to be used in performing the activities.
2. They develop relationships with each other through exchange processes. Each actor is embedded in a network of more or less strong relationships which gives the actor access to others' resources.
3. Their activities are based on control over resources. There are two types of control. Direct control is based on ownership. Indirect control is based on

relationships with other actors and the associated dependence relations with those actors.

4. They are goal-oriented. Irrespective of the goals of specific actors, the general goal of actors is to increase their control over the network. For such control enables them to control resources and knowledge and therefore to have the possibility of achieving other goals.

5. They have differential knowledge about activities, resources and other actors in the network. This knowledge is a function of their experience with activities in the network and therefore the knowledge of nearer parts of the network is greater than knowledge of more distant parts.

Actors combine, develop, exchange or create resources by utilising other resources when performing activities. There are two main kinds of activities: (i) transformation activities, which change resources in some way and are always directly controlled by one actor; and (ii) transfer activities, which transfer direct control over a resource from one actor to another and link transformation activities of different actors to each other. In contrast to transformation activities, transfer activities are never controlled by only one actor. In addition, transfer activities affect and are affected by the relationship between the actors involved. A complete activity cycle always contains both transformation and transfer activities.

Performing different kinds of activities requires different resources. Resources are heterogeneous and the use and value of a specific resource is dependent on how it is combined with other resources. According to Håkansson and Johanson, knowledge and experience of resources are important. On the one hand, the joint performance of combined heterogeneous resources will increase through experimental learning and adaptation. On the other hand, when heterogeneous resources are combined, new knowledge emerges which creates possibilities for new and improved combinations (Håkansson and Johanson, 1992). It is worth noting that control over resources is very important and the importance of such control will increase as the resource in question becomes scarcer.

5.1.3. Characteristics of networks

A business network has the following characteristics:

1. *Division of work.* In a network, each firm supplies its specific resources to meet other firms' needs and in turn gets access to other firms' resources which it needs. A relationship of dependence upon each other is thus established (see for example, Easton, 1992; Johanson and Mattsson, 1985, 1988). This interdependence is a necessary condition for the operation of modern firms and the necessity for such interdependence increases with the level of roundabout in production and the advancement of technology.

2. *Resource complementarity.* Basically, there exists both competition and complementarity between firms in a network. While competition exists mainly between firms having the same or similar positions in a specific transaction, for example, between possible suppliers or among possible buyers, complementarity exists mainly between firms which have a possible seller-buyer relationship in a specific transaction. Complementarity between firms is more important for the functioning of a network (Håkansson and Snehota, 1995). This is not only because the realisation of the seller-buyer relationship determines the functioning of relevant firms and competition serves this realisation, but also because competition between firms can create opportunities for cooperation between them. For example, two firms may produce similar goods but each may have its own specific intangible assets. Both firms may be able to improve the quality or reduce the cost of their products if they can pool each other's specific advantages.

3. *Relative Stability.* To function smoothly, a firm's relationships with other firms in a network should be stable. Business practice shows that individual business transactions between firms usually take place within the framework of established relationships, as the existing relationships have been tested over time and firms have knowledge of their counterparts through the established bonds between them. However, totally stable relationships in business transactions are rare for several reasons (Johanson and Mattsson, 1988). When a firm engages in a new business, it is most likely to establish new relationships with new counterparts or add a relationship to the existing ones with existing counterparts. On the other hand, business relationships are sometimes disrupted due to new competition or other changes in business. However, such disruptions are relatively small and normally leave relationships in the network relatively stable.

4. *Cumulative process.* The logic of relatively stable networks is that relationships in a network are the result of a cumulative process which involves continuous resource inputs to search, maintain, develop and sometimes break relationships with other firms.

As each firm is engaged in a number of exchange relationships with other firms, and as these relationships define the position of each firm in the network, positioning is important to individual firms. According to Thorelli (1986), a position (which is a location a firm occupies in a given network) depends on at least three major factors: the domain of the firm (indicating its role in the division of labour), the position of the firm in other networks, and the power of the firm relative to other participants in the focal network. He stresses that 'position, – like power itself – is inherently a relational, relativistic concept'.

Johanson and Mattsson (1988) hold that there are micro-positions and macro-positions. A micro-position refers to the relationship with a specific individual counterpart. It is characterised by the role the firm has for other firms, its importance to other firms and the strength of its relationship with the other firms. A macro-position refers to the relationships to a network as a whole or to a specific section of it. It is characterised by: (1) the density of the firms with which the firm has direct relationships and indirect relations in the network; (2) the role of the firm in the network; (3) the importance of the firm in the network; and (4) the strength of the relationships with the other firms. They stress that 'the macro-positions are also affected by the interdependencies in the whole network as well as by the complementarity of the micro-positions in the network. Thus, in the context of the whole network, the macro-position is not an aggregation of micro-position' (Johanson and Mattsson, 1988, p.293).

It may be helpful for a better understanding of position to refer to Kutschker's (1982) interpretation of the following five characteristics of power:

1. *The basis of power*. Kutschker refers to Dahl (1957) for distinguishing between power based on reward, coercion, reference, legitimacy, expertise and information.
2. *The means of power*. These are activities by which a firm uses its inert resources in order to influence other organisations, including such activities as advertising and promotion, sales effort, persuasion, promises and even threats.
3. *The scope of power*. This refers to a set of specific actions in which a firm can influence a second organisation to perform by using the power at its command.
4. *The extension of power*. This is the set of organisations over which a firm has power.
5. *The cost of power*. This refers to the cost in terms of total resources required for the power holder to wield that power.

5.2. FDI AND NETWORKS

Although networks have been a major research subject in many studies, this subject has not attracted as much attention in the literature of FDI. Nevertheless, existing publications on FDI with the network approach carry meaningful implications for further theoretical investigation.

5.2.1. Internationalisation

Foreign direct investment is the necessary approach for a national firm to become multinational and the growth of most multinational enterprises is normally an evolutionary process. Based on this observation, some researchers treat FDI to the evolutionary process approach, especially when they investigate the phenomenon of the internationalisation of small firms. The most widely accepted conclusion is that firms become international in a slow and incremental manner (Andersen *et al.*, 93). It is also acknowledged that the internationalisation process of the firm involves a varying number of stages. There are several reasons for this. On the one hand, when firms start their overseas operations, they often lack sufficient international business resources, such as international business experience, firm-specific assets, financial resources, etc. They have to accumulate these resources through long-term operations. On the other hand, international business is a long-term innovative course of action and hence a question of adopting new ways of doing business. This argument therefore implies that FDI is likely to start from countries with economic, geographical and cultural proximity to the investing countries. As firms gain more competitive advantages through international operation, they can go further away. This phenomenon is like 'rings in the water'.

However, some researchers have noticed a different phenomenon where some firms skip different stages of internationalisation. For example, Welch and Luostarinen (1988) found that many small English, Australian and Swedish firms engaged in FDI in their early stages of growth. Brush (1992) found in a nationwide study of small US manufacturers that 13 per cent of the sample had started international activities during the first year of operations.

Masen and Servais (1997) incorporate the existing findings and attribute the rise of the so-called 'born global' mainly to three important factors: (1) the new market conditions – increasing international specialisation; (2) technological development – basic changes in technology resulting in specialisation and small production; and (3) more elaborate capabilities of people – increased ability of human resources to exploit the possibility of technological changes in international markets.

Some other researchers specially stress the impact of changes in the world economy from internationalisation to globalisation on the behaviour of firms: with globalisation, both the dominant actors and the dominant forms of the internationalisation process have changed (Michalet, 1991). Michalet argued that the new strategy of the global firm is very different from the multinational strategy of previous decades. Previously, the multinationalisation process began with exports, moved on to the creation of a local distribution subsidiary and then a manufacturing plant. This consequence is no longer relevant. Instead, the global firm first identifies carefully its specific competitive advantage *vis-à-vis* all of its current and potential competitors worldwide. Secondly, it tries to eliminate most of them through takeovers and mergers so as to become the world leader in a specific world market. Competition being more intense, the key factor of success is to be faster than others. 'As a result, the global multinational can be called an "instant" multinational on the model of "instant coffee"'(Michalet, 1991, p.57).

Also focusing on the process of internationalisation, Johanson and Mattsson (1988) take a network approach. They view the internationalisation of a firm as a process of establishing and strengthening international relationships. They argue that as a firm internationalises, the number and strength of the relationships between parts of the business network increase. By internationalising, the firm creates and maintains relationships with counterparts in other countries. This occurs in different ways. The first is by forming relationships with counterparts in countries that are new to the firm (international extension). The second is by increasing commitment in already established foreign networks (penetration). And the third is by integrating their positions in networks in various countries (international integration).

Johanson and Mattsson (1988) view markets as networks of relationships between firms that engage in production, distribution and use of goods and services. Individual firms have positions in the networks, and those positions are developed through activities in the network and define important possibilities and constraints for present and future activities. Investments are processes in which resources are committed to creating, building or acquiring assets that can be used in the future. By overseas direct investment, a firm establishes and develops positions in relation to its counterparts in foreign networks. This argument implies that a national market is a market node in the international networks of markets; an investment project is a business node in the networks of the investing firm's business and this node not only ties different business activities of the firm but also ties the firm's business network to the market networks.

Under the purview of the network approach, resources can be grouped into two types: one is firm-specific internal resources, and the other is network resources which are resources within the network. The sole purpose of linking to a foreign network via FDI is to access the network resources there (Chen and Chen, 1998). For this purpose FDI subsidiaries have to adapt to local networks as interdependent production, logistics, development and administrative activities and resources need to be modified and coordinated to bring about a better match between the firms in the network (Hallen *et al.*, 1991; Chen and Chen, 1998).

As to the features of foreign direct investment, Johanson and Mattsson (1988) identify four categories of firms:

1. *The early starter*. A firm in this category is one with few international relationships and whose competitors and suppliers are also in the same position. Consequently, the early starter has little knowledge about foreign markets and it cannot count upon utilising relationships in the domestic market to gain such knowledge. As a result, the firm is inclined to use agents rather than subsidiaries to enter foreign markets. By doing so, it can reduce costs and uncertainty, as it can benefit from the agent's previous knowledge and investments in that market.
2. *The lonely international*. A firm in this category is one which is highly internationalised while its market environment is domestically focused. It has acquired knowledge and means to handle different environments. Therefore it can easily break into new markets by using such knowledge and resources.

As an internationalised firm, its established position in the business network provides it with a comparative advantage over its domestic competitors.

3. *The late starter*. A firm in this category is in a market environment that is already internationalised. Consequently, the firm has indirect relationships with foreign business networks through its suppliers, customers and competitors. The firm can be 'pulled out' by customers or suppliers and thus market investments in the domestic market are assets which can be utilised when going abroad. Therefore it is not necessary to start overseas business in nearby markets moving to more distant markets and the step abroad can already be rather large at the beginning.

4. *The international among others*. A firm in this category is a highly internationalised firm operating in a highly internationalised market. Given the fact that a highly internationalised firm has enormous knowledge about international business as well as strong positions in many markets, it is quick at setting up sales subsidiaries, as it needs to integrate its global business activities by coordinating activities in different markets.

While the network approach normally stresses the external relationships of a firm, some researchers turn to internal relationships of MNEs. They conceptualise MNEs (normally large ones) as an inter-organisational grouping rather than as a unitary 'organisation'. Therefore, a multinational enterprise in their view is an international network, because the large physical and cultural distances between the owned and owning units within an MNE have weakened the linkage between ownership and hierarchical power in complex organisations. Such linkage is particularly weak when some subsidiaries control critical linkages with key actors in their local environments, particularly the host government (Ghoshal and Bartlett, 1993).

5.2.2. International strategic alliances

In the past two decades or so, international strategic alliances among multinational enterprises have become a popular international business approach, especially in high-tech and capital-intensive industries. The ranges of the strategic alliances vary from purely contractual cooperation to cross-share-holding between the partners. As international strategic alliances are increasing in number and importance for multinationals (either as supplementary to FDI or as a form of FDI), literature about collaborative business strategies has also increased sharply.

The main body of the literature on international strategic alliances challenges the existing theory of MNEs and tries to advance new explanations of the nature of international strategic alliances and the factors behind them. Most contemporary theorising stresses that multinational enterprises favour internalised hierarchies and prefer wholly owned subsidiaries to joint ventures. These preferences, it is argued, stem from the potential that hierarchies afford for a reduction in transaction costs and, in a context of market imperfections, for enhancement of the ability to appropriate rents from tangible or intangible assets (Hymer, 1960; Teece, 1981; Dunning, 1979; Buckley and Casson, 1988). While the internalisation hypothesis suggests that ownership is the critical means by which firms control access to economic rents, it stops short of considering the possibility that such rents can be appropriated by means other than ownership, such as international strategic alliances (Oman, 1989).

There are three broad explanations in the literature as to why MNEs form international strategic alliances. One explanation focuses on resource dependence and technical coordination. According to Richardson (1972), cooperation among firms stems from the need to coordinate closely in complementary but dissimilar activities. Gaps in knowledge make market arrangements insufficient for that purpose. If an industry carries out a large number of activities, such as research, development and design, production and marketing of goods, different organisations will specialise in subsets of these activities, accumulating activity-specific knowledge, experience and skills. Coordination between these different subsets can be maintained through hierarchical, market or cooperative arrangements that bind partners together through mutually agreed plans and long-term obligations. Cooperative coordination would be required when activities are dissimilar but economies of scale or matching R&D efforts are required and cannot be left to the vagaries of the market. In such cooperative coordination, each partner is most likely to take advantage of the partner's resources as well.

Another explanation is grounded on transaction cost saving. According to Williamson (1975, 1985), the selection of the most appropriate governance mechanism in a competitive environment is determined by its efficiency in managing transactions with the lowest possible cost, contingent upon a set of behavioural and environmental factors – bounded rationality and opportunism on the one hand and complexity and a small numbers of players on the other. Asset specificity and the complexity of the task and service exchange favour the internalisation of transactions as the mechanism whereby fewer resources would be consumed in coordinating separate activities. The standardisation of goods and services and the correspondingly large number of producers and buyers suggest that a market arrangement would perform better. Strategic alliances fall somewhere in-between. In fact, successful multinational growth increases the size of the firm and the bureaucratic costs of managing it. Ultimately, the marginal benefit of internalised structures becomes lower than the marginal bureaucratic cost (Jones and Hill, 1988). Then the organisational structure has to be re-examined and some kinds of strategic alliances with other firms may be valuable.

The third explanation pays close attention to global competition. This stream of explanation is mostly empirical in nature. In the era of globalisation and growing knowledge intensity of production, firms are facing a set of contradictory dynamics that have increased the costs, risks and uncertainties of knowledge production and intensified competition over market shares.

International strategic alliances enable MNEs to pool resources while they share the costs and the risks. According to Porter and Fuller (1986), strategic alliances permit firms:

- to obtain superior economies of scale, or ride down the experience curve faster;
- to gain more effective access to knowledge;
- to reduce the risks of costly projects; and
- to shape competition by *inter alia* modifying the number of actual competitors and creating new barriers to entry.

They further suggest that the alliance could be affected by transaction costs stemming from:

- coordination between the partners, contingent upon their respective strategy and configuration;
- lack of trust between the partners that makes coordination more difficult;
- erosion of the competitive position: coalitions can strengthen the position of the allied competitors; and
- an adverse bargaining position: coalitions can expose one of the partners to extraction of profits by the other because of a weaker bargaining position.

Thus, an international strategic alliance is adopted as a result of the trade-off between the benefits and costs of alternative arrangements.

Strategic alliances between MNEs are featured by collaborative and competitive behaviour throughout the whole process. The logic of this is twofold. If there is no competition between partners, firms must be under the same owner. If there is no collaboration, there is no alliance between firms at all. The essential requirement is that there should be some type of mechanism to structure collaboration and competition organically. An empirical study by Ciborra (1991) shows that there are two kinds of costs which are crucial to international strategic alliances: transaction costs and change costs. Changing partners would incur change costs, including the costs of locating new partners and the loss of speciality investment for the existing partnerships. If transaction costs were low, an arm's length relationship between firms would do. However, if transaction costs are high, change costs discriminate between internal development/acquisition and alliances. The stability and longevity of alliances are thus determined by transaction and change costs. If the former are very high, alliances may break up. If the latter are very low, partnerships will be transitional devices that ultimately lead to internalisation.

Considered from the aspect of the benefit of strategic alliances, there are three basic ways for international partners to benefit from alliances: (1) to improve collaboration to yield higher 'value' (to make a bigger cake); (2) to extract more benefit from the existing 'value'; and (3) to internalise the other party's competence. The benefits and costs for any firm in an alliance lie in its relative market position before and after the alliance.

Generally speaking, the proliferation of international strategic alliances is attributed to the emergence of some very significant changes in the way organisations are structured and how their evolving organisational forms are managed. These changes have their genesis in a range of trends and events that have dramatically affected the economic, political, technological and social context in which organisations are structured. Indeed, as market complexity and instability are increasing and competition intensifies, go-it-alone policy may limit or even impair the ability of the MNEs to gain or sustain competitive advantage. In turn these proliferating cooperative arrangements among MNEs from different countries and regions are transforming the global business environment.

5.3. CONCLUDING REMARKS

This brief survey has attempted to present the theoretical conceptualisation of issues regarding the basic nature of network relationships and their relevance to foreign direct investment in the literature of networks. It shows that the network approach to FDI is in the embryonic stage and a formal theory is still non-existent (Gilroy, 1993, p.105). Nevertheless, as indicated by Dunning (1993b, p.92), 'network analysis would seem to have a lot more to offer than it has so far been able to demonstrate, but it needs to be integrated with work now being done by industrial organisational economists'. This book is an attempt at such integration, with special reference to China's outward FDI.

6. A Network Model of Foreign Direct Investment

The analysis in Chapter 4 shows that it is difficult to provide a convincing explanation of the pattern of China's outward FDI by using a mainstream theory of FDI. With the aim of providing such an explanation, this chapter develops a network model of FDI by combining the network ideas of business analysis with the economic theory of business organisation.

6.1. CHOICE OF ECONOMIC ORGANISATION

While business networks are an important topic in the management literature, they are not an integrated part of the mainstream economic theories of business or business investment. Therefore, there is a need to integrate these concepts and views of business networks with a more formal theory of economic organisation. Such a conceptualisation is attempted in this section.

6.1.1. Networks as an institutional form

Economic activities involve two integrated configurations: technological configuration and governance configuration. The first configuration exhibits an industrial logic of interconnected activities and resources. In terms of economic organisation, one of the most important aspects of technological configuration is related to the spatial distribution of resources, products, as well as productions. The second configuration relates to the institutional approach to the first configuration. For convenience, we first sketch the second configuration and construct a model of 'spaceless' economic organisation without considering the first configuration. Then we will bring the technological configuration back into the model in Section 6.2.

Economic organisation involves methods of organisation and economic institutions that use those methods. Mainstream economic theory deals with this subject mainly under two sets of conceptions, namely, price and hierarchy, and the market and the firm (Hennart, 1993a). Following Williamson's (1975) conception of equating hierarchy with the firm, most existing theories treat markets and hierarchies, and therefore the market and the firm, as two alternative forms for organising economic activities. It is basically held that the market uses the price system to organise transactions between firms while each firm organises its internal activities via hierarchy.

It is further held that market-based transactions will be most efficient in organising exchanges when the market is perfect. When the market is perfect, price signals operate in a low-cost manner to transmit information about costs of production and distribution and about the value of resources in alternative uses. In other words, in a perfect market it is the price mechanism, a function of the supply and demand, that organises the economy. Here, firms in the neoclassical microeconomic theory are merely production units that result from demand for a product and from the economies of scale needed to produce that product efficiently. In the market, firms are faceless, 'sharp in' by clear agreement and 'sharp out' by clear performance; and the boundaries between 'in' and 'out' at the beginning and 'in' and 'out' at the end, are clear (MacNeil, 1974, p.750).

However, where the market is not perfect, the costs of organising and monitoring market transactions are quite high. Unfortunately, contrary to what neoclassical theory presumes, market imperfection is the norm and perfect markets are rare exceptions. First, the quality of competition cannot be maintained where a transaction requires investment in assets specific to the deal. The parties are then stuck with each other and the discipline of competition is lost. Secondly, a transaction becomes more complex where the exchange of information and knowledge is involved. Information asymmetry between the transaction parties and difficulties in describing the trading object may hinder proper monitoring of the transaction. Thirdly, it is difficult to satisfactorily specify a contract term when the future becomes unpredictable.

When two parties to a transaction are within the same firm, that is, under common governance of hierarchy based on common ownership, difficulties stemming from market imperfections can be overcome and therefore transaction costs due to the existence of market imperfections can be avoided. This occurs for two reasons. First, by bringing assets specific to each party to the transaction under common ownership, the firm is able to provide a central contracting agency for the multitude of resource owners (of labour and capital) to define precisely the products, process and task. Secondly, common ownership also enables the firm to centralise the monitoring function which is needed to prevent shirking and to maintain quality.

The property of the above two types of transactions has been extensively explored by economists. Coase's 'The Nature of the Firm' (Coase, 1937) and Williamson's 'Market and Hierarchies' (Williamson, 1975) are classic works in this respect. Such abstracting is very important to capture the basic characteristics of the modern economy. However, it ignores the transactions between these two alternative forms of organisation. In the real world, a significant portion of economic activity, or in Hennart's (1993b) words, a 'swollen middle', is organised outside the firm but does not fit into the market either. For example, hierarchical forms of corporate governance have to an increasing extent been complemented by, and in some cases replaced by, a variety of inter-firm cooperative agreements in the leading market economies in recent years. Obviously, it is quite difficult, if not impossible, to label inter-firm relationships such as strategic alliances between competitors as a form of organisation of market or hierarchy. In fact, Williamson (1991) has noticed the limitation of such understanding and posited an organisational category between firms and markets, which he calls the *hybrid*, and in which he deposits those cases that do not fit into either the market or the firm.

But if we go a step further, three interesting features of activities lying between the market and the firm, that is, the so-called *hybrid*, can be revealed. First, these activities are organised via a mode which incorporates both price and hierarchy instead of one or the other. The reason is simple: the organisation of these activities stretches over the market characterised as 'sharp in and sharp out' via the price system and over the firm characterised as hierarchy. In other words, as they are organised neither entirely in the market nor entirely within the firm, their method of organisation must be some kind of hybrid of price and hierarchy corresponding to the market and the firm. The fusion of price and hierarchy may vary for different activities and under different conditions. While an activity may mainly rely on a price mechanism complemented by a weak role for hierarchy, another activity may rely heavily on hierarchy complemented by a limited role for price. Theoretically, if *a* is the market transaction representing the incorporation of the entire price mechanism and no hierarchy and *b* the transaction within the firm representing no price mechanism and the entire hierarchy, these activities are located in the area (*a*, *b*) in terms of the mode of their organisation. Here, *a* (market) and *b* (firm) are seen as poles in a continuum for the distribution of all economic activity (Figure 6.1).

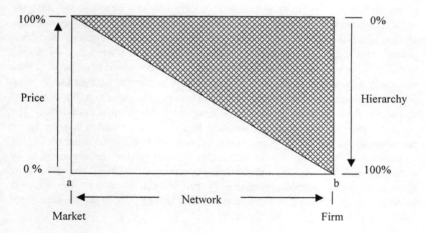

Figure 6.1 Modes and institutions in economic organisation

Secondly, the organisation of the hybrid activities involves at least two firms on a basis other than a spot basis. The reason is that where a part of any hybrid activity is organised outside a firm, there must be another firm(s) to join in the activity. However, for the same reason which leads to integrating functions within the firm explained in transaction theory, the remaining part lying within the firm implies that the firm has 'longer' arrangements, such as investment in specialised assets, in the relations with its counterpart(s). In the meantime, the counterpart(s) has behaved in the same way (but possibly to a different degree) in the activity. Therefore, a particular interlocked relationship between the involved firms has come into being. The number of relationships will increase as the firm engages in more hybrid activities with more counterparts. This leads to the formation of external networks around the hub firm.

Thirdly, the organisation of the hybrid activities reshapes the boundaries of the firm. Here we suggest that the firm has two boundaries, namely, an economic boundary and a governance boundary. While the economic boundary is derived from ownership and leads to the position of a firm in relation to other firms, the governance boundary is shaped by the internal hierarchy of a firm. In the classic market, these two boundaries coincide with each other. There, each firm minds its own business and transacts with others on a spot basis for its own interests. However, this is most likely not to be the case for hybrid activities. For these kinds of activities, the involved firms are interlocked. One of the basic reasons for such an interlocked relationship lies in the institutionalised context in reality: only a range of specific options and an array of specific economic organisations are present. Therefore, though participants in market economies reach decisions based on rational means and calculations of interests, 'in any given institutional environment, economic organisations attempt to dictate the terms of exchange, and those in charge of these organisations, if they have the ability, will quickly alter their organisational structure to achieve greater market power' (Hamilton and Feenstra, 1997, pp.63-4). The asymmetry of ability between firms will result in changes in these firms' economic boundaries. Those that own advantageous assets will move their economic boundaries forward from their governance boundaries. Correspondingly, the economic boundaries of the weak firms will be pushed back from their governance boundaries. The overlap between one firm's economic boundary and another's governance boundary forms the ties, links and bonds between firms in business networks.

It follows that there are in fact three institutions for the organisation of economic activity, namely, the market, the network and the firm. While the market organises economic activity by price mechanism and the firm via hierarchy, the network organises economic activity through a mechanism involving a blend of price and hierarchy.

6.1.2. Choice of economic organisation

When the network is acknowledged as an institution for organising economic activity, the firm has three basic choices regarding the organisation of economic activity: through the market, within the firm, or via the network. The decision about choices can be made by calculating the relevant Total Costs[1] or Total Benefits associated with the alternative organisations. Mainstream theory approaches the choice of activity organisation mainly via cost calculation. We also follow suit.

A different organisation of activity incurs different costs. Assume a firm needs the output of an activity. If the activity is totally organised by itself, it will incur an Internal Cost I. If the firm buys the output of the activity from an outsider supplier, the firm will incur an External Cost (EP) (the price charged by the supplier) plus a Transaction Cost (TC), which comprise the Total External Cost (S), that is, $S = EP + TC$. However, if the firm chooses the method of network organisation, the firm will incur a Network Cost (N) for the networked activity, where:

$$N = \alpha I^{\beta} + (1 - \alpha)(EP + TC)\gamma \qquad (6.1)$$

Here α ($0 < \alpha < 1$) is the proportion of the activity which is carried out by the firm, and $1-\alpha$ is the remaining proportion of the activity which is carried out by the outside partner(s). β ($0 < \beta \leq 1$) and γ ($0 < \gamma \leq 1$) capture the cost-saving effects of networking for the hub firm and its partner firm(s) respectively. For simplicity, we suppose that networking has the same cost-saving effect on both the external supply price and the transaction cost involved, therefore:

$$N = \alpha I^{\beta} + (1 - \alpha) S\gamma \qquad . \qquad (6.2)$$

The choice for network-organising the activity concerned would occur under the following condition:

$$\begin{cases} \alpha I^{\beta} + (1-\alpha)S^{\gamma} < I \\ \alpha I^{\beta} + (1-\alpha)S^{\gamma} < S \end{cases} \qquad (6.3)$$

Obviously, whether or not to choose a network organisation mainly depends on whether the network organisation can achieve sufficient cost-saving effects for the participants in the networking. There are the following conditions:

- Where the Internal Cost is larger than the Total External Cost, that is, $I > S$, the network organisation of the activity would be a beneficial choice for the firm if $\beta < \dfrac{\ln S}{\ln I}$ and/or $\gamma < \dfrac{\ln(S - \alpha I) - \ln(1 - \alpha)}{\ln S}$. This implies that even if $\beta = 1$, which means that the networking has no positive effect on the reduction of the hub firm's internal cost for the proportion of the activity carried out by itself, so long as the networking can have a sufficient cost-saving effect, that is, $\gamma < \dfrac{\ln(S - \alpha I) - \ln(1 - \alpha)}{\ln S}$, for the reduction of the partner's supply price and transaction cost, networking will remain an economic choice for the hub firm.

- Where the Internal Cost is equal to the Total External Cost, that is, $I = S$, the network organisation of the activity would be a beneficial choice for the firm if $\beta < 1$ and/or $\gamma < 1$. In particular, even if networking has no effect on the reduction in the firm's internal cost, that is, $\beta = 1$, so long as networking can reduce the partner's supply price and transaction cost to a level which is lower than I, networking will remain an economic choice for the hub firm.

- Where the Internal Cost is smaller than the Total External Cost, that is, $I < S$, the network organisation of the activity would be a beneficial choice for the firm if $\beta < \dfrac{\ln[I - (1 - \alpha)S] - \ln\alpha}{\ln I}$ and/or $\gamma < \dfrac{\ln I}{\ln S}$. In particular, even if networking does not have a cost-saving effect for the hub firm, that is, $\beta = 1$, the hub firm would also be able to benefit from networking if such networking can give the partner firm a cost-reduction effect to the level $\gamma < \dfrac{\ln I}{\ln S}$.

These terms are summarised in Table 6.1.

Table 6.1 Ranges of values of β and γ for the choice of networking*

	Value of β		Value of γ
$I > S$	$\beta < \dfrac{\ln S}{\ln I}$	and/or	$\gamma < \dfrac{\ln(S - \alpha I) - \ln(1 - \alpha)}{\ln S}$
$I = S$	$\beta < 1$	and/or	$\gamma < 1$
$I < S$	$\beta < \dfrac{\ln[I - (1 - \alpha)S] - \ln\alpha}{\ln I}$	and/or	$\gamma < \dfrac{\ln I}{\ln S}$

Note: Refer to the appendix to this chapter for the calculations.

As the effective domains of β and γ for the choice of networking are inverse functions of S, I and α, the ranges of the values of these three variables affect the possible effective domains of β and γ. Therefore from the above discussion we can also draw the following corollaries regarding the range of values of β and γ:

- When the Internal Cost I is larger than the Total External Cost S, the larger $I - S$ is, the stronger are the cost-saving effects required for both the hub and partner firms for the choice of networking; the smaller $I - S$ is, the weaker the cost-saving effects required for the choice of networking. In the meantime, the larger the proportion of the activity carried out by the hub firm, the larger is the cost-saving effect required for the partner firm for the choice of networking; the smaller the proportion of the activity carried out by the hub firm, the smaller is the cost-saving effect required for the partner firm for the choice of networking.

- When the Internal Cost I is smaller than the Total External Cost S, the larger $S - I$ is, the stronger are the cost-saving effects required for both the hub and the partner firms for the choice of networking; the smaller the $S - I$ is, the weaker are the cost-saving effects required for the choice of networking. In the meantime, the larger the proportion of the activity carried out by the hub firm, the smaller is the cost-saving effect required for the hub firm for the choice of networking; the smaller the proportion of the activity carried out by the hub firm, the larger is the cost-saving effect required for the hub firm for the choice of networking.

The terms of the corollaries are summarised in Table 6.2 and an example of the cost structure is shown in Figure 6.2.

Table 6.2 Changing trends of β and γ in Table 6.1

		β	γ
When $I > S$	if $(I-S)\uparrow$	$\downarrow$	$\downarrow$ (for $\alpha < S/I$)
	if $(I-S)\to 0$	$\to 1$	$\to 1$
	$\alpha\uparrow$		$\downarrow$
	$\alpha\downarrow$		$\to 1$
When $I < S$	if $(S-I)\uparrow$	$\downarrow$	$\downarrow$
	if $(S-I)\to 0$	$\to 1$	$\to 1$
	$\alpha\uparrow$	$\to 1$	
	$\alpha\downarrow$	$\downarrow$ (for $\alpha > 1 - I/S$)	

6.1.3. Rationales for engaging in networking

Whether a firm chooses to engage in networking to organise an activity rather than undertaking that activity totally within the firm or obtaining the output of that activity solely in the classic market, it essentially depends on whether networking can bring about positive cost-reduction effects for the firm. Networking can realise cost reductions in two ways, that is, through reducing governance costs and saving transaction costs, all of which stem from the overlap of economic and governance boundaries between firms.

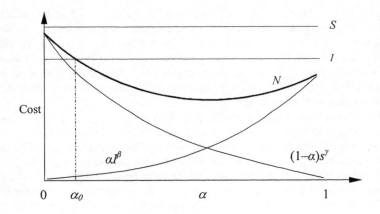

Note: Network has cost-saving effects when $\alpha > \alpha_0$

Figure 6.2 Structure of costs (Case of S > I)

One of the most noticeable benefits of networking is the overlapping of the economic and governance boundaries of the firms involved, which forms a good environment for more effective transaction and transfer of information between firms. The interlocked relationship between two firms helps ease transactions between them, therefore bringing the transaction cost down. Information flows occur between people rather than the plants themselves (Casson and Cox, 1997). Boundary overlapping can: (i) maximise the number of non-redundant contacts in the network to maximise the yield in structure holes[2] per contact; and (ii) maximise the number of contacts clustered around a limited number of primary contacts (such a structure is ports), and the firm can focus on properly supporting relations with primary contacts (Burt, 1992, pp.67-9). Therefore, the social bonds sustained by networks reduce the cost of both communicating information and assuring its quality. And the consequent reduction in information costs encourages greater sharing of information.

In addition, networking can also help the realisation of economies of scale and/or scope, such as joint research, marketing or production (Contractor and Lorange, 1988; Håkansson and Snehota, 1989). In the era of globalisation and the knowledge-based economy, the accelerating increase of R&D expenditure and the shortening of the technological life span have greatly increased the importance of sharing R&D costs as well as R&D benefits among relevant firms.

In short, the separation of the economic and governance boundaries of the firm in the networked activity creates possibilities of overlapping economic and governance boundaries between firms and forms the rationale for combining the price mechanism and the hierarchy mechanism to save transaction costs and governance costs (Thorelli, 1986; Hennart, 1991).

6.2. FDI AND NETWORKING

6.2.1. Organisation at home and abroad

In the above analysis we did not consider the role of physical factors in economic organisation. These factors can be grouped under the categories of technology and geography. Technology determines what inputs are required and in what proportion to generate a given output, and whether or not this transformation affords economies of scale and scope. Geography represents the spatial distribution of resources which determines the degree of difficulty (and thus the cost) of obtaining the required inputs or marketing the outputs. If a required resource is located in a country other than where the firm is located, transaction costs are likely to be higher. These two groups of factors affect the spatial features of economic activity.

Considering that the market is not universal and homogeneous, but that it consists of different markets at different locations for different resources and products, economic activity can take place in a firm's home country or abroad. As the organisation of economic activity has three institutional choices, that is, solely via the market, through networking or solely within the firm, the firm has six possible choices for the organisation of an activity regarding where and how to carry out this activity (Figure 6.3). The relevant costs for different types of organisation at home and abroad are shown in Table 6.3.

Costs for overseas economic organisations are denoted by adding quotation marks to the corresponding ones at home. This captures the possible difference between each pair of costs due to the following factors:

1. Both natural assets and created assets are geographically scattered, and different distances to the required assets have different transaction costs.
2. The increasing share and importance of created assets in economic activity call for effective organisation to use and get access to them. In the real world, created assets have now replaced natural assets as a dominant factor in economic activity; and the higher the technological intensity of an industry is, the larger the share of created assets in its total input. However, created assets are basically firm specific. Different forms of organisation may have quite different cost effects.
3. Social context, including cultural features and social norms, differs from country to country and has important impacts on economic organisation.
4. Coordination between firms in activities, especially those involving the transfer and use of created assets, becomes very complex and subtle.

Similarly, we denote the cost-saving efficiency coefficients of networking in a foreign country by adding quote marks to the relative ones at home.

The choice among the forms of organisation for an activity can be made by a two-step calculation and comparison. First, the relevant costs of different organisations for home country and foreign country are calculated separately. The calculation and analysis are the same as discussed above. Secondly, the lowest cost organisational form at home and the lowest abroad are selected and a decision is made by choosing the lower cost option between these two.

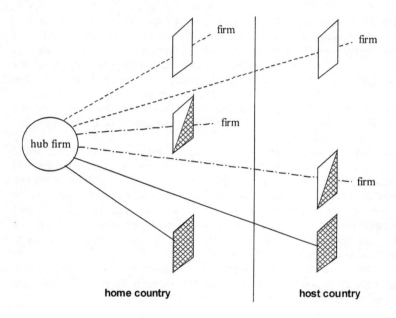

Figure 6.3 Transaction modes and location

Table 6.3 Costs for different types of organisation at home and abroad

Institution	Home country	Foreign country
Market	$S = EP + TC$	$S' = EP' + TC'$
Network	$N = \alpha I^\beta + (1 - \alpha) S^\gamma$	$N' = \alpha I'^\beta + (1 - \alpha) S'^{\gamma'}$
Firm	I	I'

Specifically, the terms for the choice of the network organisation of an activity in a foreign country are:

$$\alpha I'^{\beta'} + (1 - \alpha)S'^{\gamma'} < Min\{I, I', S, S'\} \tag{6.4}$$

By solving this inequality we can obtain the ranges of values of β' and γ' for the choice of location of networked activity.

6.2.2. Foreign direct investment

In the light of the above discussion, FDI can be defined as a form of international economic organisation by using methods ranging from partial to total involvement of hierarchy based on the degree of ownership. Thus FDI leads to an expansion of the investing firm's boundary into the host country and serves as a node, which can be used for further networking.

Therefore, an FDI project is a node (in the case of initial investment) or an improvement of an existing node (in the case of subsequent incremental investment) in the network of the investing firm's global business. This node ties not only the different business activities of the firm but also the firm's business network to the market networks of the host country. So a high quality investment project is one which is able to: (i) tie organically the different activities of the firm so as to improve the firm's strength and thus improve the firm's position in the market; (ii) tie dynamically the firm's business network to the market networks so as to lay a good foundation for the operation and further growth of the firm; and (iii) operate at the minimum possible cost.

If it can be said that FDI is pushed by the internationalisation of commodity chains, the benefits of networking are the driving forces which stimulate firms to go international. The cost-saving effects of FDI can thus be calculated using the framework discussed above.

The motives for FDI vary from one firm to another and between projects. Following Dunning (1992), the existing literature generally classifies the main motivations for FDI as follows:

1. *Labour-seeking*. The motivation here is to utilise the host country's cheaper labour (normally unskilled or semi-skilled labour) to produce relatively cheap finished consumer goods. This motive is captured by the standard Heckscher-Ohlin model of international exchange, which suggests that capital will tend to flow to relatively capital-poor and labour-abundant countries. As differences in relative factor endowments are an important source of differences in comparative advantage, in this type of investment country-specific endowments (capital and labour) are decisive determinants of investment flows. In the meantime, as the products are normally standardised and their process technology is matured and simplified, while the investing firm's marketing skills are relatively important, its firm-specific know-how plays only a minor role in the investment.

2. *Natural resource-extracting*. The motivation for this type of investment is to take advantage of comparative advantages of the home and host countries, so that capital will tend to flow to relatively capital-poor and natural-resource-abundant countries. However, as resource-extracting activities are normally large in scale and relatively capital-technology-intensive in nature, compared with labour-seeking investment, the MNE's firm-specific assets in production are more important in resource-extracting investment.

3. *Component-outsourcing*. This FDI aims at utilising the host country's relatively cheap labour as well as the high productivity of factors in the host country for the MNE's international production network. The products involved are more expensive and their production is more roundabout in nature. This investment cannot be fully captured by the standard Heckscher-Ohlin model and is attracted to countries that possess not only comparative, but also absolute advantages in production.

4. *Horizontal investment in differentiated products*. This investment involves the production of more expensive consumer goods and intermediate goods, such as automobiles, consumer durables, pharmaceuticals, etc. In this investment, whereas low wages alone are not sufficient to attract FDI, sufficient economies of scale in production and distribution and firm-specific assets play very important roles. In this sense, this type of FDI to some degree goes beyond the explanation of traditional Heckscher-Ohlin model.

5. *Service-related investment*. This kind of FDI involves capital accumulation in the usually called non-traded or non-tradable sector of the economy, including business services, construction and financial services. This investment is usually driven by market size and thickness and geared to the domestic market. For foreign investors, the quantity and quality of their firm-specific assets, especially know-hows of various kinds, are essential; this is why most foreign investors in this type of FDI are from developed countries.

6. *Technology seeking*. This type of FDI aims at establishing a channel in the host country to absorb local current and future advanced technology. As the pace of technology advancement is getting quicker and technology plays a more and more important role in competition, how to obtain the most advanced technology becomes a major concern for firms. However, besides patent protection, cultural and geographical distances still hinder technology diffusion internationally. Foreign direct investment on the spot is an effective way to bypass the relative barriers. For foreign investors, the major concern is their technology-assimilating ability and the success of an investment project is most likely to be judged from the point of view of the whole operation of the MNE group.

Considering the context of the networks, this classification has not told the whole story. As in the modern economy, firms operate through networks and the establishment and maintenance of network relationships are very important for business activities. FDI is motivated by not only the obtaining or using of particular factors, nor the production of particular products or services, but also by deeper considerations about the operation of the firm's business networks. In business networks, the most important issues for a firm are: (i) to take advantage of networks in resource exchange and sharing; (ii) to enforce transactions via the market by filling the gap between the minimum enforceable performance and a quality performance; and (iii) to improve the firm's position in the networks. Therefore motivations for FDI can be better classified as follows below.

6.2.2.1. FDI for resource exchange

The motivation for resource exchange includes (from the above list) motivations (1), (2), (3), (6) and part of motivations (4) and (5) which are recognised in the existing literature, as noted above. Here resources are defined in the network perspective and therefore in a much broader sense. Resources in this sense include tangible and intangible resources. Tangible resources include real physical factors such as natural resources, labour (in its basic sense), components and capital, whereas knowledge at different levels of abstraction, such as knowledge of the technical, administrative or logistical characteristics of a partner, information about technological development in a specific field in the host country, and a good industrial relationship are examples of intangible resources. Time as a resource, on the other hand, has received little attention in the economic analysis of FDI. However, in the financial analysis of FDI, time is a decisive factor in the projecting and selection of FDI projects. In an era of accelerating technological advances, the weight of time in business choices is ever growing. This is one of the reasons why inter-firm strategic alliances have become worthwhile nowadays: to gain time by cooperating with competitors via giving up some other resources at the cost of reducing internal integration and control.

Conventional theory generally puts emphasis on the acquisition of tangible resources *in* the host country and the transferring *to* the host country of the investing firm's intangible assets (referred as ownership advantage in conventional theory) either to overcome disadvantages or to obtain quasi-rent there. The acquisition of intangible resources in the host country is no less important in a network perspective. This is not only because of the important role of intangible assets in the knowledge-led economy, but also because of the importance of positive inter-firm relationships which are path-dependent and need long-term relationship-specific investment as well as relationship-development investment (Easton and Araujo, 1994).

6.2.2.2. FDI for enforcing transactions via market

As stated above, there is a gap between the minimum enforceable performance and quality performance. The impacts of this gap on the firm's business will be magnified by the three characteristics of the transactions involved, namely, frequency, uncertainty and asset specificity. If any of these characteristics is high, the firm is likely to be at bay if it has not applied some means to fill the gap. Specifically, high frequency implies the firm's circulating process is highly attached to its partner's operation and exchange behaviour. Therefore the firm's circulating process will face a slowdown or suspension risk when changes occur in its partner's exchange behaviour and operation. Similarly, high asset specificity implies that the transaction assets are non-tradable to a significant degree; the firm will be exposed to opportunistic behaviour as well as poor management. In the meantime, uncertainty, which can result from various institutional events and/or competition behaviour, will widen the gap instead of reducing it.

One of the important approaches to reduce the gap between minimum enforceable performance and quality performance is to establish a node in the place closest to the partner in the network or to improve the existing node in the network where the partner is located. The reason for this effect is the fact that such a node will benefit the firm in information obtaining and network positioning. When the firm has established such a node in the market networks, it can obtain more information at a quicker speed and with more accuracy in content, for the firm is now able to contact the partner as well as the partner's networks more directly.[3] This is most likely to increase the adaptive and innovative capacity for the firm as well as its partner. As information increases in volume, the firm is able to select investment options that are less risky (Gilroy, 1993, p.110). In the meantime, the direct presence of the firm in the network where the partner is situated increases the firm's network position relative to its partner. This reduces the possibility of contract violation by the partner.

FDI for enforcing transactions via the market aims at improving the performance of transactions where gaps between the minimum enforceable performance and a quality performance are relatively large. This kind of investment mainly occurs in these conditions. First, transactions for the investing firm are large in volume and/or important for its business and reducing the uncertainty in the transaction is one of the first priorities on the management agenda. The firm can either expand its boundary by FDI to cover overseas production or distribution of products previously transacted via the market or just set up a 'small' node in the foreign market to tighten its relationships with partners in the transactions. Secondly, external transactions are carried out in economies dominated by networks.

6.2.2.3. FDI for improving the firm's position in networks
Foreign direct investment aimed at improving the investing firm's position in networks is to increase the firm's power in the networks so as to enable the firm to get access to external resources in foreign countries on more favourable terms. The rationale behind this is that business networks rely on strongly normative social bonds and operate in a hierarchy of some kind (see below). By investing abroad, a firm establishes and develops positions in relation to its counterparts in foreign networks.

According to Hamilton and Feenstra (1997, pp.69-72), there are two types of network hierarchies, that is, vertically controlled networks and horizontally controlled hierarchies. Vertically controlled networks are a feature of modern economies whereby extensive networks of legally independent firms (business groups) are controlled by some core firms upon systems of authority. The core firms are very large companies dominating the markets for intermediate inputs, labour-intensive operations and services. They have positions of considerable economic power *vis-à-vis* thousands of small- and medium-sized firms that supply goods and services to them.[4] Horizontally controlled networks are formed based on the same associational (organisational) rules aimed at defining the terms of doing business and the quality of products and services. Inside horizontally controlled networks, associational rules do not facilitate individual strategies leading to vertical and horizontal integration, for transaction rules are defined collectively and monopolistic strategies threaten the groups themselves[5] (Hamilton and Feenstra, 1997, p.72). While these two types of network hierarchies are different in terms of business organisation, they are similar in one respect – long-term close relationships between firms are essential for the functioning of networks as well as for the firms involved.

Foreign direct investment into either vertically controlled networks or horizontally controlled networks has two main meanings for the investing firm in terms of the perspective of improving its position in the networks. First, the firm becomes an insider in the networks of the host country and will not be treated as an outsider thereafter. Compared with those non-involved firms which can only receive lower priority from firms in the network, an insider will be given a higher priority (Hertz, 1992, p.117). Secondly, when a firm establishes or improves its position in one network, its positions in other networks will be improved for two reasons: (i) it can now get access to more resources; and (ii) it is given more opportunities to disperse risk among the participants in a network value system when using contractual arrangements.

6.2.3. Types of Foreign Direct Investment

When foreign direct investment is viewed as a sequential process with various motivations as described above, it can be classified into three basic types: network-stretching FDI, network-widening FDI, and network-integrating FDI.

6.2.3.1. Network-stretching FDI
Network stretching FDI is the investing firm's first-round initial investment in a foreign country. Through this investment, the investing firm has set up its first ownership-based node in that country and this node couples the firm's business network with networks in the foreign country. As foreign direct investment is a sequential process stemming from the advantages of flexibility of a multinational system (Kogut, 1983) and having operational consequences for the firm in the future, network-stretching FDI is crucial for the development of the investing firm's networks.

From a network perspective, a firm's FDI is determined by the internationalisation (or globalisation) of both the market of the industry and the firm itself. The former reflects the scope and intensity of international division and cooperation in that industry. And the latter reflects the degree of international growth of the firm.

The internationalisation of the market of an industry can be captured in the framework of global commodity chains. Global commodity chains, according to Gereffi, are rooted in transnational production systems that give rise to particular patterns of coordinated international trade. Commodity chains have three main dimensions: an input-output structure (a set of production units of different sizes linked together in a sequence of value-adding economic activities); territoriality (spatial dispersion or concentration of production and marketing networks, comprising enterprises of different sizes and types); and a governance structure (authority and power relationships that determine how financial, material and human resources are allocated and flow within a chain) (Gereffi, 1994a, pp.96-7).

> A 'production system' links the economic activities of firms to technological and organisational networks that permit companies to develop, manufacture and market specific commodities. In the transnational production systems that characterise global capitalism, economic activity is not only international in scope; it is also global in its organisation. While 'internationalisation' refers simply to the geographical spread of economic activities across national boundaries, 'globalisation' implies a degree of functional integration between these internationally dispersed activities. The requisite administrative coordination is carried out by diverse corporate actors in centralised as well as decentralised economic structures. (Gereffi, 1994b, p.215)

Similarly, the internationalisation of a firm is also rooted in the system of the industry in which it is situated and implies corresponding changes in the internal organisation of the firm's business activity. Welch and Luostrarinen (1988) suggest that the internationalisation of a firm has four dimensions: (i) *how* to engage in overseas business; (ii) *what* content of products to market overseas; (iii) *where* the market is; and (iv) the *capacity* of the internal organisation.

Therefore, good network-stretching FDI connects a firm's activity with the international industrial system in those places where useful bits of information are likely to be available and provides reliable flows of information to and from those places. In practice such places should: (i) maximise the number of non-redundant contacts in the network to maximise the yield in structure holes per contact; and (ii) maximise the number of contacts clustered around a limited number of primary contacts (such a structure is ports), and the firm can focus on properly supporting relations with primary contacts (Burt, 1992, pp.67-9).

Such places vary across firms, industries, and markets with different hierarchies. The choice is mainly a function of the following variables.

First, there are the firm's business activities which are about to be internationalised via foreign direct investment. For a firm, its business activities can be divided into primary activities and supporting activities. Primary activities are the production and marketing of physical products or services. These activities are the basic activities of the firm and are aided by supporting activities such as human resource management and procurement. Together they form the value chain, which runs through the firm and links to other firms. Value will be created everywhere close to these activities (Porter, 1986). Therefore a firm has to locate different activities in the most favourable places so as to maximise or secure the maximisation of the value. Most foreign direct investment is used to expand the basic product line internationally, leaving the operation of minor product lines and support activities more open to the market. For the basic product line embodies the firm's most competitive advantages. Such competitive advantages are most valuable to the firm and form the competitive basis for improving or maintaining the firm's position in relation to its competitors in the market. However, it may be better for a firm to undertake FDI involving minor product lines or some part of its supporting activities for various reasons. One reason may be that the main product line is very developed; hence FDI in this product may overexpose the firm. Also if the firm has limited international business experience, it could gain experience through FDI involving minor activities.

Secondly, features of the global commodity chain in which the investing firm is situated should be considered. According to Gereffi (1994b), there are two types of commodity chains, namely, producer-driven or demand-creating commodity chains and buyer-driven or demand-responsive commodity chains. Producer-driven chains refer to those industries in which large, usually transnational, corporations play key roles in coordinating global production systems. They are found most often in capital- and technology-intensive industries, such as automobiles, computers, aircrafts and electrical machinery. The main companies control the entire production and distribution process. Subcontracting of components involving labour-intensive processes is carried out around the main companies. Buyer-driven commodity chains refer to industries in which large retailers and trading companies play the central role in shaping decentralised production networks. This type of commodity chain prevails in industries such as garments, footwear, toys and household goods. Here the organisers of the commodity chains are not giant manufacturers, rather branded mass merchandisers. Many commodity chains are not typically producer-driven or buyer-driven, rather they lie in between these two extremes. In the globalising world economy, the organisation of a commodity chain is not the legally defined, clearly bounded corporation, rather it is defined through loosely defined networks of firms sharing some form of ownership or asset control. And the configuration of the commodity chains overlaps with some types of hierarchical configuration of ownership and asset-control-linked networks of firms (Hamilton and Waters, 1995, p.91). Such configurations shape firms' foreign direct investment. In the first place, firms as 'drivers' (driving producers or driving merchandisers) in commodity chains will differ from driven firms in FDI. While FDI from drivers is likely to penetrate the clusters of producers or distributors to establish themselves in local networks, FDI from driven firms would go in the direction of fastening ties with the drivers. In the second place, firms in vertically controlled network hierarchies would emphasise improving the division and resource exchange in the network when undertaking FDI, while firms in horizontally controlled network hierarchies are likely to focus on expanding information flows and rapid response when undertaking FDI.

Therefore, in the network perspective, decisions are made from the perspective of improving the firm's relationships and positions in market networks. The following factors are important in this regard:

- the actors (that is, customers, suppliers, competitors or public agencies) and the important relationships which are decisive in the target market;
- the relative positions of the actors in the network;
- the relationships of the focal firm to actors in the potential country market; and
- the way that resources of other actors can be mobilised in support of market entry.

6.2.3.2. Network-Expanding FDI

Network-expanding FDI is the subsequent incremental investment which aims at improving the position of the node established by previous FDI. Specifically, this type of FDI normally takes place in the following situations:

1. *Expanding the existing project to the scale required by economies of scale or optimum network position.* Sometimes due to environmental risk or lack of international business, the initial investment might have been made on a smaller scale. When the business environment has improved or the firm has gained experience in international business through learning by doing, the firm now seeks to expand its business in the host country. Another case is where the established node is not large enough to establish the investing firm in the host country's network, therefore the exchange of information and other resources are limited and the terms for transactions via market are not very favourable.
2. *Undertaking other FDI projects.* These projects are likely to differ in location, product line, ownership structure or legal identity. However, they all serve the objective of improving the investing firm's position in the host country's networks. For host countries with a large market or proximity to large markets, such investment is the normal case and very important for improving the investing firm's position.
3. *Establishing a node in a third country by FDI from the existing node.* Such FDI is a first-round initial investment for the investing firm but only a second-round investment for the parent firm.

Through network expansion FDI, a firm can gain an improved position in overseas networks. In order to obtain efficiency and effectiveness, such investment should be made in places with the largest market thickness.

6.2.3.3. Network-integrating FDI

Network globalisation FDI is the highest level of foreign direct investment for forming and improving a firm's global business networks. The multinational corporation itself is an inter-organisational network formed around a headquarters and the focal units.[6] The advantages of such an internationalised inter-organisational network lie in: (i) the ability to arbitrage institutional restrictions, for example, tax codes, antitrust provisions, financial limitations, and even national security; (ii) the ability to capture externalities in information; and (iii) the ability to realise joint production economies occurring in both marketing and manufacturing (Kogut, 1983). However, because of the large physical and cultural distances between the owned and the owning units, the link between different units within the multinational corporation is particularly weak (Ghoshal and Bartlett, 1993, p.82). Therefore, some kind of FDI is needed to improve the functioning of the internal inter-organisational network within the MNE and to improve the contacts between the MNE network and market networks.

FDI can be undertaken to establish necessary ownership integration while keeping a necessary degree of coordination integration. The requirement for ownership integration varies across industries, from the lowest (activities within Marshallian district) to the highest (Chandlerian firms). Similar situations exist in coordination integration.[7] For firms in industries with a high ownership integration requirement, the establishment of wholly owned or majority owned overseas subsidiaries might be of vital importance. However, for firms in industries with a high coordination requirement but low ownership integration requirement, relationship-specific investment and relationship-development investment might be crucial.[8]

6.3. CONCLUDING REMARKS

This chapter has developed a network model of foreign direct investment by integrating network ideas from business analysis with those of economic organisation. In this model, FDI is defined as a form of international economic organisation using methods ranging from partly to wholly-owned involvement of hierarchy based on ownership. It leads to the expansion of the investing firm's boundary into the host country and the formation of a node there. This node can be used for further networking.

This model acknowledges that the network, along with the market and the firm, is an institution for economic organisation. While the market uses the price system to organise transactions between firms and the firm organises internal activities via hierarchy, the network organises activities across the market and the firm by using a blend of price and hierarchy. Through the network, a certain kind of interlocked relationship between the firms concerned is formed due to the overlapping of economic and governance boundaries between these firms.

This leads to the formation of external networks around the hub firm. On the other hand, the heterogeneity of market and the industrial logic of interconnected activities and resources are the determinants of where to organise an economic activity. FDI is the case in which economic organisation takes place in the host country by using hierarchy alone or by using a blend of hierarchy and price.

It follows that FDI essentially depends on the proper functioning of market economic elements, including price and hierarchy. As FDI leads to the formation of international networks for the investing firm and the network has the function of resource exchanges and information flows, FDI can be used not only to exploit the firm's assets, but also to obtain strategic resources and important information. In this respect, this model differs from most of the mainstream models and paradigms, which often stress the supply side of FDI (that is, asset exploitation) but ignore the demand side (that is, resource seeking).

NOTES

1. Including sunk costs.
2. According to Burt (1992, p.65), a structure hole is the separation between non-redundant contacts. Non-redundant contacts are connected by a structure hole and a structure hole is a relationship of non-redundancy between two contacts. As a result of the hole between them, the two contacts provide network benefits that are in some degree additive rather than overlapping.
3. According to Burt, information benefits occur in three forms: access, timing and referrals. Access refers to receiving a valuable piece of information and knowing who can use it. Given a limit to the volume of information that anyone can process, the network becomes an important screening device. In terms of timing, personal contacts can give a person early access to information. When a person has insider contacts in another group, the insiders can promote that person's interests in decision making process within that group (Burt, 1992).
4. Typical giants dominating network hierarchies are Japanese business groups (keiretsu): large firms at the top of the hierarchy are mutually owned through overlapping shareholding (Aoki, 1988, 1990). A similar hierarchical network structure has also developed in the German economy (Orrù, 1993).
5. In modern economies, stock markets and commodities exchanges can be seen as typical horizontally controlled networks. They represent organisationally encompassed firms, the brokerage houses with seats on the exchange that work under a common set of rules defining the terms of trade and the conditions of entry (Abolafia, 1984). Household-based economies established by overseas Chinese and the Taiwanese economy are another example.
6. Some scholars hold that, parallel to the external network, a firm is also a network of similar attributes, as organisation within a firm is no less a contractual matter than organisation through markets, and a 'firm' is nothing more than a particular dense intersection of contracts (Cheung, 1983). We admit the network attributes of firms but stress the production process aspect rather than the legal aspect.
7. For details on the degree of ownership integration and the degree of coordination integration, see Robertson and Langlois (1995).
8. Williamson holds that investment in transaction-specific assets renders the adapting firm vulnerable to opportunistic behaviour by its counterpart (Williamson, 1985). Easton and Araujo (1994) have expanded Williamson's concept and proposed a hierarchy of investments within relationships: (1) minimal investment; (2) relationship-specific investment; (3) relationship-development investment; (4) secondary investment; and (5) marketing and market investment.

APPENDIX

Specification of the model:

The determination of the range of value for β when $I > S$:

$$\begin{cases} \alpha I^{\beta} + (1-\alpha)S^{\gamma} < I \\ \alpha I^{\beta} + (1-\alpha)S^{\gamma} < S \end{cases}$$

Assume $I > S$, then the conditions for networking would be

$$\alpha I^{\beta} + (1-\alpha)S^{\gamma} < S.$$

Let γ be 1; solve the above inequality by substituting γ with 1, then:

$$\alpha I^{\beta} + S - \alpha S < S$$
$$I^{\beta} < S$$
$$\beta < \frac{\ln S}{\ln I}$$

With the same method, we can obtain all the relevant values for γ and β.

PART III

China's Outward FDI: A Descriptive Analysis

INTRODUCTION

From the analysis in Chapter 4 we conclude that the existing mainstream theory of foreign direct investment is inadequate for explaining the phenomenon of the rapid expansion of China's outward direct investment. Therefore, an alternative paradigm of FDI, namely the network model, has been developed in Chapter 6. This model suggests that FDI is a form of international economic organisation which involves a hierarchy based on ownership, and which depends on both forms of the market system, namely, exchange and hierarchy. As FDI leads to the formation of international networks for the investing firm and the networks perform the function of resource exchange and information flows, FDI can be used not only to exploit the firm's assets, but also to obtain strategic resources and information.

Against this background, this part investigates the rationale underlying China's outward FDI in the framework of the advanced model. As outward FDI by Chinese firms has a very short history, comprehensive data, especially on industrial composition and overseas subsidiaries' operations, are not yet available. This rules out the possibility of more specific testing with the aid of formal econometric analysis. Accordingly, the analysis in this case is basically of descriptive nature.

7. Economic Transition and Outward FDI

The model developed in the previous chapter suggests that FDI is a form of organising economic activity internationally and essentially depends on the proper functioning of market economic elements, including price and hierarchy. In the framework of that model, this chapter analyses the determination, in the respect of governance configuration, of China's outbound FDI in the context of economic organisation in China.

7.1. ECONOMIC ORGANISATION IN THE MAOIST ECONOMIC SYSTEM

7.1.1. Microeconomic environment

It is not until the beginning of the economic reforms in late 1978 that China began to engage in international direct investment in a normal sense. For three decades before the reform, China had a planned economy with a quasi-autarky in the 1950s and near-autarky from the 1960s to mid 1970s.

Domestically, after the conversion of private and foreign enterprises into state-owned enterprises by 1953, central planning and 'public ownership' dominated the national economy. Mandatory central planning covered not only important microeconomic issues such as the aggregate investment ratio and regional development but also basic operational activities such as financing, production, sourcing and sales. Activities of the so-called collective enterprises and communes (agricultural units) were also highly controlled by central planning bodies through integrated political networks of top to bottom administration and the Communist Party systems, though collective enterprises and communes were theoretically and politically not state-owned. As central planning covered both macro and microeconomic activities, market mechanisms were generally excluded from the functioning of the economy. In the meantime, the establishment of public ownership was taken as a central task and state ownership was emphasised as the highest form of public ownership. The more important an activity was, the more rigorously state ownership was established and advantageous resources were intensively injected. As a result, state-owned enterprises, especially the large ones, enjoyed being allocated the most advantageous resources but had the least freedom to operate.

Table 7.1 China's economic development stages and activities (1949-80)

Period	Activity
Economic rehabilitation (1949-52)	Postponing socialisation of industry Land reform in the agricultural sector
The First Five-Year Plan (1953-57)	Adopting the planned economy model of the Soviet Union Collectivisation of agriculture Socialist transforming of industry
The Second Five-Year Plan (1958-62)	The Great Leap Forward of Production The People's Commune Movement The withdrawal of Soviet assistance The rise of Liu Shaoqi to power
Economic readjustment (1963-65)	The agriculture-first policy Changes in the commune system Changes in industry management
The Third Five-Year Plan (1966-70)	Power struggle between Mao Zedong and Liu Shaoqi Phase I of the Cultural Revolution
The Fourth Five-Year Plan (1971-75)	Formulation of the Four Modernisations The open-door policy (improving relationships with the United States and Japan) Phase II of the Cultural Revolution The Gang of Four
The Fifth Five-Year Plan (1976-80)	The rise of Hua Guofeng to power The Ten-Year Economic Development Plan The Three-Year Adjustment Plan The Third Plenum of the Eleventh CCP Central Committee The rise of Deng Xiaoping to power

Source: Liou (1998), p.13.

Internationally, China adopted the principle of self-reliance in its foreign economic relations, and such relations were politically coloured and tuned. First, foreign economic relations were subjected to political and ideological needs and often characterised as 'leaning to one side'.[1] In the 1950s, China excluded (or was excluded from[2]) foreign economic relations with Western countries whilst maintaining certain dependent economic relations with the Soviet bloc. For over a decade from the 1960s to mid 1970s, when Sino-Soviet relations turned sour after the Soviets had withdrawn their assistance while the United States still maintained an economic embargo against China, China opposed their international 'revisionism' and 'imperialism' respectively and 'self-reliance' (*Zili Gengsheng*) became an important principle for China in developing its limited foreign economic relationships with other countries. The third world became the main focus of these initiatives, while the 'second world' – industrialised countries excluding the United States – remained secondary.

Secondly, foreign economic relations were generally confined to foreign trade, and higher-level international economic activities, such as foreign direct investment, were basically proscribed. The formal ban on inward FDI was lifted in 1972 in the wake of the visit to China of US President Richard Nixon. This opened the door for the resumption of diplomatic relations with some major industrialised countries. However, the severity of restrictions on foreign investment remained unchanged.

Thirdly, foreign trade was permitted to the extent that imports were restricted to meeting shortages in domestic production, while exports were only a means to raise the foreign currency required to pay for imports. As a result, China's share in the total value of world trade decreased from 1.4 per cent in the 1950s to 1.1 per cent in the 1960s and further to 0.8 per cent in the 1970s (Teng, 1982).

Several factors contributed to this de-linking of China's economy from the world market system, especially: (1) the degree of adherence to communist ideology; (2) the difference in attitude to the benefits and costs of interdependence with the world economy; and (3) relations with major countries. While the goal was the same throughout the period: development rapid enough to enable China to catch up economically with the major advanced countries, strategies and policies changed following changes in these factors from time to time.

Essentially, the pursuit of its foreign economic relations was deeply rooted in the Chinese Communist Party's understanding of China's bitter experience in the past 100 years and orthodox Marxist theory. For the Chinese government, if international economic relations were unequal, then they must be associated with cross-country exploitation. It followed that if China developed international economic relations, then it must either exploit or be exploited by other countries, except for its relationships with other socialist countries, which were based on comradeship or those with other developing countries with similar experience and conditions, which served to help each other. In addition, the pursuit of economic independence was a main concern throughout the period. Even in the honeymoon period with the Soviet Union, China viewed dependence as a means of achieving independence. Zhang Huadong, China's Minister of Trade, said in 1955, 'The purpose of importing more industrial equipment from the Soviet Union is to lay the foundation of China's industrial independence, so that in the future China can make all of the producer goods it needs and will not have to rely on imports from the outside' (quote in Ross, 1994, p.438).

7.1.2. Economic organisation and arranged networking

Under the Maoist economic system, the organisation of economic activity was totally different from that in market economies. The Chinese government ran the country as a planned economy, similar to the Soviet Union. The state was the owner, operator, and employer – thus planned, directed and funded all enterprises (Kidd and Lu, 1999, p.213). First, a broad division of labour was realised through the establishment of different types of enterprises, with each type of enterprise specialising in particular activities. Roughly speaking, there were production enterprises and commercial enterprises. Production enterprises carried out manufacturing, mining and other non-commercial activities. They were further divided into different industries and came under the governance of relevant ministries or their lower level agents. Commercial enterprises fell into two subtypes, domestic commercial enterprises and foreign trade companies. The former specialised in the trade of finished goods (mainly consumer goods) of production enterprises, and the latter specialised in the export and import of both intermediate and commercial goods. There were basically no enterprises that had cross-industrial diversified activities such as exist in market economies.

Secondly, the government set output quotas for each production enterprise and similar tasks for commercial enterprises. The sources and quantities of supply of input for production were arranged by government planning, so were procurement and supply in commercial enterprises.

Thirdly, the enterprises operated within a peculiar system of dual financial flows with the government, which acted like a financial straitjacket. Enterprises turned over their revenues (profit) to the state, and the state in turn allocated funds to cover the costs of enterprises. Each type of fund the government allocated to enterprises had its specified purposes and was not allowed to be used for other purposes, as conveyed in the figurative saying, 'the money for buying cooking oil could not be used to buy vinegar'. Fixed capital investment and investment for technological improvement in enterprises were appropriated by the state through a separate system – planned by the State Planning Commission and administered by the People's Construction Bank of China.[3] Small investment projects were planned by lower agents of the Commission.

Fourthly, firms were generally embedded in the grid of the state administrative system: they were controlled by relevant industrial ministries and/or commissions vertically regarding their business activities, and by local government horizontally with regard to administration. The smaller and less important an enterprise was, the more power the central government delegated to local government to regulate it. On the opposite side, the bigger and more important an enterprise was, the less power local government had in the regulation of the enterprise.

As a result, price and market in the sense of a market economy were basically excluded from the economy. Though there were 'prices', they were mostly set by the state. They neither revealed information about the relationship between demand and supply, nor reflected the quality of products. As price became a kind of quota, the 'quota' took pride of place in economic organisation. In the same sense, market was replaced by planning. In addition, firms in this system had limited autonomy. For a firm, internal activities were organised via a '*hierarchy*' which was specified by and attached to the government.

Correspondingly, the external transactions of a firm were arranged by government via *planning*, and the volume of transaction and the prices for goods involved in the transactions were set by the government as a *quota*. This feature of economic organisation is illustrated in Figure 7.1.

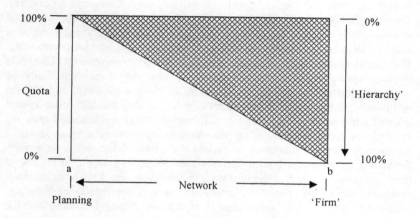

Figure 7.1 Economic organisation in the Maoist economic system

Nevertheless, there was still scope between the real planned transactions and transactions within the hierarchy of the firm. For a firm, there were external and internal reasons for this. The external reason was that there was a lack of a sufficiently and stable codified bureaucratic order. This to a large extent was rooted in the structure of society in China, which was featured as 'the nation or the state'. As Boisot and Child (1996) indicated, there is a 'contrast between the concept of a "nation state" and that of "the nation and the state", even "the nation or the state"'. The former assumes that there is a positive balance between government and society, with the state being the codification of the nation through the constitutional and legal system. This approximates to the Western model. The latter concept envisages a sharp distinction between government and nation, where the state may be oppressive and fail to secure popular legitimacy. It may be conjectured that in the former Soviet Union and in China by 1976, the situation was one of 'the state or the nation', and that this contributed importantly to the failure of the planning system. As China is a segmented society, in China's case this mainly existed in the relationship between the central government and local government, with local government having some legitimacy to run local communities. As a result, there was 'a collection of local systems in competition with each other but co-ordinated by government at the next level up. At this higher meso level the co-ordinated group could find itself in competition with other meso level groups, with government at the next level up resolving the competition'. A similar situation also existed among different government departments within an industry or sector.

The internal reason was that firms had incentives to carry out external transactions in a way that deviated from strict planning. There were two types of incentives, that is, technological incentives and managerial incentives. Technological incentives stemmed from the requirements of the industrial system, which aimed at reducing the mismatch between supply and demand as well as division of labour which were arranged by mandatory planning. Managerial incentives aimed at obtaining more freedom and fewer difficulties in business operation. In a planned economy, such incentives could only be realised ultimately through the arrangements of the government. The lack of a sufficiently stable codified bureaucratic order in the administrative system allowed firms to carry out economic activities in a way that deviated from the strict planning (at least the central planning), for different agencies or levels of government also had incentives to expand their controllable economic activity for various purposes, such as to increase their ability to compete in the higher level government, to show performance in improving the well being of local residents, and so on. Therefore, enterprises were active in obtaining support from the relevant level of government by strengthening the relationship with the government through various measures, including improving personal relationships with officials in charge.

A brief description of the traditional planning system and economic management system may be useful for a better understanding of the situation. Planning was generally based on the principle of 'two top-downs and one bottom up' (*Liangxia Yishang*). The first step was top down where the State Council transmitted general directions and control targets during a planning round which were drawn up by the State Planning Commission after a process of research and consultation with the regions, ministries and basic level units. The second step was bottom up. Plans at the basic enterprise level were negotiated and drawn up on the basis of these directions and control targets. Then these plans were submitted to the planning agencies of local government or ministries according to the subordinating status of each firm. These agencies in turn made pooled plans based on received plans and submitted them to higher level planning agencies, and so on, up to the provincial planning commissions (regional plans) and planning agencies of ministries (industrial plans). Regional and industrial plans were then submitted to the State Planning Commission for reconciliation to ensure consistency across regions and ministries and then formed a draft aggregate central plan which was submitted to the State Council. Once the State Council adopted the central plan, it was submitted to the National People's Congress for approval. The approved plan would be transmitted downwards level by level to the basic enterprise units for implementation under the joint supervision of the Party and the state.[4]

In this system, while planning agencies had to decide the output that could be delivered from firms (the output quota) and the inputs that had to be provided to enable these outputs to be produced (the input quota), firms were inclined to seek low production quotas but high input quotas. The quotas would be determined after a process of bargaining between planning agencies and firms. In the implementation of plans, production targets supported by planned inputs and allocated to other organisations were less likely to be exceeded than production targets that did not meet these criteria. An enterprise in this situation had no reason to exceed its target output. Any over-achievement would only lead planners to increase the target output in the next planning period. The enterprise would therefore have the incentive to disguise its true production potential (Liew, 1997, p.60). For similar reasons, local government was also inclined to under-report the hidden production potential and scrambled for more resources when dealing with higher level government.

With regard to carrying out external transactions deviating from strict planning, firms could use various methods. Firms were inclined to barter with the aim of adjusting excess demand and supply due to the absence of markets and price signals. For this purpose, a firm would hoard any materials that it did not currently need before being able to exchange them for materials that it had a shortage of (Liew, 1997, p.63). Sometimes several transactions would be required before the desired good was obtained. As the number of possible barter partners was very limited due to the absence of markets and price signals, the relationship with trading partners was important for the possibility of and better terms for bartering. On the other hand, a state-owned enterprise could set up a 'collectively owned enterprise' with the local government. Investment was jointly financed by this state-owned enterprise and the local government, employees were recruited from both the dependants of the employees of the state-owned enterprise and local residents, and that collective enterprise served as a manufacturer and supplier of some kind of spare parts for the state-owned enterprise. Due to the *de facto* ownership relationship the state-owned enterprise had over the collective enterprise, the state-owned enterprise had options in and influence on the demand-supply balance between the two firms. Similarly, a local government, under pressure from a state-owned enterprise, would seek approval from the central government to establish a new enterprise in its region to manufacture and supply some kind of spare parts for that state-owned enterprise. In such a way, the existing state-owned enterprise expanded and improved networks with other firms and local communities.

Under the planning system, the expansion and improvement of networks in most cases would ultimately depend on the arrangement of the government; we call the formation of such networks as 'arranged networking' (Figure 7.2).

The Maoist economic system not only gave the enterprises incentives to transact through arranged networking which deviated from strict planning, but also had incentives to internalise activities within the hierarchy of the firm. The latter enabled the firm to reduce its dependence on outsiders. This can be seen as a response by the firm to the rigidity of bureaucratically quota-based planning and soft budget constraints. Enterprises intended to expand the range of activities within their hierarchy, so as to deepen the internal division of labour. Enterprises would not outsource by choice. The internalisation could reach an extreme, and could cover not only production activities, but also non-production activities. Thus, there was a trend in the pre-reform period for every enterprise to be established as a pocket-like self-contained society. All large- and medium-sized enterprises had at least several internal welfare facilities ranging from internal medical clinics or hospitals, kindergartens, education facilities (from primary schools to high schools), shops, clubs, canteens and restaurants, bathhouses and swimming pools, to housing for employees, and so forth. Small enterprises ran their 'small societies' on a much smaller scale, but even they had at least medical clinics and kindergartens. This model was jokingly referred to as the 'large and self-contained', 'small and self-contained' enterprises that 'had every facility except for a crematorium'. These were the origins of the so-called social burden for state-owned enterprises.

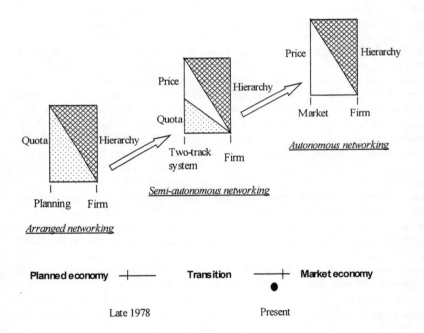

Figure 7.2 Evolution of economic organisation in China

It should be noted, however, that during this period the space for arranged networking was limited due to the rigid planning system. In most cases, such networking was unlikely to be expanded beyond the local region and relationships between nodes in networks were relatively weak.

7.2. ECONOMIC ORGANISATION DURING THE TRANSITIONAL PERIOD

7.2.1. Economic reform and the firm

Important changes to the system of the closed planned economy in China have been formally taking place since December 1978 when the Third Plenum of the Eleventh Central Committee of the Chinese Communist Party announced it would reform the economy. The reforms were initiated by Hua Guofeng, the then head of the Party, the State Council and the Army, and generally acknowledged to be led by Deng Xiaoping as Hua gradually lost his power in the following few years.[5]

The core of the reforms consisted of the introduction of the market mechanism into the economy and engaging actively in the global economic system, also referred to as 'internal revitalisation and external opening up' or 'reform and opening up' in short.

7.2.1.1. Internal revitalisation

(1) *Introducing a market mechanism into the economy.* One of the basic changes during the economic reforms was to introduce a market mechanism into the economy and to reduce the range and degree of central planning. The last two decades have witnessed the growing role of the market mechanism and the decreasing role of central planning in China's economy. In other words, China's economy has been developing more and more in the direction of a market orientation since the late 1970s. However, in the early years of economic reform, while the importance of introducing a market mechanism was stressed, there were no identical views as to how far the market mechanism should function in the economy. Debates centred on two issues, the relationship between the market mechanism and planning, and the scope of the market mechanism.

Generally, there were three different points of view on the relationship between the market mechanism and planning. Some argued that market mechanisms and planning are equally important in the sense that they are complementary to each other and correct each other's imperfections, therefore they should be 'rubber-glued together' (Liu and Zhao, 1979). Others advocated that planning has precedence over market mechanisms and their relationship is similar to 'a bird in a cage', that is, economic agents can only be granted the freedom to function according to market rules within the limits set by planning, just as a bird can only fly in a cage (Chen, 1986).[6] Others held that neither planning nor market mechanisms are essential attributes of economic systems but merely methods which can be used by different economic systems, socialism and capitalism alike (Gao, 1988). As the reforms progressed, in 1992 the nature of China's economic system was for the first time officially acknowledged as a *socialist market economy* and the previously admitted term of a planning economy supplementarily adjusted by market was abandoned. This change signified a fundamental breakthrough in China's economic system in that the nature of the firm was finally acknowledged.

(2) *The expansion of the dimensions of the market.* For a long time in China the market was restricted to a very limited commodity market while factors of production including capital, labour and other inputs were excluded. This ruled out the possibility that enterprises obtained essential inputs, sold intermediate products, and avoided risks through market mechanisms. Therefore, carrying out international trade and joining in international production through inward and outward direct investment were beyond their scope. By 1988, the market economy had expanded and the factor markets started to emerge. Significant changes have taken place since then, especially after 1992. Stock markets, real estate markets, foreign exchange markets and futures markets are now open to the public. Other factor markets have also spread all over the country. The volume of transactions is huge and expanding rapidly. For example, the Shanghai Metal Exchange, which opened in May 1992, has organised futures markets in which transactions during the first seven months of operation were more than 45 billion *yuan*. By 1998, market mechanism covered prices of more than 85 per cent of factors, 90 per cent of manufacturing products and 95 per cent of commercial goods (IIE, 1998). The emergence and boom of factor and product markets have paved the way for enterprises to regain their nature.

(3) *Diversification of ownership.* Before the start of the economic reforms, there were generally only two types of ownership of the means of production in China's economy, namely, state ownership and collective ownership. In industries and services, state-owned enterprises were the main body and collective enterprises were relatively small in size and weak in role. Agriculture basically consisted of collective ownership organisations: communes. Forms of ownership other than these effectively did not exist. The success of the experimental rural reform of the 'family contractual production responsibility system' in Anhui and Sichuan provinces in 1978 had given empirical grounds to believe that state ownership was the main root or cause of all problems in China's previous economic development and therefore spurred the reform of ownership in other sectors of the economy. The approach that separates ownership rights from management rights through various measures was initially adopted in collective enterprises and later extended to most medium-sized state-owned enterprises by the late 1980s.

Further measures have been adopted to reshape the patterns of ownership in industrial and services sectors and to develop modern organisations of enterprises. First, ownership structures for different types of enterprise have been legally established. Besides the originally existing state-owned enterprises and collectively owned enterprises, private enterprise, shareholding corporations, foreign-funded enterprises and self-employed (individual) business[7] have come into being, and now account for a growing share in the national economy. Table 7.2 shows that, from 1985 to 1995, 'other types' of enterprises (mainly enterprises funded by foreigners and by entrepreneurs from Hong Kong, Macau and Taiwan) increased 1522, 1120 and 967 per cent in their share of national total assets, employment and industrial output, respectively. In comparison, in 1985 the state-owned industrial enterprises accounted for 74.6 per cent of total assets and 64.9 per cent of industrial output, but these shares dropped to 53.7 per cent and 34 per cent respectively a decade later.

Table 7.2 Patterns of ownership in industry (%)

Ownership	Total assets			Employment			Output		
	1985	1995	Δ %	1985	1995	Δ %	1985	1995	Δ %
State	74.6	53.7	-28.0	41.1	31.6	-23.1	64.9	34	-47.6
Collective	24	23.8	-0.8	49.5	39.8	-19.6	32.1	36.6	14.0
Private		1			3.3			2.6	
Individual	0.5	1.9	280.0	8.9	17.5	96.6	1.8	10.5	483.3
Shareholdings		5			1.7			3.5	
Other types	0.9	14.6	1522.2	0.5	6.1	1120.0	1.2	12.8	966.7
Total	100	100		100	100		100	100	

Source: Main Data from the Third National Industrial General Survey. *China Industrial and Commercial Times* (Zhonghua Gongshang Shibao), 20 February 1997.

Secondly, state-owned enterprises have been granted greater autonomy. They have more freedom to plan and manage production, the purchase of inputs, marketing, pricing, distributing salaries and bonuses, and hiring and firing workers. Some state-owned enterprises have been granted the autonomy of direct exporting.[8]

Thirdly, the formation of industrial concerns (conglomerates) and the establishment of a stock exchange system have advanced to a relatively large scale. The development of industrial conglomerates in China formally started in 1987 when economic reforms gradually cut off the existing supply and demand arrangements between enterprises that had existed under central planning. But prices had not yet kept pace reflecting the interests of different enterprises. In particular, raw materials and intermediate products were under-priced and final products were over-priced. These had given the under-paid firms incentives to evade the central planning-assigned supply quotas one way or another, which affected, in many cases seriously, the production of firms downstream. In order to secure supply and smooth business, many large downstream manufacturers sought to establish conglomerates of reverse integration with former suppliers, or some firms established conglomerates with other related firms to compete with larger conglomerates. Therefore there was a boom in the establishment of conglomerates in the 1980s. In 1988 there were 1630 self-styled conglomerates of different types (La Croix *et al.*, 1995, p.37). The trends in setting up conglomerates have later moved to developing 'pillar' industries, pushing forward technological advancements, expanding exports and competing with foreign-based multinational enterprises. With these aims central government pushed the development of conglomerates and selected 57 conglomerates in 1991 and added another 63 conglomerates in May 1997 as 'experimental conglomerates' to test the way of forming China's industrial giants. Local governments also followed suit in this respect. The average size of some experimental conglomerates is shown in Table 7.3. The main approaches to forming conglomerates are assets-licensed operation, establishing financial companies, buying shares of other companies, and merging with or taking over other companies. As the core firms in forming conglomerates are relatively large and strong, and large enterprises are the main body of enterprises to be reconstructed into shareholding corporations, the development of conglomerates in China has been accompanied by the development of the stock exchange system. For example, among the 120 experimental conglomerates in Table 7.3, 45 enterprises are listed stock corporations.

Table 7.3 Average size of 120 experimental conglomerates

Industry	Number of conglomerates	Total assets (100 million yuan)	Net assets (100 million yuan)	Sales (100 million *yuan*)	Realised profit and tax (million *yuan*)	Export (US$ million)
Metallurgy	8	357.0	192.1	178.2	2760.4	228.0
Energy	11	412.9	203.4	147.0	1719.2	31.0
Chemical	7	76.7	29.3	34.9	484.2	25.5
Automobile	6	262.9	90.2	219.4	2437.6	42.1
Engineering	14	43.5	13.4	24.7	244.7	26.2
Electronics	10	43.1	14.7	42.8	357.5	103.6
Communication	8	234.4	81.2	102.9	605.0	256.1
Pharmaceutical	5	39.0	13.0	23.8	305.6	31.4
Construction	3	155.0	31.3	106.0	533.9	48.3
Foreign trade	8	119.4	22.7	135.5	308.8	764.7
120 Average		133.8	54.3	77.5	711.5	117.3

Source: IIE (1998), p.122.

7.2.1.2. External opening up

The direction of China's policy of opening up, which was introduced in 1978 by the Third Plenum of the Eleventh Central Committee of the Chinese Communist Party, was to expand economic cooperation actively on terms of equality and mutual benefit with other countries and to strive to adopt the world's advanced technologies (*Beijing Review*, 29 December 1978, p.11). This official endorsement of opening up the economy signified the casting away of China's former principles that regulated interaction with the global economy. This was indeed a watershed. The principle of self-reliance was no longer to be understood to exclude international intercourse, and economic interest was no longer to be subjected to politics in foreign affairs. Rather, it was acknowledged that self-reliance did not contradict expanding economic cooperation with foreign countries in the fields of trade, finance, labour, aid, technology and science, etc. It was also acknowledged that foreign economic relations based on comparative advantage were able to make the best use of the international division of labour to actively promote national economic development, in the sense that 'exports are not only the means of earning foreign currency necessary for imports, but also the means of promoting technological transformation and structural reform of the national economy' and that 'imports not only meet the needs in domestic market and production but also actively serve in expanding exports' (Wang *et al.*, 1992).

Based upon the positive acknowledgement of foreign economic relations, an outward-looking export-oriented development model was advocated. Different regions and different business organisations were to be given different priorities because of China's large size and huge internal divergence as well as lack of experience. Deng Xiaoping's famous phrase 'crossing the river by touching the stones'[9] represented the gradualism in China's policy of opening up, rather than a big bang approach.

(1) *Regional opening up.* China's economic reforms have been carried out in a gradual way and the regional open-door policy was implemented in the same way as well. The regional opening up began with the establishment of the four Special Economic Zones (SEZs) in the southeast coast and then expanded to some other parts of the southeast region, and later to north and west China.

In 1979, a new Law on Joint Ventures was passed that provided a basic framework under which foreign firms were allowed to operate. Four SEZs were established along the coast of Guandong and Fujian provinces close to Hong Kong, Macau and Taiwan.[10] SEZs (including their home provinces in some respects) enjoyed financial subsidies and were granted higher autonomy in economic affairs and a more freely market-oriented system. Additional preferential tax and administrative treatment were granted to foreign-invested firms there. For example, on the basis that the applicable income tax rate for foreign-invested firms in China was 33 per cent while the rate for domestic firms was 37 per cent, foreign-invested firms in the SEZs all enjoyed a tax holiday for the first and second profit-making years; a 50 per cent reduction of income tax (that is, applicable rate: 33% × 50%) in the following three years; and a 15 per cent reduction of income tax (that is, applicable rate: 33% × 85%) afterwards. Those foreign-invested firms were also granted exemption from income tax on the remitted share of profits, exemption from export duties, and from import duties for equipment, instruments and apparatus for producing exports.

The success in economic development and foreign investment in the special economic zones had increased the confidence of the Chinese central government in economic opening up and other regions had alerted to the benefits of opening up. Therefore regional opening up was expanded to other regions in China. In May 1984 the concept of SEZs was extended to another fourteen coastal cities and Hainan Island.[11] Their local governments were delegated similar status to that of SEZs in regulating FDI. In these cities the Economic and Technological Development Zones (ETDZs) were set up and ETDZs gave foreign investment projects similar incentives to those in SEZs. Foreign invested firms there were levied a 24 per cent tax rate, and local authorities were granted the right to approve foreign investment for projects under US$30 million.

As the economic reform proceeded, more cities were granted a similar status to the SEZs. The so-called 'high and new technology development zones' and 'economic development zones' were established in nearly every provincial capital city and afterwards extended to medium-sized cities or even small cities or towns. As different regions competed with each other to attract foreign investment by offering tax incentives and surcharge reductions for foreign-invested firms, the opening up of the whole economy of China was realised.

(2) *Liberalising export and international business of local firms.* Before the economic reforms, China's domestic industrial firms were essentially manufacturing plants. They were not only granted very limited freedom to respond to domestic markets but were also cut off from international markets. Twelve state-owned foreign trade companies, each with responsibilities for a specific category or specific categories of commodities, were the only mediators between domestic firms and the international markets. However, the monopoly status of these trade companies made them 'poor conductors' in functioning between domestic firms and overseas markets, especially in respect of market information supply and response. In the meantime local governments had no autonomy in foreign trade.

Since 1979 several measures have been adopted in reforming the foreign trade system:

- decentralising the right to conduct foreign trade and permitting local governments, some industrial sectors, many large- and medium-sized enterprises and business conglomerates to engage in foreign trade in combination with their products and technology;
- reducing imperative planning, increasing instructive planning and strengthening macro-regulation over exports and imports through the leverages of exchanges rates, tariffs, credits, licences and quotas; and
- eliminating export subsidies, rectifying the disparities of foreign exchange retention between regions, and standardising enterprise management behaviour.

With the above measures there are now roughly three separate trade regimes in China. The first regime is for foreign-invested enterprises, which are allowed to engage in international trade directly. In addition, export-oriented foreign-invested firms enjoy duty-free import of raw materials, components and capital equipment for export production. The second regime is for local foreign trade companies. These companies have the licence to engage in international trade, and the international trade of ordinary local producers has to be undertaken through these foreign trade companies. The third regime is for larger local enterprises which have been granted independent import and export rights. These firms are normally the parents or important subsidiaries within conglomerates. They also have the autonomy to decide upon setting up production joint ventures of US$30 million or less with foreign investors and a certain degree of autonomy to engage in other international business such as project construction.

7.2.2. Economic organisation and semi-autonomous networking

The above description has revealed two important facts about the Chinese economy. One is that before the economic reform, enterprises lost their essential character of a firm and each of them was attached to a specific location, an industry and a government institution. Another is that the method of economic system transition in China can be characterised as a dual track approach, setting out from a condition without a market mechanism towards the restoration of a market mechanism by gradually shortening the 'non-market track' while gradually lengthening the 'market track'.

During the transition, the two tracks co-existed in every aspect of China's economy, and the relative 'length' of the two tracks at a particular time differed among different aspects of the economy. Based on an econometric analysis involving eleven groups of 76 indicators, Chen *et al.* (1998) show the marketisation in different sectors between 1979 and 1997 (Table 7.4). Theoretically, the range of marketisation is 0–100 per cent. While the marketisation of government behaviour and the technology market was quicker in the early stages of economic reform, the marketisation of the product market was very slow at first but faster in the later stages. In the meantime, the marketisation of the financial market lags far behind that of other factor markets. For example, up to 1997, the marketisation of the product market reached 85 per cent, but the financial market only reached 10 per cent. The marketisation of the firm was very slow in the early stages of the reform and is now just halfway through.

The gradual restoration of the nature of the firm during the economic reform means that enterprises are slowly breaking their attachment to government institutions and single locations and evolving towards the institutionalisation of their own interests and the marketisation of their operations. At any particular time in the process of the marketisation of the firm, firms of different types, that is, different in size, ownership, industry and location, enjoy different treatment.

In the meantime, a firm can also be differently treated if it uses different channels of input and output. Therefore, different firms are not on a level playing field in terms of their operation and competition.

Table 7.4 Trends of marketisation in the Chinese economy (%)

	1979	1985	1990	1995	1997
Firm	0	10.0[a]	15.0	46.4	48.0
Government behaviour	4.0	50.8[a]	62.2	73.0	72.0
Product market	2.25	15.0[a]	54.5	84.5	85.0
Labour market	5.1	24.3	34.8	64.7	65.0
Financial market	1	3.6[b]	6.3	9.1	10.0
Technology market	0	46.3	54.1	70.8	71.0
Agriculture	7.67	49.7	51.6	65.0	66.0
Industry	0	23.5	37.3[c]	49.9	50.0
Foreign trade	1.5	9.0	22.3[c]	41.4	54.4
East region				70.3	
Central region				64.4	
West region				64.9	
North region				54.9	
South region				67.9	

Notes: [a]. figure for 1984; [b]. figure for 1986; [c]. figure for 1991.

Source: Chen *et al.* (1998).

As the dual track approach is discriminatory in nature, it inevitably leads firms to form business networks actively, so as to exploit the dual tracks as well as to explore the ordinary benefits of networking. On the one hand, the dual track reform gives enterprises more space in forming networks: enterprises can not only carry out activities through approaches between price and hierarchy or between quota and hierarchy, but also hedge between the price and the quota with some methods. On the other hand, the incentives for enterprises to form networks are much stronger than that in the traditional planning system: a firm will enjoy more favourable treatment if it can operate in a specific region, or in a specific industry, or simply is involved in a specific type of ownership. In the meantime, the dual track price system affects the performance of enterprises. Therefore, firms are keen to expand or change their facilities or operations into the regions or industries or activities in which they can enjoy more favourable treatment. Similarly, enterprises are also actively going into favourably treated types of ownership. As enterprises have obtained some autonomy through the reform, such networking is semi-autonomous networking (Figure 7.2).

The following pattern of networking behaviour is commonly observed during the economic transition.

First, inland enterprises actively set up subsidiaries or other types of affiliates in the coastal areas. This is one of the major forces behind the economic boom in SEZs such as Shenzhen, Zhuhai and Haikou, which were either remote villages or backward regions before the economic reform. Through the expansion of business facilities enterprises have greatly expanded their business networks from previously geographically concentrated ones into networks extending over several regions or provinces. The expanded networks have several functions. They serve not only as a method for the newly established affiliates to take advantage of more favourable treatment in the newly entered regions but also as a method of leverage for whole enterprises in transfer pricing and financial flows. In addition, parent enterprises can benefit from the expanded networks to improve management through learning by doing and gathering important information which benefits by the closeness of the established facilities to international markets (for example, Hong Kong) as well as a huge number of foreign-invested firms in the coastal areas.

Secondly, many enterprises are very enthusiastic about forming industrial concerns (conglomerates). Developing industrial concerns is one of the methods of economic reform aimed at expanding the ranges of enterprises' business and improving utilisation of existing advantageous assets (including intangible ones) of different member firms by mobilising these assets among members of the same industrial concern (IIE, 1996, ch.15). For this purpose the government grants industrial concerns preferential treatment in various ways, ranging from reduced income tax rates to additional loans and even subsidies for technological improvement projects. Government support is offered in a variety of ways to firms trying to build international brand names (Richter, 1999, p.245). Besides favourable treatment, the main reason for the enthusiasm of enterprises for engaging in the formation of industrial concerns is that this is a good way for them to expand their networks. Expanded networks enable them not only to get access to the advantageous resources of other firms, but also to get rid of administrative and policy restrictions remaining in other aspects of or for some firms. Generally speaking, vertical conglomerates are formed mainly as a result of enterprises' concerns about dual pricing, as price reform in factors is behind that in consumer goods, and horizontal conglomerates are mainly formed out of concern by the segment of the market at the institutionalised opportunistic behaviour of government in different regions.

Firms' strong response towards developing industrial conglomerates is further increased later by intensified competition in the domestic market as well as implementation of the bankruptcy policy. Above all, large industrial groups have gained in market power as well as bargaining power against the government, and non-member firms hope to attach to these industrial groups, to enjoy such power. On the other hand, facing intensified competition, local governments also encourage local enterprises to form industrial groups to compete with foreign-invested firms and large industrial conglomerates headquartered in other regions. For example, Dalian Municipality of Liaoning Province has formed ten industrial concerns via the restructuring of state-owned assets. The ten industrial concerns involve total assets of 17.73 billion *yuan* and

150 enterprises. Their assets and output account for 65 per cent and 60 per cent respectively of those of the industries within the budget of the city. Of course, local governments are basically concerned with the segment of local market and local interests, as we stated in Section 1.2 on arranged networking.

Thirdly, domestic enterprises actively seek to establish joint ventures with foreign investors. During the 1979-96 period, 76 per cent of foreign investment, in terms of the number of projects as well as foreign capital actually used, consisted of Sino-foreign joint ventures, including equity joint ventures, contractual joint ventures and contractual joint development. In comparison, foreign wholly owned enterprises accounted for only 24 per cent of total inward FDI (Wang, 1997, p.4). This reflects the active attitude of domestic firms towards forming joint businesses with foreign investors. In fact, it is common that the most competitive domestic enterprises, including industrial concerns, have set up joint ventures with foreign investing firms. A typical example is the detergent manufacturing industry, where all Chinese firms which had famous brands merged or established joint ventures with foreign firms had their brands either replaced by foreign brands or confined to selected products after the introduction of foreign capital. The main motives for local firms to set up Sino-foreign joint ventures are to enjoy favourable treatment for foreign-invested firms and to get indirectly into the networks of overseas market. These two motives to a large extent stem from the dual track policy and restrictions on free international business of domestic firms.

The above analysis shows that during the economic transition, due to the dual track policy, firms responded to the strong incentives to establish and expand their networks. Firms cannot only enjoy the benefits of networking which are typical in market economies, but also exploit the dual tracks. However, there are also limitations for firms in establishing and expanding networks in the economic transition. First of all, they cannot be completely free of administrative interference in their networking expansion and business operation. Of course there is a dilemma. In cases where they are weak in competition and have small networks, they may need government support and interference to improve their status in the market and expand their networks. However, once they have obtained some market power and network penetration, they prefer freedom in their operations. Secondly, compared with foreign-invested firms, local enterprises are still unfavourably treated in terms of taxation, though discrimination has been lessening over time. Thirdly, their networks are not large enough to compete with foreign firms, especially the large MNEs headquartered in Western industrialised countries. In short, in the economic transition enterprises cannot fully realise efficiency and legitimacy, the two instrumental purposes of networking (Jansson *et al.*, 1995, p.35), if their networks are confined to the domestic market. Intensified competition in the Chinese market and changing industrial structure in the development of the economy are imperatives for firms to perform on a larger stage.

7.3. OUTWARD DIRECT INVESTMENT IN ECONOMIC TRANSITION

7.3.1. Motivations for international networking

While Chinese firms have strong incentives to establish and expand their networks during the process of economic transition, they cannot benefit fully from networking if their networks are confined within the boundary of the national economy.

First of all, a firm might be in an unfavourable situation in global commodity chains. For industrial firms, if they do not have their own networks in foreign markets, they are in an awkward position in gathering information about international trade and changes in technology and choosing a better position in global commodity chains, which means that they have difficulties avoiding being unfairly treated in their exports and imports either by foreign firms or by Chinese foreign trade companies. Tseng has quoted one of his experiences to illustrate this situation:

> The author (that is, Tseng) had a personal experience of this when he represented a US Fortune 500 firm in negotiating the purchase of a number of mixing tanks for its chemical plant in Shanghai. At the time of negotiation, the US firm was asked to negotiate the commercial terms and price with the import and export corporation, and the specifications and delivery date with an iron-work factory. After the start-up of the chemical plant (considered as a domestic firm in Shanghai), the author approached the iron-work factory for additional mixing tanks and discovered that the price was only 20 per cent of that of the previous purchase. As can be expected, the iron-work factory was equally upset that the import and export corporation had made such a huge profit. (Tseng, 1994, pp.122-3)

For ordinary industrial firms, the problem is that they do not have the right to engage directly in foreign trade if they have not been included in one of the three separate trade regimes in China, that is, the regimes for foreign-invested enterprises, for local foreign trade companies and for larger local enterprises which have been granted independent import and export rights respectively. For a firm outside these regimes, even if it has set up a joint venture with a foreign firm, it may still be in a disadvantageous position, as in most cases only a part of a firm goes into joint venture and only the joint venture concerned has the right to undertake foreign trade. The foreign parent is also most likely to use its knowledge of and channels in overseas markets to increase its control over the joint venture.

Foreign trade companies are facing problems as well. The increasing autonomy of enterprises and the decentralisation of the foreign trade system have increased the bargaining power of manufacturing firms in foreign trade through specialised foreign trade companies and other firms alike. Industrial firms have more and more leeway in choosing foreign trade agencies and negotiating terms of trade, leaving foreign trade companies and other licensed foreign trade agents to compete for sourcing and supplying. Tseng's experiences also include such a situation:

> The import and export corporations are sometimes on the losing end. The author had a very different experience when representing a Korean conglomerate to explore the feasibility of setting up a joint venture factory with a hardware factory in Fuzhou, China, to produce iron nails for the United States market. We helped the factory to calculate the direct cost of the iron nails and found out that it was much higher than the export price quoted by the import and export corporation. This means the export price of iron nails was heavily subsidised. (Tseng, 1994, p.123)

Secondly, foreign-invested firms still enjoy more favourable treatment. It is well known that since the launching of the economic reform in late 1978, China has attracted a huge amount of FDI. Annual total FDI flowing into China grew rapidly. From under US$2 billion in 1985 it jumped to over US$11 billion in 1992 and further to over US$41 billion after 1996. Since 1992 China has been the largest host country for FDI next to the United States. Besides the huge domestic market and low labour costs, preferential treatment for foreign-invested firms is an important attraction.

Up to the mid 1990s, China offered investment incentives to FDI firms that locate in particular areas (such as SEZs and ETDZs) and engage in particular sectors or activities (in particular manufacturing, infrastructure and agriculture). On the one hand, different taxation treatment was applied to domestic and foreign-invested firms. For example, the corporate income tax rate for domestic and foreign-invested firms were 37 per cent and 33 per cent respectively before the taxation reform in 1994. In addition, foreign-invested firms were entitled to enjoy tax exemption and a 50 per cent reduction for a certain period (normally a tax exemption for the first two years commencing from the first profit-making year and a 50 per cent reduction for the three subsequent years). In 1994, the turnover tax regime and individual income tax regime were unified. As a result, both domestic and foreign firms are now governed by a unified set of rules on value-added, consumption, business operations and individual income taxation.[12] However, the preferential treatment on corporate income tax to foreign-invested firms remains unchanged. Foreign-invested firms can also enjoy other incentives including favourable land prices, various surcharge deductions, subsidies, favourable loans, etc. All this treatment puts local firms in a disadvantageous position.

Thirdly, Chinese firms face increasing competition at home. Essentially, reform does not only mean an expansion of markets, but also greater competition among firms (Jefferson and Rawski, 1993), as market forces create a tendency to equalise financial returns to factors employed in different lines of business. Market forces and non-market forces have both contributed to the intensification of competition. In pursuing high financial returns, capital has flowed to activities where supply falls short of demand, leading to an end to the shortage economy, a consequence all centrally planned economies bear. Moreover, as the abolishment of the soft budget constraint lags behind the granting of autonomy in investment to various institutions (including firms) in the process of the decentralisation of investment system, over-investment has occurred in activities with high profit. Specifically, for a long time since the commencement of economic reform, most of the state-owned enterprises, collective-owned enterprises and local government agencies have more and more leverage in investment decisions, but nobody bears responsibility for investment failures in the meantime. In such a situation, firms and local governments are more active than ever in competing for state investment funds and banks' loans to finance their investment projects. High information imperfection in the transitional period further fuels such behaviour. The situation was particularly bad in the 1980s: 'the decentralisation of decision-making promoted by reform resulted in a period when neither central planning nor market forces were in a position to discipline their financial demands adequately' (Hannan, 1998, p.10). As a result, duplicate projects have mushroomed all over the country, and the situation in industries with low entry barriers is particularly serious. This leads to highly intensified competition and production undercapacity. For example, while less than 50 per cent of production capacity for most household electric products is realised, there are still a lot of projects under construction (Table 7.5).

Table 7.5 Production capacity of household electrical appliances (1995)

Product (1000 sets)	Production capacity	Utilisation of production capacity (%)	Additional capacity under construction
Washing machines	21830	43.4	2280
Vacuum cleaners	12840	43.2	200
Electric fans	142530	65.1	2550
Refrigerators	18210	50.5	2170
Air conditioners	20350	33.5	3800
Colour TVs	44680	46.1	2600
Smoke absorbers	8920	40.2	170
Video recorders	5170	41.7	1900
Camcorders	350	12.3	10
Microwave ovens	2590	38.6	–

Source: China Business Daily, 5 May 1997.

Another contributory factor to the intensified competition in China has been the inflows of FDI. Inward FDI is now playing an important role in China's economy. This can be seen from the contributions of foreign-capital-invested firms to the growth of the national economy. In 1997, actually used FDI accounted for 15.04 per cent of China's total fixed assets investment; the amount of imports and exports by foreign-invested firms accounted for 46.95 per cent of the nation's total foreign trade; and the tax paid by foreign-invested firms accounted about 13.16 per cent of China's total industrial and commercial taxes (Table 7.6).

Table 7.6 Role of inward FDI in China's economy (%)

Year	FDI/Total fixed assets investment	Output by FDI firms/National total output in industry	Foreign trade by FDI firms/National foreign trade	Employees in FDI firms/Non-agricultural population	Tax from FDI firms/National industrial and commercial taxes
1991	4.15	–	21.40	–	–
1992	7.51	–	26.42	–	–
1993	12.13	–	34.27	–	–
1994	17.08	9.47	37.02	–	–
1995	15.65	11.66	39.10	–	–
1996	15.14	12.02	47.30	–	–
1997	15.04	12.66	46.95	10.00	13.16

Source: NBS, various issues.

Huge foreign capital inflow and active operations of foreign-invested firms have greatly affected China's institutional environment and intensified market competition. These exert enormous pressure on local firms and force them to find ways to survive and develop.

Foreign capital invested firms have seized a large portion of China's market, though their market shares vary from industry to industry and from region to region. In 1997, among 39 industries, there was one industry (electronics and communication equipment manufacturing) in which FDI firms accounted for 61.33 per cent of the broad market share;[13] four accounted for 40-50 per cent (clothing and other fibres; leather, feather and their products; cultural, education and sport products; and instrument, meter and office machinery); eleven accounted for 20-30 per cent (food; beverage; timber, bamboo and rattan works; furniture; paper and paper products; duplication of recording media in printing industry; medicine; rubber products; metal products; transport equipment manufacturing; electric machinery and equipment manufacturing); and one accounted for 18 per cent (textiles). In the same year, of the provinces and municipalities directly under the Central Government, there were two where FDI firms had a broad market share of between 50-60 per cent (Guangdong and Fujian); one had 40-50 per cent (Tianjin); one 30-40 per cent (Shanghai); one 20-30 per cent (Beijing); and one 18-20 per cent (Jiangsu).

The general trend in foreign-invested firms is an inclination to control high-tech industries and high profit industries. In the new and high-tech industries, the market share of foreign-invested firms keeps increasing; some firms even dominate the market. For example, in the micro-electronic industry, of the eight biggest integrated circuit manufacturers, five are Sino-foreign joint ventures, one is a wholly foreign-owned enterprise, and only two are local firms. IBM has established a wholly owned subsidary and six joint ventures, 72 partners, and 200 PC speciality shops around the country. Motorola, after having monopolised the mobile communication market, set up one wholly owned integrated circuit chips manufacturing firm and eight joint ventures in Shanghai, Sichuan, Jiangsu and Liaoning. In 1998 Motorola (China)'s sales was more than RMB 19.6 billion *yuan* (about US$2.4 billion).

Foreign-invested firms tend to invest in downstream industries and focus on those consumer products which have great market and profit potential. Therefore, the upperstream industries with high costs and low profits are left for local firms. For example, in the machinery industry, automobile, electrical engineering, engineering machinery, and petroleum chemical general machinery together account for 75 per cent of FDI in the industry. In the medical industry, FDI firms are mainly concentrated in the production of preparations of drugs, while the producers of raw materials are almost all local firms. In the detergent, beer, bicycles, refrigerators, washing machines and air conditioners industries, FDI firms account for a large share of the market.

Inward FDI also affects the existing brands of local products and hinders the development of local brands. This occurs mainly for three reasons. First, with the aim of penetrating into the Chinese market and reducing competition, many established foreign firms seek Chinese firms with brands established in China to form joint ventures to produce and market existing or similar products with their foreign brands. Chinese firms, due to difficulties such as capital shortage, redundant employees, heavy internal social burden, heavier tax burden, less autonomy in operation which stem from either the old economic system or changes in economic regime, take the forming of joint ventures as a measure to tackle these difficulties and are therefore willing to form joint ventures with foreigners. In some cases, local brands, though still used, are losing their identification in the market as available resources for promotion are limited or production volume is reduced. Detergent, soap and electrical appliances are typical examples.

Secondly, former local brands face strong challenges from foreign brands. On the one hand, in contrast to most Chinese firms which had not begun to operate in a market economic environment until the start of the economic transition, foreign firms have grown out of mature market economies and therefore are more skilful in marketing and management. Many foreign investors have internationally sound brands and high quality products, which directly challenge the brands of local Chinese firms when they carry out business operations in China. On the other hand, even in the case of joint ventures where foreign brands have not replaced local brands, local brands are still severely challenged as the Chinese partner in a joint venture is normally not the whole Chinese firm involved but only a part of the firm, leaving the other part of the firm to operate separately with its own brand(s). Therefore a portion of the existing market share of the Chinese firm has been ceded to the foreign brand(s) after the forming of the joint venture. Examples include several famous Chinese bicycle manufacturers, such as Phoenix, Forever, and Golden Lion, each of which has formed a separate joint venture with a foreign firm on a 50-50 or 49-51 equity base. These Chinese parent firms' products labelled with their local brands have been competing directly with the joint ventures' products labelled with foreign partners' brands.

Thirdly, the presence of famous foreign brands in the Chinese market has not only reduced the market share of local brands, but also hindered the development of sound local brands, though many products have world-class quality and technology. The main reasons for this include: some foreign firms invest in China with subsidies from their home governments, Chinese firms are weaker in their financial strength than those foreign firms, and FDI firms enjoy more favourable tax and surcharge treatments.

7.3.2. Outward direct investment

Motivated by the desire to escape the above pressures and to search for more network benefits, Chinese firms began to undertake outward direct investment almost at the same time as foreign investors began to invest in China. The locus of the development of China's outward direct investment coincides with the evolutionary process of firm-related reform in China. Whenever there is a major reform, there is a big increase in outward FDI (Table 7.7). This suggests that Chinese enterprises have made use of the autonomy granted by government and changed policies to engage in outward direct investment, just as they have in establishing and expanding domestic networks.

Before 1984, the urban and industrial reform measures introduced basically focused on the reform of the industrial management system and the expansion of enterprise power (or *Jianzheng Fangquan* in Chinese – simplifying administration and decentralising the power). The major reform during this period was the profit-retention system adopted by the government in 1979. It allowed profit-making enterprises to retain part of their profits to set up three internal funds, that is, funds for production development, welfare of employees, and bonuses respectively. The aim of this measure was to transform enterprises from traditional cost centres to profit centres. In the following year, this system was modified to become a two-tier package combining a fixed base of profit retention plus a flexible extra-base proportion of profit retention, which further enhanced the incentive of enterprises to make profits.

As reforms during this period were partial ones and only covered some experiments in state-owned enterprises, ordinary enterprises had neither enough authority to engage in international business, nor were there relevant market mechanisms for such activity. Only a very limited number of enterprises invested abroad and the investment was small in both volume and number of projects. The investors were some ministry-rank companies plus a few enterprises directly under the administrative management of provinces (Li, 2000, p.15).

Table 7.7 Firm-related economic reforms and outward direct investment

	Firm related reforms	Number of FDI Projects	Total Investment (US$M)	Chinese Investment (US$M)
1979-82	Profit-retention system (1979)	43	82	37
1983		33	8	13
1984	Tax-for-profit system	37	120	100
1985		76	88	47
1986		88	109	33
1987	Contractual management system	108	1373	410
1988		141	118	75
1989	(Tian'anmen Square incident and economic adjustment)	119	325	236
1990		156	167	77
1991	Reform resumes, with focus on revitalising state-owned large- and medium-sized enterprises	207	759	367
1992	Endorsement of a 'socialist market economy'	355	351	195
1993		294	187	96
1994	Deregulation of foreign exchange; Overall taxation reform: central-local fiscal arrangements, income taxation on enterprises and reforms of indirect taxes	106	124	71

Note: Since the mid 1990s, economic reform has entered the period of overall reform and comprehensive measures have been adopted. Therefore no single measure has as strong effects on enterprises as before. So no measures are listed in the table after 1995.

Source: MOFTEC, various issues.

The urban-industrial reforms expanded significantly in 1984. The reform programmes were stressed and outlined in 'The Decision of the (CCP's) Central Committee on the Reform of the Economic System', adopted in October 1984. The programmes emphasised an expansion of enterprise autonomy and incentives and the reduction, but not elimination, of the government within-plan allocation of resources.

A tax-for-profit system was instituted in two successive steps in 1983 and 1984. Under this system enterprises were required to pay tax instead of profit remittance and were able to fully retain their after-tax profits. This gave firms stronger incentives to use possible means to expand their profits, and improved operations would in turn increase their financial ability to carry out investment.

In 1987, the contractual management system was applied to Chinese enterprises against a background of falling enterprise-realised profits and state budget revenue. It followed the comprehensive economic reform begun in late 1984, aiming at coping with the problems of soft-budget behaviour. This system set out to personalise enterprises amid their taking up of rights and duties and therefore replaced the traditional party committee-dominated enterprise leadership system. Under this system managers were designated as the legal representatives of enterprises and were responsible for the fulfilment of business tasks (for example, profit, remittance and taxes) set in multi-year management responsibility contracts. With regard to internal operation and management, the reforms allowed enterprise managers to use their authority to choose the level of production, to sell output and acquire material inputs on the market, and to set or negotiate prices. With regard to external business activities, the reforms gave enterprise managers the right to develop lateral economic associations across different trades and regions as well as to permit the exchange of capital and technology and to cooperate in production matters. In addition, enterprise managers had the right to control activities related to employment, including, for example, the right to recruit labour openly and to determine the level of skill or qualifications required.

In the meantime the government abandoned the pursuit of a single rate of state-enterprise division of profits which would be applicable across the board. It required enterprises to ensure a steady increase in tax and profit remittance (or a decrease in subsidies and/or tax exemptions for loss-making enterprises) over the pre-contract remittance which was taken as the base. In addition to the requirement of increasing current profits, firms had to ensure the fulfilment of another two tasks: technical renovation investment and the linking of the wage bill with total realised profits, the latter being set as a device both to enhance enterprises' incentive and to avoid bonus expansion at the expense of state assets accumulation (Lo, 1997, p. 108).

In the meantime the country's foreign trade system underwent drastic reform. The national import and export corporations delegated functions to their local branches; certain industrial firms were encouraged to form holding companies and were given authority to import and export; and certain big industrial firms were also granted such rights.

The important firm-related reform in 1984 and 1987 significantly increased the autonomy and internal incentives of enterprises, which in turn led to big jumps in overseas investment in the years concerned. In terms of the amount of investment flows, China's outward investment in the two years had increased about 669 per cent and 1142 per cent respectively on the previous year's base. In comparison, the number of investment projects had increased about 12 per cent and 23 per cent respectively. As the latter are much lower than the former, it is obvious that the average size of outward FDI projects increased greatly in the two years.

Economic reform slowed down in 1989 and 1990 due to several interrelated factors, including different views on economic reforms between the conservatives and the reformers in the Party leadership, problems associated with economic growth and modernisation, and especially, the incident in Tian'anmen Square. Behind the notorious political troubles, there was a serious economic crisis. From 1985, China's economy had experienced high rates of inflation, with the retail price index ranging from 8.8 per cent in 1985 to 7.3 per cent in 1987, and further skyrocketing to 18.5 per cent in 1988. The direct outcome of these factors was a change of leadership in economic management, the beginning of hard-line dominance of economic policy (Liou, 1998, pp.36-7), and the economic adjustment. Therefore outward direct investment in 1990 fell to the level of 1988. It is interesting that in 1989 outward investment increased significantly. It is certain that a part of the increase was due to the lag between the approval and undertaking of outward investment – investment projects were improved in previous years but carried out in 1989. Some of the increase was most likely to be due to capital flight behaviour by investors out of concern over political uncertainty.

Economic reform was regenerated in mid 1991 and accelerated in 1992 after Deng Xiaoping's trip to South China. During that trip, Deng attacked conservative options and called on the country to pursue reform and opening up more vigorously. In October 1992, the Fourteenth National Congress of the Party endorsed Deng's view and called for the establishment of a 'socialist market economy'. The goal of establishing a socialist market economy was adopted in China's constitution during the first session of the Eighth National People's Congress in March 1993.

The reform plans and measures introduced in the 1990s attempted to broaden and deepen the reform process. These plans and measures covered not only the reform activities emphasised in the earlier stages of reform but also major issues related to China's macroeconomic structures, including, for example: (1) reforming the exchange rate system (allowing the RMB to be devalued without formal government action); (2) adjusting the fiscal system (introducing a new tax assignment system that separates central and local taxation authorities); (3) reforming the bank system (intended to establish an effective central banking system and to commercialise the state banks); (4) opening the stock markets (in Shanghai and Shenzhen); (5) emphasising state-owned enterprises' reform to improve the efficiency of SOEs; (6) adopting systems of accounting, laws on property rights, and patent protection; (7) reforming the social security system; (8) reforming the circulation system; and (9) accelerating housing reforms (Liou, 1998, p.32).

Such comprehensive measures have changed markedly the whole economic system in China in the direction of a market economy and therefore affected enterprises' investment behaviour. While firms have gained more freedom to engage in overseas direct investment, the maturing of the market economic mechanism means that the benefit from international networking was to some extent reduced due to the decreasing benefit from exploiting the two-track system. In other words, as marketisation in nearly all aspects of the economy proceeds, more and more enterprises are able to carry out overseas investment with fewer difficulties (easier to obtain the government's approval of and more capability to engage in outward direct investment), being able to invest abroad is becoming less proprietary in taking advantage of the segment (or barriers) between the domestic and international markets and between those with and those without overseas investment. For example, when it is very difficult to be granted a 'licence' to invest abroad and only a very limited number of enterprises have such 'licences', those enterprises which have overseas subsidiaries could relatively easily undertake roundabout investment in the home market in the name of their overseas subsidiaries. They could then enjoy the preferential treatment specifically for *foreign* investors as well as establishing internal international commodity chains with one end in China and the other in overseas markets. Through these chains foreign goods badly needed in China can be supplied and overseas markets supplied with the products of the parents with very low wage labour. The reduction of both international and internal barriers due to marketisation as well as the entering of a large number of competitors inevitably reduce the profit margin of such activities. Of course, the normal benefit of international networking still remains. As a result of the interaction of the two forces, the growth of China's outward direct investment in the 1990s was rapid at first and relatively smooth afterwards, with obvious increases after a few years when major measures were adopted in the reform.

The first big increase of the 1990s occurred in 1991. A part of this increase resulted from the approval of some FDI projects which were suspended in the 1989-90 period. In addition, the further deepening of the reform in 1991 also contributed to this quick growth. In the following year, 1992, China for the first time claimed to be developing a market economy, though for political reasons a tag of 'socialist' was still attached. That year the number of outward direct investment projects reached 355, an increase of more than 71 per cent from the previous year, and the amount of investment was relatively large.

The tax reform in 1994 represented the Chinese government's intention to re-construct its overall tax system and covered three major aspects: central-local fiscal arrangements, income taxation on enterprises, and reforms of indirect taxes. In the central-local fiscal arrangement, the old fiscal contract system (the central and local governments shared revenues according to a pre-agreed ratio) was replaced with a new tax system which divided taxes into three categories: central taxes (for example, tariffs, income tax on central enterprises, tax on revenues from railways, banks and insurance companies, and consumption tax), local taxes (for example, business tax, income tax from local enterprises, personal income tax, capital tax on land and property sales, estate duty, and stamp duty), and share taxes (for example, value-added tax for central and local governments and stock transaction gain tax for central and local governments). The reform introduced income (profit) tax at a uniform rate of 33 per cent for all enterprises (state and non-state). This measure to some extent has clarified state-firm relationships and has therefore indirectly increased the autonomy of firms.

On 1 January 1994, the previous two-tier foreign exchange rate system was replaced by a single foreign exchange rate system, and the RMB under the current account could be freely changed into foreign currencies. In addition, the Chinese government abandoned mandatory planning over revenue and expenditure of foreign exchange. This was a significant change for firms entering international business.

The two big reforms in the areas of taxation and foreign exchange in 1994 also pushed the development of outward FDI in the following years. However, as these reforms were not directly related to the autonomy and strategic development of enterprises, and and the market was maturing, their effects on FDI were not so strong as the previous major measures of reform.

7.4. CONCLUDING REMARKS

Since the late 1970s, China has been experiencing fundamental changes from a basically closed planning economy to a gradually internationally oriented market economy. The process of such changes accompanies the diversifying of industrial organisational forms, the enhancing of the market mechanism, and the acceleration of the integration of the economy into the global economy. During the process of change, Chinese enterprises at any particular time tried to establish and expand their networks, so as to gain the benefits of networking.

The two-track system in the economic system transition enabled enterprises to obtain benefit from hedging the two tracks in addition to the normal benefits of networking. Therefore the benefits of networking in the two-track system were larger than in the single-track system, that is, the matured market economic system. However, for a particular enterprise, the precondition for obtaining such 'bigger' benefits is that it has autonomy as well as the capacity to expand its networks to reach foreign markets. Enterprises faced an awkward condition in their efforts for such expansion. On the one hand, it was difficult for them to realise such networking when the market track was very short but the non-market track was very long. On the other hand, once it was easy to expand their networking due to maturing marketisation, the specific benefits of networking stemming from hedging the two tracks were reduced. Therefore, the firms were most actively engaged in international networking when they had sufficient autonomy and yet marketisation was not too mature. They were most sensitive to measures introduced in economic reform when carrying out foreign direct investment. Before that, marketisation was not mature enough for ordinary enterprises to sustain such motivations for international networking. And after that, enterprises would consider factors other than hedging the two tracks in their international networking. As a result, the locus of the growth of China's outward direct investment was very closely interrelated with firm-related reforms some time after the start of the economic reform and the interrelationship became less strong as the marketisation matured.

NOTES

1. As Mao Zedong put it, 'all Chinese without exception must lean either to the side of imperialism or to the side of socialism' (Mao, 1968, p.416).
2. For example, the United States put China under the same export restrictions as the Soviet satellite states in Eastern Europe when the Chinese Communists proclaimed their new government in October 1949. 'This embargo was broadened twice again before the Korean War, whereupon Chinese assets in the United States were frozen and virtually all US trade with China was outlawed until 1972' (Roy, 1998, pp.77-80).
3. The People's Construction Bank of China was once merged into the Ministry of Finance.
4. Prior to the reforms, firms fell into three broad categories according to their status: central controlled, dual controlled and local controlled. Firms in the first category were big and important enterprises, such as oil fields, the First Automobile Works (Jiefang) and the Second Automobile Works (Dongfeng). They served the national market. In contrast, local controlled firms were normally small and basically served only the local market, though their size and importance also varied depending on which levels of local government they were subordinated to (provincial, city or county). Dual controlled firms lay in between. Local firms were coordinated and controlled by local plans and only their aggregated quotas and targets went into the central plan as quotas and targets for the local economy.
5. The brewing of the economic reforms can be traced back to the mid 1970s when Zhou Enlai, the Premier, and others started questioning China's policy of isolation, saying that the effect was to perpetuate Chinese weakness by cutting off access to advanced science and technology, the same mistake the last emperors of the pre-modern era had made. After Mao's death and the downfall of the radical 'Gang of Four' led by Jiang Qing (Mao's wife), Hua Guofeng became Chairman of the Central Committee of the Chinese Communist Party, Chairman of the Military Commission of the Central Committee of the Chinese Communist Party and Premier of the State Council. Though showing no intention to undertake political reform for the time being, he was active and determined in starting the programme of the Four Modernisations (modernisations of industry, agriculture, science and technology and national defence) and the opening up to the rest of the world. Before the Third Plenum of the Eleventh Central Committee of the Chinese Communist Party, the Chinese government had sent many delegates to visit Western economies and Hong Kong and Macau. For example, in May 1978, a senior delegation headed by Gu Mu, Deputy-Premier, visited eleven cities in France, West Germany, Switzerland, Denmark and Belgium. After their return, Hua Guofeng held an over-20 days' meeting discussing guidelines for the 'four modernisations', in which Gu Mu expressed his views upon their observation. In the meantime, the observation group of Hong Kong's and Macau's economies appointed by Gu Mu returned and raised a proposal for setting up an exporting base in Bao'an and Zhuhai (in Guangdong Province), a region close to Hong Kong and Macau. On 3 June 1978, they reported to Hua Guofeng, Hua gave 'general approval' right away and instructed them to act without delay. His instruction initiated the establishment of the Shekou Industrial Base and other activities regarding the opening up in Bao'an and Zhuhai.
6. Chen Yun was a high-ranking official in the Chinese Communist Party and had been in charge of economic affairs in the central government for decades. His basic view on the relationship between planning and market mechanisms is jokingly referred to as a theory of birdcage economics. As to the cage, he especially stressed the so-called four balances – the macro balance of the supply and demand of factors (materials), national revenue, investment and foreign exchange individually as well as all together. He and Deng Xiaoping had similar seniority until the mid 1990s when he died. His point of view had therefore influenced the process and direction of China's economic reform until his death.
7. Enterprises in China are classified into the following broad categories in statistics: (1) State-owned and state holding majority shares enterprises, referring to the sole state-owned enterprises and the enterprises in which the state holds majority shares; (2) Collective-owned enterprises, referring enterprises where the assets are owned collectively, including urban and rural

enterprises invested by collectives; (3) Private enterprises; (4) Shareholding corporations Ltd, with total registered capital divided into equal shares and raised through issuing stocks; (5) Enterprises invested by investors from Hong Kong, Macau and Taiwan, including equity joint ventures, contractual joint ventures, wholly owned enterprises and stock holding corporations; and (6) Enterprises funded by foreigners (NBS, 2000, pp.462-4).

8. The state-owned enterprises have experienced four stages of reform so far. The first stage (1978 - September 1984) is the experimental stage of expanding the autonomy of enterprises: the main measures were government transfer to state-owned enterprises of some powers in the latter's planning, marketing and profit sharing. The second stage (October 1984 - end 1986) signifies the beginning of the formal reform of state-owned enterprise and focused on the separation between government and enterprises, and between the ownership and operation of firms. The main measures adopted were various types of contractual operations. The third stage (1987 - end 1993) centred on the transformation of enterprises' operating mechanisms. Through particular legislation state-owned enterprises were legally granted fourteen autonomy rights in operation. The fourth stage (from 1994) centres on establishing enterprises in the sense of the firm in a market economy.

9. 'Crossing the river by touching the stones', is a well-known phrase of Deng Xiaoping to describe as well as to guide China's economic reform. It reflects the fact that economic reform in China is experimental in nature: it proceeds step by step, moving forwards at the rate the government deems appropriate at any given time.

10. These SEZs are Shenzhen (across the border from Hong Kong), Zhuhai (across the border from Macau), Shantou (on the Guangdong coast facing Taiwan) and Xiamen (across the Taiwan Straits from Taiwan).

11. In May 1984 the central government announced fourteen coastal cities as Outward Open Cities: Dalian, Qinhuangdao, Tianjin, Yantan, Qingdao, Lianyungang, Nantong, Shanghai, Ningbo, Wenzhou, Fuzhou, Guangzhou, Zhanjiang and Beihai. Hainan Island was given same status in 1984 and became a special economic zone and province in 1987. Afterwards many important inland cities – especially those locating along the Yangtze River and Yellow River – became the Outward Open Cities (*duiwai kaifang chengshi*) where Economic and Technological Development Zones (ETDZs) were set up. By 1993 the central government had approved 30 ETDZs: Dalian, Yingkou, Changchun, Shenyang, Harbin, Qinhuangdao, Tianjin, Weihai, Yantai, Qindao, Lianyungang, Nantong, Shanghai Minhang, Shanghai Hongqiao, Shanghai Caojinghe, Kunshan, Ningbo, Wuhu, Wenzhou, Hanzhou, Xiaoshan, Fuzhou, Fuzhou Rongqiao, Fujian Dongshan, Guangzhou, Nansha, Huizhou Dayawan, Zhanjiang, Wuhan and Chongqing.

12. In early 1997 the State General Taxation Bureau made a clear stipulation that directors in foreign-invested firms would be taken as dual positions of directors and employees if they actually assumed managerial positions. While their income of dividend and extra dividend, according to the Circular of the State General Taxation Bureau on the Income Taxation on Dividend and Share Transfer Income Received by Foreign Invested Firms, Foreign Firms and Foreign Nationals, will be exempt from individual income taxation, they have to pay individual income tax for their income of director commission, wages and salaries.

13. Value added of foreign-invested firms as percentage of the national total value added in this industry.

8. Economic Development and Outward FDI

The previous chapter analysed the institutional aspects of the rationale for China's outward FDI and showed that there was a close relationship between the growth of outward direct investment and economic reforms. Such a relationship reflects the intrinsic dynamics of the Chinese firms engaged in networking. Specifically, the emergence and development of China's outward direct investment from the late 1970s reflect a change in firms' behaviour in networking as China began to be transformed from a centrally planned economy towards a market economy. The limited arranged networking in the previous planning system was replaced by semi-autonomous networking during the transition. Due to the co-existence of the two tracks during the transition, engaging in outbound direct investment enabled relevant firms not only to obtain normal international networking benefits but also to exploit the existence of the two tracks. As a result, the growth of outward FDI was very rapid when the benefits from exploiting the two tracks were plentiful and returned to a normal speed when such benefits were reduced due to the maturing of marketisation.

The purpose of this chapter is to analyse the main aims of Chinese firms in using international networking via FDI. Section 8.1 analyses the opportunities provided by the development of the economy for the growth of firms. Section 8.2 analyses the major constraints on exploiting the opportunities for Chinese firms. Section 8.3 analyses Chinese firms' exploitation of opportunities by tackling the constraints via outward FDI.

8.1. CHINESE FIRMS IN ECONOMIC DEVELOPMENT

The Chinese economy is a large developing economy with a comprehensive complex industrial and economic system. While some sectors or parts are advancing rapidly in catching up and some are lagging behind, the economy as a whole is now in the process of industrialisation: secondary and tertiary industries are growing at an above average rate while the share of the primary sector is decreasing proportionally. It is worth noting that the pace of industrialisation is quite fast and economic structure upgrading, especially in more developed regions, is remarkable. Rapid urbanisation in coastal areas and economic belts along the Yangtze River and major railway routes signifies such changes. Huge foreign investment inflow and fast expansion of the non-state sector are two of the major driving forces for the development. In addition, worldwide technological advancement and the spread of the knowledge economy are helping the process.

8.1.1. Size and growth potential of the economy

China is currently the world's seventh largest economy and the biggest developing economy by GDP. In 2004, it realised a GDP of US$1649 billion, behind major developed countries (that is, the United States, Japan, Germany, the United Kingdom, France and Italy), but much larger than other developed countries (Table 8.1). Within the developing country group, China's GDP in 2004 was respectively 2.38 and 2.43 times that of India and South Korea, the world's second and third largest developing economies by GDP.

Table 8.1 Gross domestic product of selected countries (US$ billion)

	1980	2004		1980	2004
China	201.69	1649.33	Spain	213.31	991.44
US	2709.00	11667.52	Russia	–	582.40
Japan	1059.25	4623.40	India	186.39	691.88
Germany	–	2714.42	Indonesia	78.01	257.64
UK	537.38	2140.90	Thailand	32.35	163.50
France	664.60	2002.59	South Korea	62.54	679.67
Italy	449.91	1672.30	Mexico	223.51	676.50
Canada	266.00	979.76	Brazil	235.03	604.86
Australia	160.11	631.26	Argentina	76.96	151.50

Source: World Bank (2000, 2005).

China is the world's largest producer of many agricultural and industrial products (Table 8.2). Its output of cereals, meat, cotton lint, groundnuts in shell, and rapeseeds accounted for 21 to 38.2 per cent of the world's total output. It also produces the lion's share of several industrial products in the world, and for some industrial products, its output is much larger than that of the second largest country. For example, in 1999 China produced 536 million tons of cement, nearly 5.7 times that of the United States, the second largest cement producer in the same year. China also produced 36.37 million sets of television, nearly twice as much as South Korea and 3.18 times as much as the United States, the second and third largest television producers in the world. This suggests that China is not only a big agricultural country, but is also becoming a big industrial country.

Judging from its current industrial output and technological level, the country seems to be in the middle stages of industrialisation. In 2001, China's industry value added reached US$591.11 billion, larger than that of the United Kingdom (US$384.51 billion) and Germany (US$572.29 billion). In the same year, its manufacturing value added was US$405.66 billion, almost as large as South

Korea's GDP. The industry and manufacturing sectors' share in GDP was 51 and 35 per cent respectively, higher than that of South Korea (43 and 30 per cent), a newly industrialised country (World Bank, 2003, pp.190-92). This shows that China is close to newly industrialised countries in the position and structure of its industry. As China has established a comprehensive industrial complex and economic system, it produces a large range of products with multi-level technologies, some of which are advanced.

Table 8.2 Output of major agricultural and industrial products (1999)

Product	China	World	China/World (%)
Cereals (million tons)	453.04	2064.18	21.9
Rapeseeds (million tons)	10.13	42.53	23.8
Cotton lint (million tons)	3.83	18.24	21.0
Groundnuts in shell (million tons)	12.64	33.07	38.2
Meat (million tons)	59.49	225.94	26.3
Fruit (million tons)	62.38	444.65	14.0
Fishery (million tons)	36.02	122.14	29.5
Crude steel (million tons)	115.59	727.55	15.9
Cement (million tons)	536.00	1507.60	35.6
Coal (million tons)	1250.00	4763.55	26.2
Fertiliser (million tons)	28.21	149.96	18.8
Electricity (billion kwh)	11670.00	137457.00	8.5
TV sets (million sets)	36.37	137.14	26.5

Sources: United Nations FAO database.

But judging from per capita industrial output and per capita production of major industrial products, China is still in the initial stage of industrialisation. With about one-fifth of the world's population, the per capita figures of China are very small. In 2004, the per capita GNI of China was US$1290, only about 3.12 per cent of that of the United States, 3.47 per cent of Japan's, 9.23 per cent of South Korea's, 27.74 per cent of that in Malaysia, and 20.50 per cent of the world level[1] (World Bank, 2005). In fact, as labour productivity is higher and increases more rapidly in industry, and hence people in developing countries flock to cities seeking employment in industries (Riedel, 1988, pp.15-16), a developing country with low per capita income must have a large proportion of people outside the industrial sector. This is just the case currently in China.

In the process of modernisation, a developing country has to experience industrialisation and sufficient expansion of the services sector. Industrialisation is essential for economic growth in most countries (Riedel, 1988, p.6). If the share of industry in GDP shows the progress that a developing country has made towards the completion of industrialisation, the share of the services sector in GDP demonstrates its distance from developed countries. With economic development, China's agricultural share in GDP reduced from 30 per cent in 1980 to 15 per cent in 2001 and the services' share increased from 21 per cent to 34 per cent (Table 8.3). However, compared with newly industrialised economies, there is still a long distance. For example, the share of services in GDP fifteen years before, that is in 1983, in Singapore, Taiwan, South Korea and Malaysia was already 62, 47, 47 and 44 per cent, respectively (World Bank figure, quoted by Riedel, 1988, p.8), much higher than that of China in 1998. Therefore, there is huge scope for the development of industries and services in China, as there was for the newly industrialised countries decades ago.

Since the start of the economic reform in the late 1970s, China's economy has been booming and becoming one of the fastest growing economies in the world. China's GDP grew at an average annual rate of 10.3 per cent between 1980 and 1990 and 10 per cent between 1990 and 2001 (Table 8.3), 7 percentage points and 7.3 percentage points higher than the world average annual growth rate in the two periods respectively (World Bank, 2003, pp.186-8). In 1980, China's GDP was about US$202 billion, smaller than that of Canada (US$266 billion), Brazil (US$235 billion), Mexico (US$224 billion) and Spain (US$213 billion). Two decades later in 2001, China had overtaken these countries (World Bank, 2003). Many analysts have projected that, if its current trends in economic development continue, China could overtake Japan and the United States to become the world's largest economy sometime between 2020 and 2030.[2]

Table 8.3 China's GDP and population

	Amount		Average annual growth rate (%)	
	1980	2001	1980-90	1990-2001
GDP (US$billion)	**201.69**	**1159.03**	**10.3**	**10.00**
Agriculture value added	60.51	173.85	5.90	4.00
(% of GDP)	(30)	(15)		
Industry value added	98.83	591.11	11.10	13.10
(% of GDP)	(49)	(51)		
Manufacturing value added	82.69	405.66	10.80	12.10
(% of GDP)	(41)	(35)		
Services value added	42.35	394.07	13.50	8.90
(% of GDP)	(21)	(34)		
Population (billion)	**0.99**	**1.27**	**1.48**	**1.20**

Sources:
GDP from World Bank (2000, 2003); population from NBS (2000); Annual progressive growth rate calculated by the author.

It is reasonable to hold that China will continue its catching up process in the coming decades. 'Countries in China's situation of relative backwardness and distance from the technological frontier have a capacity for fast growth if they mobilise and allocate physical and human capital effectively, adapt foreign technology to their factor proportions and utilise the opportunities for specialisation which come from integration into the world economy. China demonstrated a capacity to do most of these things in the reform period, and there is no good reason to suppose that this capacity will evaporate' (Maddison, 1998, p.95).[3]

8.1.2. Growth of Chinese firms

A rapidly growing economy provides more opportunities for the growth of firms, including more chances for the emergence of new firms as well as for the expansion of existing firms. The chances for growth of new firms are especially good under the following conditions: (1) in industries which have not been dominated by large firms; and (2) where the opportunity for the growth of firms provided by the economy is too large for existing firms, especially large ones, to capitalise on fully, therefore there is room for small firms to expand and new firms to emerge.

The Chinese economy was in just such a situation in the last two decades – the 1980s and 1990s, especially in the early days of the reform. Before the economic reform, the Chinese economy was not only backward as a whole but also ill-structured: heavy industry weighed too 'heavy' in the economy and light industry was too 'light'. As a result, consumer goods were in severely short supply and there was a major lack of variety. Most durable consumer goods were either not available or produced on a very small scale. Examples include motorcycles, automobiles, washing machines, refrigerators, freezers, colour television sets, video recorders, hi-fi, tape recorders, air conditioners, etc. So the economy of those days was characterised as a shortage economy. The start of the economic reform exposed the big gap between China and the outside world in the manufacture of many consumer goods as well as the associated huge profit margin for such manufacturing. Driven by the prospect of huge profit and fuelled by the soft budget constraints due to lags in financial reforms, firms engaged in manufacturing and supply of short supply goods mushroomed all over the country after the start of the economic reform, and the investment craze had lasted for at least fifteen years. These firms were basically set up with advanced technology and equipment imported from abroad. This boom has brought about several changes. First, along with existing firms, many large new firms involving the production of the durable goods and other short supply goods have emerged. Secondly, it brought to an end the shortage economy in around 1996, intensifying competition ever since. Thirdly, due to the lags in financial reforms and local (basically provincial) opportunism (local government supports the development of the local economy by various means), many of these firms operated below capacity for quite some time.

Penrose (1995, p.248) argues that 'if an economy (or industry) is growing at a constant rate, the larger firms must be growing at a faster rate'. This phenomenon of industrial concentration has also accompanied the rapid growth of the Chinese economy. During the 1980-97 period, the number of China's large- and medium-sized industrial enterprises increased from 4 700 to 24 000 (ITD, 1998, p.18), at an annual progressive growth rate of 10.07 per cent, higher than the 9.05 per cent annual progressive growth rate for GDP between 1980 and 1998.[4] As a result, the proportion of large- and medium-sized enterprises has been increasing. In 1980, China had 377 700 firms, of which 4 700 were large- and medium-sized ones, accounting for 1.4 per cent. In 1997, China had 534 400 enterprises, of which 24 000 were large- and medium-sized enterprises, accounting for 4.5 per cent (Table 8.4). The share of large- and medium-sized firms in China trebled in less than two decades. In the sense that firms are collections of resources (Penrose, 1995), the larger average size of enterprises implies that the capability of Chinese firms has improved.

Table 8.4 Number of industrial enterprises in China (thousand)

	a. Number of enterprises	b. Number of large- and medium-sized enterprises	b/a (%)
1980	377.3	4.7	1.2
1985	463.2	7.9	1.7
1990	504.4	13.5	2.7
1995	592.1	23.0	3.9
1997	534.4	24.0	4.5

Source: ITD (1998).

Accompanying the faster growth of large- and medium-sized enterprises, industrial conglomerates are developing rapidly in China. The changing pattern of market competition is the major environmental force in the development of industrial conglomerates, though the specific motives for different industrial conglomerates may be different. In the process of the transition of the Chinese economy from a shortage economy to a buyers' market economy, those which have gained in capability want to expand their market share and market power as quickly as possible, so as to explore the market opportunities ahead of their emerging followers; and those which are losing their competitiveness want to merge with stronger conglomerates for survival and development. Many industrial conglomerates are therefore formed between these two kinds of enterprises with the stronger firms as the core. Such formation enables the core enterprises to expand their business quickly and often economically. This may be because the centralised command can smooth the previous external relationships among these firms or because the existing facilities of the weak enterprises can function properly once the needed resources, normally the intangible assets and financial resources supplied by the core enterprise become available. There are also industrial conglomerates which are formed between competitive enterprises rather than between strong and weak enterprises. Such formation mainly aims at enhancing their competitiveness in relation to foreign-based multinational enterprises by pooling the resources of the enterprises involved. A meaningful feature of the formation of industrial conglomerates is that many of them are cross-regionally organised, which has broken through firms' localised behaviour, a common phenomenon attributable to the old economic system.

The development of industrial conglomerates in China has also been supported by the government. With the aim of improving firms' international competitiveness, the Chinese government has adopted specific measures to encourage the development of industrial conglomerates. On 14 December 1991, the State Council issued the No. 71 instrument of 1991, which approved the request by the State Planning Commission, State System Reform Commission and the Production Office of the State Council for an experiment involving selected large-sized conglomerates. This signalled the government's efforts in pushing the development of China's industrial giants. Besides specified incentives, conversions of the selected conglomerates into joint stock companies were the main focus in the instrument. Industrial conglomerates were given preferential treatment in listing the stocks of their core firms on the Shanghai and Shenzhen stock exchanges, which greatly facilitated their ability to raise capital. On 16 May 1997, the State Council further approved the proposals of the State Planning Commission, the State Economic and Trade Commission and the State System Reform Commission about deepening the experiment of large-sized conglomerates. The new instrument gave experimental conglomerates further autonomy in investment, international financing (including listing on foreign stock exchanges), foreign trade, and employment. The state also subsidised innovation activities in these experimental industrial conglomerates. For example, Baosteel, Qingdao Hier, Founder, Changhong, North China Pharmaceutical Group Corporation (NCPC) and Jiangnan Heavy Industry Co. are now entitled to obtain at least RMB 20 million *yuan* every year as an innovation subsidy (IIE, 1998, p.120).

The growing large enterprises and industrial conglomerates in China form the core competitiveness of the economy. While the average profitability of industrial firms is declining, large-sized firms are much better off. For example, in 1997, the rate of return to capital for large-sized enterprises was 8.51 per cent, much higher than the 4.63 per cent for medium-sized firms and 5.71 per cent for small firms (IDT, 1998, p.82). According to the central bank's report on its successive monitoring of 1254 large-sized enterprises, the sales and profits of these firms grew simultaneously and earnings were concentrated towards some super big enterprises and industrial conglomerates. At the end of November 1997, 23 firms of the 1254 enterprises realised sales over RMB 10 billion *yuan* per firm. Thus 2 per cent of firms realised RMB 480 billion *yuan* of sales and over RMB *yuan* 40 billion of profit, and accounted for 31.5 per cent of sales and

56 per cent of profit respectively of the 1254 firms (IIE, 1998, p.115; 1999, p.438).

8.2. MAJOR CONSTRAINTS ON THE GROWTH OF FIRMS

Although economic reform and development in China have provided firms with opportunities for growth, and most of them have exploited the opportunities, a survey by the World Bank shows that there are many factors that prevent firms from raising productivity and growth. Firms are commonly confronted with shortages of raw materials, technicians, skilled workers, and capable managers. In addition, while shortage of capital and technology is another unfavourable factor for non-state-owned enterprises, the problem of outdated equipment is serious in state-owned enterprises (Table 8.5). As outdated equipment will certainly result in outdated technology in the production process, in this respect both state-owned enterprises and non-state-owned enterprises face the same problem: shortage of technology.

All these disadvantages can be attributed to two factors: the lack of certain critical resources, including created assets, and intensified domestic competition.

8.2.1. Natural resources shortage

China has a large land area, and so far 162 kinds of minerals have been discovered and the potential value of proven reserves amounts to around 10 trillion *yuan* (calculated on the basis of the potential value of 45 minerals), placing China third in the world ranking (Guo, 1996). However, there are some serious problems relating to China's natural resource endowment. First, while the total amount of natural resources is huge, per capita natural resources are very low. Though China's total resource base accounts for 5-10 per cent of the world's total for each of many types of natural resources, with one-fifth of the world population, China's per capita resource base is only 20-50 per cent of the world's per capita average. For example, China's per capita output of mineral resources is only one-half of the world's average (of this, petroleum is around one-fifth, phosphorus four-fifths, and iron two-fifths). Per capita forest resource is one-sixth and per capita forest reserve one-eighth. Per capita cultivated land is one-third and per capita water resource one-fourth (Guo, 1996).

Secondly, most natural resources are poor in quality. Over 75 per cent of China's land is on hills or mountains over 500m high. Half of its total land area is arid or semi-arid. Two-thirds of cultivated fields produce low or medium yields. Irrigated land accounted for only 37.7 per cent of cropland in the 1995-7 period (World Bank, 2000, p.118). Similarly, China's poor quality mines outnumber high quality ones. For example, 95 per cent of iron mines are of poor quality, containing less than 50 per cent iron. A mere 2 per cent of proven iron ore

Table 8.5 Impediments to raising productivity (percentage of sample)

Impediment*	SOEs			Urban cooperatives			Township & village enterprises		
	I	II	III	I	II	III	I	II	III
Shortage of raw materials	14.6	5.5	4.3	17.2	3.7	5.8	14.3	7.4	5.3
Shortage of electricity and other energy inputs	5.7	6.3	4.4	3.0	5.4	4.4	7.7	11.2	10.6
Shortage of technicians and skilled workers	9.7	14.7	10.5	16.8	22.1	8.5	12.2	13.3	20.1
Shortage of good managers	10.7	14.1	12.2	17.8	21.1	10.5	17.5	16.1	9.5
Lack of effective incentives	7.0	6.7	9.0	4.4	5.4	7.8	0.7	0.4	1.4
Poor market conditions	15.7	8.0	11.2	14.1	9.4	13.6	13.3	9.5	9.9
Shortage of capital or technology	8.5	12.6	10.7	12.5	14.1	16.6	21.3	23.9	12.7
Too much production under mandatory plan	1.8	2.4	1.1	0	1.0	0.3	1.4	2.5	2.5
No authority to set prices and production	3.1	5.0	3.6	1.0	1.7	2.0	2.1	4.9	5.3
Excessive profit handed over to the state	5.5	6.2	6.8	3.7	4.4	4.4	0.3	0.4	2.8
Little authority over personnel	3.3	4.0	3.9	3.0	2.3	2.4	6.6	10.2	19.0
Outdated equipment	14.4	14.5	21.3	6.1	9.1	22.4	2.4	–**	0.7

Notes:
* I – most important; II – Second most important; III – Third most important.
** Negligible

Source: World Bank (1992).

reserves can be melted directly; and the average national grade of iron ore is 31.8 per cent, which means that 3.8 to 4 tons of ore have to be mined to melt each ton of iron. In contrast, in many other countries the grade of iron ore is over 50 per cent and 1.5 to 1.6 tons of ore can produce a ton of iron. The grades of Chinese manganese, lead and zinc are also very low.

Thirdly, the geographical distribution of natural resources mismatches demand or complementary factors. There is a serious disparity between the distribution of cultivated land and water resources. While 63.9 per cent of China's total cultivated land lies on the plains north of the Yangtze River, only 17.2 per cent of the country's total water resources and 9.5 per cent of the country's annual precipitation are in that region. On the contrary, with 36.1 per cent of China's total cultivated land, the land south of the Yangtze River possesses as much as 82.8 per cent and 90.5 per cent of the country's total water resources and average annual precipitation respectively. Similarly, north of the Yangtze River lie 75.2 and 84.2 per cent of the country's coal and oil deposits, respectively, but south of the Yangtze River energy reserves are in severely short supply. In the meantime, there also exists regional disparity between the distribution of mine resources and industrial development. Geographically, the ratio between the potential value of the proven deposits of 45 minerals in the eastern, central and western regions is 1:2:2, but the ratio of gross industrial output between the three regions is 1:0.3:0.2 and that of mining output is 1:0.47:0.28. More particularly, the lower reaches of the Yangtze, despite the lack of iron resources, currently shoulder one-third of the nation's steel production. The five provinces of Yunnan, Guizhou, Hubei, Sichuan, and Henan possess 80 per cent of the nation's phosphorus mines while the vast northern and eastern regions are short of this resource.

As to individual resources, research by nearly 300 Chinese specialists indicates that 45 major minerals are crucial for the development of the Chinese economy but many of them are or will be in serious short supply (Guo, 1996). They classified these resources into four groups according to the degree of security up to the end of last century (Table 8.6). Except for the first group in which China has abundant reserves, China faced shortages in supply and the shortage was especially severe for the third and fourth groups of resources. The situation will become worse as economic development proceeds. Guo's projection shows that, from 2000 to 2020, one-half of the 45 minerals will not be sufficient to meet domestic needs. Of the 15 major staple minerals used in large amounts and on which economic development depends (that is, coal, oil, natural gas, uranium, iron, bauxite, copper, lead, zinc, gold, sulphur, phosphorus, sylvite, sodium and cement raw materials), seven (oil, natural gas, gold, copper, sylvite, iron and coal) have either insufficient deposits or shortfalls. The shortages in the supply of these resources are as follows: oil: 10 billion tons; natural gas: 1.5 trillion M^3; proven coal reserves: 61 billion tons; proven gold deposits: 3000 tons; copper: 250 to 300 thousand tons annually; and sylvite: 80 per cent of demand. At the same time, rich iron ores need to be imported in large quantities. In 2020, China will become a net importing nation in resource-type products and raw materials (Guo, 1996, p.15).

Table 8.6 Security of 45 major mineral reserves until 2000

Type	Mineral
1. *Abundant reserves*: sufficient for domestic needs and some export	Coal, beryllium, tin, molybdenum, antinomy, rare earth elements, graphite, fluorite, magnesite, barite, talcum, cement limestone, siliceous raw material
2. *Nearly sufficient reserves*: can meet domestic needs, but with some problems	Iron, manganese, aluminium, zinc, lead, nickel, phosphorus, sulphur, uranium, asbestos
3. *Insufficient reserves*: unable to meet the needs of domestic economic development	Petroleum, natural gas, copper, gold, silver
4. *Severe shortage of reserves*: too small to meet the domestic needs	Chromium, platinum, cobalt, sylvite, diamonds, high quality kaolin, boron, gem

Sources: Summarised from (1) Guo (1996); (2) China Map Publishing House's data: www.enviroinfo.or.cn/research/new_technologies.

8.2.2. Technology gap

With regard to technology, China is facing a challenging task in economic development: to close its technological gap with developed countries. Dynamically, this task includes two challenges, that is, to bridge the gap with advanced countries in existing technologies and to speed up the catch-up process in innovation and invention. Without sufficient improvement in the ability to innovate and invent, the gap with advanced countries in existing technologies would be hampered as these two aspects are intertwined. If this happens, Chinese firms will follow their counterparts in advanced countries passively at fixed distance. In the context of economic transition and development, China must meet these challenges while reforming its technology system.

China's scientific and technological system has been a centralised innovation system, dominated by three types of institutions: (1) the Chinese Academy of Science Institute, which was traditionally responsible for carrying out basic research and supporting major mission-oriented projects; (2) R&D institutions attached to universities, which have been responsible for a combination of research and education; and (3) R&D institutions within the industrial sector, which are responsible for solving problems within specific sectors. The role of government was to coordinate these activities (Turpin and Liu, 2000, p.193). These three groups of institutions had 1.67 million R&D employees (FTE[5]) in

1998, ranking number 1 in the world, but less than 30 per cent of R&D workers were employed by firms. In comparison, this ratio was 79 per cent in the United States, 61 per cent in Japan, 66 per cent in Singapore (CSIESR *et al.*, 1999, p.51).

The centralised innovation system enabled many breakthroughs in the 1960s and 1970s in some cases where major government projects were concerned, for example, two bomb projects and one satellite project. However, it was neither efficient nor innovative as a means of linking scientific research and activities to commercial activities. 'In terms of technological progress, despite the fact that China had been able to generate major innovations in short intervals after the industrialised world (for example the first IC and the first semiconductor-based computer in 1965, both were introduced six years later than in the USA and one year later than Japan), the application was basically confined to small-batch rather than commercialised production' (Lo, 1997, p.155). As a matter of fact, for commercial production and upgrading technology, China's enterprises relied heavily on foreign imports. More seriously, once a technology was imported, there were few incentives in place to stimulate innovation or adaptation around the technology. 'The Liberation Truck, for example, designed and manufactured on former Soviet technologies, remained virtually unchanged for forty years' (Turpin and Liu, 2000, p.194). As a result, technology in enterprises was caught in a vicious circle of import → obsolete → re-import → re-obsolete.

The features of the former centralised innovation system are characterised by Xu and Fang (quoted by Turpin and Liu, 2000, p.194) as follows:

- a self-contained system located within a rigid vertical structure;
- R&D institutions responsible to a higher authority rather than customers;
- weak links between R&D, education and production; and
- excessive management leading to lack of incentives for innovation and production.

Since the late 1970s, various measures have been adopted by the state to reform the science and technology system and for this purpose policy initiatives have been introduced progressively to remove existing rigidities (see Appendix). The focus of the reform was to introduce market mechanisms into the organisation of science and technology activity, to make R&D institutions more responsive to applied, downstream problems, and to promote active and formally organised R&D activities within manufacturing enterprises. The promulgation of the *Decision on Reforming the Science and Technology System* by the Central Committee of the Communist Party in March 1985 signalled the formal start of a comprehensive reform of the science and technology system, which was carried out simultaneously within research institutions and along government regulation lines. In 1988, the State Council promulgated its *Decision on Several Issues Regarding Deepening the Reform of Science and Technology System*. The main contents were: encouraging research institutions to engage in economic activities, including establishing business entities incorporating R&D and production; establishing high and new-tech industry development zones in areas where research and education facilities are concentrated; pushing technology changes in enterprises and the countryside; supporting the development of non-state-owned R&D institutions; and actively pursuing various forms of contract operations in R&D institutions. In September 1996, the State Council further issued the *Decision on Deepening the Reform of Science and Technology System during the Ninth Five-Year Period*, setting targets for reform: to form mechanisms which integrate research, development, production and markets; to establish two systems, that is, the technology development system with enterprises as the main body, and the scientific research and technological service system with science research institutes and universities as the main body.

In the meantime, the government carried out a series of science and technology development programmes with quite specific objectives, including:

- *The 863 High-tech Research and Development Programme*. It started in 1986 with the target of tracing world frontiers in selected applied research areas, including biotechnology, space technology, information, laser technology, automation, energy and advanced materials. So far considerable progress has been made, examples including the integrated circuit and hybrid rice.
- *The Torch Programme*. It was established in 1988 with the aim of commercialising discoveries from institutes and universities and creating new high technology enterprises. It was a key initiative in providing technological links for the establishment of the 53 national-class New High Technology Zones across China. By the end of 1997 these zones inhabited 13 681 new high-tech enterprises and realised a total output of 338.7 billion *yuan* (CSIESR *et al.*, 1999, p.56).
- *The Spark Programme*. This was set up in 1986 with the aim of diffusing technology appropriate for township and village enterprises (TVEs) and farming. The approach of technology diffusion in this programme is to operate directory and exemplary technology development projects.

Through the above measures, positive changes have taken place in the science and technology system. Both funding and staffing in R&D activities in firms have been increasing. For example, total funds for R&D in large- and medium-sized enterprises expanded from 9.48 billion *yuan* in 1987 to 49.98 billion *yuan* in 1997, increasing at an annual average progressive growth rate of 7.9 per cent (NBS, 2000, pp.681-8). This increase was mainly due to a large increase in firms' self-raised funds for research and development activities. As a result, firms began to consider self-innovation as another important source of technology. The ratio between expenditures on importing technology and self-innovation fell from 2.25 in 1995 to 1.24 in 1998 (IIE, 1999, p.67). All these have helped reduce the gap between China and advanced countries in technology. According to the International Institute for Management Development, the ranking of China's international technological competitiveness moved up from 23rd in 1994 to 13th in 1998 (CSIESR *et al.*, 1999, p.13).

Nevertheless, China still has a long way to go in technological catch-up. The main body of innovation as well as the relevant mechanisms for the performance of firm-centred innovation remain to be established. Innovation is 'the process by which firms master and implement the design and production of goods and services that are new to them, irrespective of whether or not they are new to their competitors – domestic or foreign. Most of the time, and in most industries, innovation is based on the continuous and incremental upgrading of existing technologies or on a new combination of them' (Ernst *et al.*, 1998, p.13). Therefore in market economies, the main source of innovation is firms. However, due to the inertia of the traditional economic and technological system, Chinese firms, especially large- and medium-sized state-owned enterprises, still lack sufficient initiatives in technological improvement and innovation. Firms are still under-equipped in human and financial resources and facilities in R&D. Total expenditure on R&D as a percentage of GDP in China is very low. The index for the sufficiency of financial resources in enterprises in China was 2.43, only about 39 per cent that of the United States (6.17), 46 per cent of Japan's (5.27), 43 per cent of Singapore's and less than that of South Korea (Table 8.7).

The shortage of staff and funding for R&D activity in enterprises is to a certain extent due to the lag of firm-related reform: enterprises have not been granted sufficient autonomy in operation. This lag not only negatively affects the incentives of firms to innovate, but also hampers the accumulation of firms' financial sources for R&D, which in turn handicaps R&D activities, including improving R&D facilities and recruiting competent R&D personnel. The innovation survey by the former State Science and Technology Commission and the State Statistical Bureau mentioned above reveals the impact of the degree of autonomy on innovation. According to the results of the survey, compared with non-SOEs, SOEs are less likely to collaborate with outside institutions. In addition, 'science-based' enterprises are very active in links with outsiders for the purpose of recruiting expert staff, but state-owned enterprises are far less likely to have links for such purposes (Turpin and Liu, 2000).

Firm size also affects ability to innovate. As noted in Section 4.1 of Chapter 4, the average size of Chinese firms is small. For example, in 1996, General Motors (US) realised sales of US$5.26 billion, which was equal to the sum of that of the 342 largest Chinese firms, or 32 times that of Daqing Oil Company, the largest firm in China by sales. Small size means that most Chinese firms only have very narrow product lines; some just manufacture a small variety of products with very limited levels of technology. Therefore many firms only have a very narrow foundation on which to carry out innovation.

Table 8.7 Technological competitiveness of selected countries (1998)

	China ranking	Value						
		China	US	Japan	Singapore	S. Korea	India	Russia
Total expenditure on R&D (US$100M)	17	39.33	1846.65	1531.81	12.71	135.22	21.88	37.60
Total expenditure on R&D as % of GDP	34	0.482	2.418	2.982	1.370	2.790	0.770	0.860
Business expenditure on R&D (US$100M)	15	24.93	1342	998.93	8.04	86.52	3.78	6.01
Total R&D personnel nationwide (1000 FTE)	1	1667.7	962.7	948.1	11.1	152.2	114.4	990.7
Total R&D personnel in business enterprise (1000 FTE)	4	477.0	764.5	573.7	7.4	96.9	37.3	671.1
Qualified engineers on the market	36	4.59	5.33	6.38	5.12	5.68	8.00	6.32
Technological cooperation between companies	19	4.73	5.65	5.99	5.60	3.17	3.72	4.43
Research cooperation between companies and universities	17	4.67	6.21	4.69	5.72	3.90	2.65	4.57
Sufficiency of financial resources in enterprises	34	2.43	6.17	5.27	5.60	2.88	2.40	1.83
Legal environment facilitating tech development and application	20	5.94	5.81	5.96	7.32	4.98	5.15	5.38
Threat to the future of economy of relocation of R&D facilities	5	6.16	7.27	5.57	5.60	5.10	6.20	5.46
Support of basic research to long-term economic and tech development	10	6.02	7.13	6.37	6.72	4.38	3.56	4.17
Science and education	25	4.96	4.4	6.19	8.16	4.26	7.07	5.71
Science & technology arouses the interest of youth	20	5.65	5.17	5.42	7.52	5.45	6.83	4.81
Patent granted to residents (1994-5)	13	1595	55903	83781	15	6175	432	18459
Average growth rate of patents granted to residents (1991-5)	19	3.94	2.15	32.83	–	26.68	3.76	–
Securing patents abroad	29	213	109146	80905	96	2434	78	403
Number of patents in force (per 100 000 inhabitants)	36	2	422	544	502	141	1	51

Source: IMD (1998).

147

In addition, current education in China is unable to keep up with economic development and technology changes. According to IMD (1998), China's position in this respect was very low, ranking 40th among the 46 surveyed countries. Higher education enrolment ranked 44th, public expenditure on education 45th and the human development index was 44th, thus placing China as one of the least competitive countries. Furthermore, on whether the education structures can meet the needs of a competitive economy, China got 4.29 (ranking 27th), though this was higher than some developed countries and newly industrialised countries, for example, Japan (3.98), the United Kingdom (3.83), and South Korea (3.79), but much below the United States (5.08), Canada (5.33), Singapore (7.09), and below some developing and transitional countries as well, for example, India (4.57) and Russia (4.72). Obviously, an uncompetitive education system will certainly weaken the basis of support for self-generated comprehensive technology changes.

For various reasons analysed above, even if firms are active in innovation, their innovation activities are basically shallow. The innovation survey by the then State Science and Technology Commission and the State Statistical Bureau mentioned above also shows, that though 92.9 per cent of the surveyed enterprises had undertaken innovation activities, only 66.7 per cent of the surveyed enterprises had new products marketed. In addition, most of the innovation items were not internationally competitive and export sales of new products accounted for only 3.3 per cent of total exports (IIE, 1999, p.68).

8.2.3. Intensified domestic competition and increasing dependence on exports

Another constraint facing many Chinese firms is that domestic competition is intensifying and dependence on exports is increasing. The intensified competition can be seen from the decline of profitability. The rate of return to capital (equals tax plus profit as a percentage of the net value of fixed assets plus working capital) for industrial enterprises dropped from about 20.5 per cent in 1986 to 6.92 per cent for all industrial enterprises in 1997. The situation was even slightly worse for state-owned enterprises (NBS, 1980-98).

The main reason for intensified domestic competition is the changing pattern of the economy. Two decades of economic reform and development have put an end to the shortage economy. Unlike in Russia, other former Soviet republics and East Europe, the reform in China led to industrial competition, not monopoly (Jefferson and Singh, 1999, p.69). The major forces for the upsurging of competition are the boom in the rural industry (notably the township enterprises), the huge number of foreign-capital-invested firms, the conversion of defence industries into civilian industries, and China's long-standing policy of building complete sets of state-owned industries in most provinces. Among them, the greatest impetus to competition comes from the growth of township and village enterprises, which accounted for about 25 per cent of GDP, 45 per cent of value added of industry and 38 per cent of export revenue for the two decades since the start of the reform (IIE, 1999, p.367).

The growth of imports of foreign goods has also contributed much to the intensified competition. During the 1980-98 period, the annual progressive growth rate of imports was 11.42 per cent, 2.37 percentage points higher than that of GDP. As a result, the ratio of imports to GDP increased from 7 per cent in 1980 to 15 per cent in 1998. In addition, Chinese firms knew that China was a high tariff country and it had been negotiating with the World Trade Organisation (including GATT) to enter this international institution since the mid 1980s. Once it became a member of the World Trade Organisation and therefore trade barriers were reduced, competition from foreign firms via imports and direct investment would inevitably increase further.[6]

In the meantime, exports from Chinese firms have also expanded dramatically. Between 1980 and 1998, China grew from the world's 26th largest exporter to the ninth, and exports grew from 6 per cent to 19 per cent of GDP (NBS, 2000). Contributions from non-state enterprises, including foreign-funded, collective and private enterprises, are especially conspicuous in this respect. For example, two-thirds of the growth in exports came from the non-state sector in the 1985-92 period. Also the share of exports from township and village enterprises increased fivefold, from 5 to 25 per cent, while the contribution from private enterprises and joint ventures rose from 1 to 20 per cent over this period (NBS, 2000).

As exports expanded, the contribution of exports to the growth of GDP increased from 0.7 per cent over the 1979-88 period to 15.8 per cent in the 1992-7 period (IIE, pp.114-115). This implies that the dependence of the economy on the world market has greatly increased. The performance of firms, especially those with export business, has become vulnerable to fluctuations in export markets. For example, affected by the 1997 East Asian financial crisis, China's exports for the first time in two decades experienced negative growth in the following year (1998) and low growth afterwards. As a result, economic growth in China slowed down and many firms experienced difficulties.

8.3. OUTWARD DIRECT INVESTMENT

The above analysis shows that while the rapid economic development in China has provided firms with opportunities to grow, it has also exposed general constraints for firms capitalising on their opportunities. In such a situation, it is an essential task for firms to pursue their growth by tackling these constraints (Andersen and Kheam, 1998). In the era of globalisation and the knowledge economy, establishing and improving international networks via outward direct investment is an important choice.

8.3.1. Seeking foreign resources

Resource-seeking direct investment is aimed at obtaining important strategic foreign resources, including natural resources and created assets. The importance of such investment is attributable to resource heterogeneity. For economic organisation, resources are not homogeneous rather heterogeneous: business firms have to collect and combine a set of different resources in their operations. The importance of a resource element depends not only on its scarcity, but also on other resources with which it is combined. Therefore, the value of a resource must be evaluated in different combinations and constellations. This is the reason why Penrose claims that individual firms are collections of heterogeneous resources (Penrose, 1995), and Alchian and Demsetz claim that the very existence of firms can be explained by resource heterogeneity (Alchian and Demsetz, 1972).

It is obvious that the lack of some crucial resources in China has, to a large extent, reduced the relative values of China's other resources, as the value of resources depends on which other resources they are combined with and must be evaluated in different combinations and constellations (Alchian and Demsetz, 1972). Also the huge growth potential of the national economy and the perceived barriers to economic development, that is, shortages of natural resources and the technological gap, have increased the pressure on firms in their operations and development as well as opportunities to explore. For the former, firms are in the shadow of uncertainty in and scarcity of resource sourcing, including natural resources and technologies. For the latter, while China as one of the world's most dynamic economies provides firms with huge opportunities for growth, those firms with scarce resources and needy technologies, due to demand and supply relationships, would gain much more in market power and competitiveness. Under such circumstances firms would be motivated to engage in activities associated with tackling the pressures.

Ever since China started to invest abroad, investment in natural resource exploitation has been a major focus. MOFTEC data show that FDI in natural resource exploitation accounted for about 30 per cent of China's total outward direct investment between 1979 and 1998. Based upon perceived shortages of certain raw materials (for example, oil, timber, metals and fishery), some Chinese firms have carried out large-scale natural resources exploitation investment. This type of investment is concentrated in Oceania, North America and Latin America. For example, the China International Trust and Investment Corporation (CITIC) spent US$140 million on buying a 10 per cent share in the Portland Aluminium Smelter Company in Australia in 1986 (Bowen, 1993). Another of its natural resource investment projects in Australia is the wholly owned Metro Meats with an investment of A$103 million. In Canada, CITIC's main investment is a pulp mill. Similarly, Shougang Corporation paid about US$312 million (including outstanding long-term company debt) to acquire 98 per cent of the stock of Herroperu SA in Peru in 1992 (Bowen, 1993). The

Ministry of Metallurgical Industry of China invested A$120 million to set up a joint venture in a mine in Mt Channer, Australia. In the meantime, local firms also joined the ranks. Tseng and Mak (1996) note that firms from the Pearl River Delta in Guangdong Province are active in natural-resource-seeking investment. For example, a cosmetic factory set up production facilities in Thailand because the essential oil produced there was readily accessible. Similarly, a furniture factory set up a subsidiary in Thailand to gain access to the timber produced there. Another overseas enterprise was set up in Alaska to carry out fish processing because of the enormous amount of resources available.

A survey covering sixteen large- and medium-sized Chinese firms and 31 of their overseas manufacturing subsidiaries carried out by Zhang and Bulcke in 1993 also provides supporting evidence for our argument. As to the relevant two factors, 'desire to be near source of supply' and 'lack of raw materials in home country', the indices for the total sample were 2.4 and 2.2 respectively (Table 8.8). Considering the fact that only a limited number of firms has, among other things, the financial ability to carry out natural resource exploitation investment as natural resource exploitation in most cases requires huge capital input, and therefore its weight in the index calculation is reduced, these figures imply that the actual motives for natural-resource-seeking investment are strong.

According to Porter's theory of competitive development, 'despite the diversity of most economies, we can identify a predominant or emergent pattern in the nature of competitive advantage in a nation's firms at a particular time' by way of four distinct stages: (i) factor driven; (ii) investment driven, which is associated with the manufacturing of intermediate and capital goods (heavy and chemical industrialisation) and infrastructural building (housing, transportation, communications and public works construction); (iii) innovation driven; and (iv) wealth driven (Porter 1990, pp.545-6). 'This evolutionary path fits the notion of an optimal sequencing of development starting from the initial stage of labour-intensive, low skill manufacturing (or from the initial stage of natural resource extraction) and moving on to the subsequent stage of relatively physical capital-intensive industrial activities and finally to the more advanced stage of human capital intensive growth' (Ozawa, 1992, p.30).

If it can be said that China's natural-resource-seeking investment is mainly motivated by considerations of developing a factor-driven economy, which is proclaimed by some economists as the initial stage of economic development, investment aimed at obtaining access to foreign technology and information is more important to firms as well as the home country as it signals the development of an innovation-driven economy which would come into being when a country is human capital abundant and active in research and development (R&D).

Table 8.8 Motives of Chinese enterprises for investing abroad[a]

Factors [b]	Most recent subsidiary	Oldest subsidiary	Largest subsidiary	Total sample ranking [c]
Expansion into new market	3.4	3.8	3.3	3.6
To advance exports of parent company	3.4	3.6	3.2	3.5
To be near export markets	3.3	3.6	3.2	3.4
Access to information abroad	2.9	3.8	2.8	3.3
Following home country's strategy	4.0	2.3	3.2	3.2
To build up international experience	3.1	3.3	2.8	3.1
Access to third country markets	2.8	3.5	2.8	3.1
Diversification of production	2.3	3.2	3.0	2.9
Higher rate of profit abroad	2.9	2.2	3.3	2.6
To use product innovation	3.1	2.2	2.7	2.6
Trade barriers in host country	2.3	2.4	2.7	2.4
Investment incentives in host country	1.8	2.5	3.0	2.4
Desire to be near source of supply	3.0	2.2	1.8	2.4
Defending existing markets	2.6	2.0	2.3	2.3
Lack of raw materials at home	2.7	1.7	2.5	2.2
To follow competition	2.0	2.5	1.7	2.1
Bilateral agreements	1.3	2.5	1.5	1.9
Cultural and language proximity	1.3	2.1	2.2	1.9
Competitive pressure at home	1.9	1.7	1.5	1.7
Lower labour cost in host country	2.0	1.5	1.7	1.7
Lower land cost in host country	1.9	1.7	1.3	1.7
To use labour-intensive technology	2.2	1.4	1.5	1.7
To exploit managerial skills	2.1	1.2	2.0	1.7
To follow customers	1.6	1.2	2.7	1.6
Lower capital cost in host country	1.0	1.6	1.3	1.4
Political instability in home country	1.0	1.2	1.5	1.2
Diversification of financial risks	1.2	1.0	1.3	1.1
Market limitation in home country	1.0	1.0	1.2	1.0

Notes:
[a]. The survey was carried out in 1993.
[b]. There were 28 responding firms, of which nine were the most recent subsidiaries, eight the oldest and five the largest subsidiaries.
[c]. The importance of each factor was ranked on a 1-5 point scale: 1 = very limited, 2 = limited, 3 = moderate, 4 = important, and 5 = very important.

Source: Zhang and Bulcke (1996b), p.150.

As indicated earlier in this chapter, judging from its current industrial output and technological level, China seems to be in the intermediate stage of industrialisation. At this stage, the improvement of technology innovation capacity becomes crucial to the further development of the economy. The rationale is that, as the technological gap between China and advanced countries gradually reduces, the efficiency of adopting the existing advanced technology to a greater extent depends on firms' ability to adapt and innovate. The required technology in most cases is more difficult to obtain, as firms begin to need 'newer' technology but owners of new technology are not as generous in technology transfer as owners of obsolete technology. Information about such technology is crucial for firms in the same trade. According to Mansfield (1985), information concerning development decisions is in the hands of domestic rivals for about 12 to 18 months and information concerning the detailed nature and option of a new product or process generally leaks out within about a year. It would be reasonable to assume that the speed of similar leakages internationally might be even slower. Therefore for firms in their higher stage of technological catch-up, one effective option is to invest in countries at the technological frontier to maintain access to sources of innovation as well as to utilise technological experts. For Chinese firms, there is another task: they not only need technology of products and processes, but also advanced organisation techniques and marketing skills in advanced market economies, which to a large degree stems from lack of experience and skills in operating under market regimes.

Against this background, many Chinese firms are active in undertaking technology-seeking investment. According to the result of Zhang and Bulcke's survey, 'access to information abroad' and 'to build up international experience' rank high in the list of investment motives of Chinese firms. According to network theory, it is natural for Chinese investors to have such motives. As Casson and Cox indicated, information flows between people. Accurate and undistorted flows of information will be characteristic of intra-firm flows created through the internalisation of markets. It is also a feature of information exchange between parties who trust each other because they belong to a well-defined social group (Casson and Cox, 1997, pp.185-6). An overseas node established by FDI will not only enable the firm to internalise the flows of information by employing local workers who are sources of the required information, but also to function as a unit for collecting and processing information through its contact with other firms and institutions, in a sense similar to the contact among members of a club. The short distance or on the spot contacting can also reduce the time for obtaining information. As for 'international experience', FDI is the unavoidable choice, as it is a type of knowledge not codifiable in nature and information needs close contact to be obtained.

Tseng's survey provides similar supporting evidence. As for acquiring foreign technology and management skills, those firms which wish to upgrade their technology think FDI is very important. What Chinese firms are equally focused on is that first-hand information of foreign technology and markets is very important, especially in product development and formulation of marketing strategy (Tseng and Mak, 1996). They quote a television factory setting up a 'window company' in Hong Kong as an information collector:

An electronic group from Shenzhen: The electronic group from Shenzhen consists of industry, science and technology, trade and finance, property development, warehouse and transportation with electronic industries as its core businesses, which include computer, television and audio-visual equipment; telecommunications, colour television tubes, semi-conductors, and so on. It is directly under the Shenzhen municipal government (Shenzhen Investment and Management Corporation). Its sales turnover amounted to RMB 4 billon.

In 1986, the group set up a department in the Shen Yep Company (a Shenzhen government company in Hong Kong) in Hong Kong as a marketing and technology information collector as well as a contact point with business associates from other parts of the world. It further set up overseas enterprises in the United States (trading); Canada (trading); Kenya (assembly of tape recorders), Thailand (production), Japan (trading) and Germany (trading).

In January 1992, the Chief Executive Officer of the electronic group announced in Hong Kong that the group had purchased 340000 sq. ft of land in the Tai Po Industrial Estate, for HK$ 48 million. The objective of acquiring the land was to build a super-integrated circuit factory in Hong Kong, with a total investment of HK$2.5 billion.

The main purpose was to acquire the latest technology from the foreign partner. The group was confident that even though the technology from the foreign partner was not the latest, they could use it as a foundation for further development. Hong Kong was chosen as the investment site instead of Shenzhen to avoid the embargo imposed by COCOM (Coordinating Committee for Multilateral Export Control) in Paris. (Tseng and Mak, 1996)

In effect, there are a number of cases of successful and unsuccessful Chinese ventures into technology upgrading through outward direct investment in the United States. For example, Shougang acquired Masta Engineering Co., a leading US designer and manufacturer of hot rolling mills and other metallurgical plants. The efforts of technology-seeking investment sometimes are not successful. An example was the proposed acquisition of Mamco Manufacturing Company by China National Aero-Technology Import and Export Corporation which was blocked by the Committee on Foreign Investment in the United States on national security grounds (Graham and Krugman, 1991).

Many firms take overseas investments, especially joint ventures outside of China, as ideal training grounds for PRC management and production personnel. Most of the large Chinese holding companies in Hong Kong, for example, the Bank of China Group, Guangdong Enterprises Holdings, and China Resources (Holdings) Co. Ltd, have their own in-house training centres there. China Resources (Holdings) Co. Ltd even organised an MBA course in cooperation with an established university in the United States for selected young high-flying executives who have the potential to be promoted to top management positions. Besides management training, this gives them the opportunity to put into practice Western management principles and production techniques in the Hong Kong environment. In addition, many Chinese executives consider an initial investment of US$0.5 million as a reasonable 'tuition fee' to learn overseas business even if the investment is ultimately lost (Tseng and Mak, 1996). Their point of view meets Peng's learning option argument that this kind of direct investment is like a financial option investment: following the intuitive notion of keeping options open, the investor makes a small initial investment to buy the option, which gives him the right for further investment without being obligated to do so (Peng, 1995).

8.3.2. Enforcing transactions and improving market positions

The major portion of transactions enforcing FDI from China is aimed at overseas market. Table 8.8 shows that this is the strongest motivation for the China's outward direct investment and the sample firms assign the relevant factors with very high weights, for example, to expand into new markets (3.6), to advance exports of parent company (3.5), to be near export markets (3.4), for access to third country markets (3.1), for higher rate of profit abroad (2.6), to bypass trade barriers in host country (2.4), and to defend existing markets (2.3). This indicates that Chinese firms are very keen to market their products to foreign countries. This, together with the fact that China is a large market with huge growth potential, implies that the domestic competition is intensifying. It is interesting that the firms surveyed have given the factor 'market limitation in home country' a very low weight. The reason may be that the domestic market still has room for these firms, but foreign markets are comparatively more profitable and more important for the future of the firms.

A large portion of China's transaction-enforcing FDI is made by industrial firms to carry out overseas manufacturing activities, though the specific motives for such investment vary from protecting an existing overseas market to developing new markets in foreign countries. From June 1999 to April 2000, a 'Go Abroad' research team incorporating researchers from the Foreign Branch of the Ministry of Finance and the Institute for International Trade and Economic Cooperation under the MOFTEC carried out a questionnaire survey about China's overseas manufacturing. This survey was taken at the Training Class for Overseas Manufacturing and Trade jointly held by the MOFTEC and the State Economic and Trade Commission and in Jiangsu, Shanghai, Guangdong and Fujian (including the SEZs of Shenzhen, Zhuhai and Xiamen) as well. Structured questionnaire sheets were sent out to about 170 firms and more than 100 firms gave effective responses. According to the results of the survey, 47.1 per cent of the surveyed firms consider 'to develop overseas market' as their main concern. About 17 per cent of the surveyed firms have the motivation to obtain higher expected profit in foreign countries. Firms that are concerned about inadequate needs and intense competition in domestic markets account for 14.5 per cent. FDI aimed at bypassing trade barriers and at tackling intensified export competition, each accounts for 12.2 per cent and 9.3 per cent respectively (Figure 8.1). The ranking of these factors confirms the findings of Zhang and Bulcke (1996a) quoted in Table 8.8.

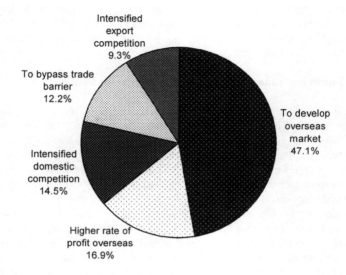

Source: Li (2000).

Figure 8.1 Motives for overseas manufacturing

As foreign direct investment can establish a node in the place closest to the firm's partners and customers and such a node can benefit the firm in obtaining information and improving network position, the firm's transactions are improved. Here we take Jincheng Motorcycles as an example. It is one of the biggest motorcycle producers in China. Due to intensified domestic competition, the overseas market is important for the company as a source of revenue. However, before 1996 it served its overseas market solely through exports. It realised that exporting only could not be a long-term strategy for the following reasons: (1) it was extremely difficult to have a satisfied imports and sales agent which was willing to provide sufficient market information and possessed rich market experience about the local market; (2) the long distance between the firm and its overseas market hampered its supply of necessary after-sales services; and (3) the firm's dependence on the imports agent was increasing as exports expanded, therefore the firm was facing growing uncertainty and risk. These factors led the firm to set up a 50-50 joint venture in Colombia in 1997 to produce motorcycles and supply the local market which had been one of Jincheng's important export destinations. The joint venture has established 25 specialised shops for the firms' products. This has greatly improved Jincheng's networks in the country. Thanks to well-structured networks and the establishment of the joint venture, Jincheng's revenue from abroad increased 69 per cent in 1997 on the previous year's base and achieved a further growth rate of 24 per cent in 1998 (Li, 2000, pp.113-26).

Not only can overseas manufacturing FDI improve firms' transaction and positions, FDI of other types also has such consequences, including natural-resource-exploiting FDI. Natural resource exploiting is a classic type of foreign direct investment. The unrecovery of most natural resources induces severe market imperfection and most of the time government behaviour would further enlarge the imperfection, resulting in uncertainty of supply. One of the key benefits of natural-resource-exploiting investment is the security of resources supply. The subsidiaries of an investing firm have access to a large set of relevant resources supplies owned by the investing firm. If there is disruption to part of the supply, action can be taken by the parent firm to minimise the effect on any one affiliate. Also, an affiliate can always renew its contracts for supplies of the specific resource. During times of crisis a firm with no ongoing relationship with a supplier may have difficulty in obtaining adequate supplies of the resource at any price. On the other hand, natural-resource-exploiting investment often results in the establishment of vertical integration within the complex of the investing firm. In such a situation, cost-saving efficiencies are most likely to be realised by coordinating activities that occur in several different countries within the networks of the firm. Therefore an international integrated firm can coordinate the exploitation, transport, refining and distribution of downstream products at lower costs than individual firms at each stage might be able to by using the market. The economies of vertical integration involve reduction in transaction costs, the cost of search and the costs of holding inventories (Aliber, 1970, pp.19-20).

8.4. CONCLUDING REMARKS

This chapter has analysed the technological configuration aspects of the rationale for China's outward FDI. As the transition of the economic system proceeds towards completion, factors relating to technological configuration in economic organisation are becoming more important for China's investors. The development and reformation of the Chinese economy have provided firms with huge opportunities for growth. However, capitalising on these opportunities requires firms to tackle difficulties related to natural resource shortages, technology gaps and intensified domestic competition. Overseas direct investment is a good means of tackling such difficulties and therefore a good means of exploiting the opportunities. With overseas investment, networks between the parent and affiliates are established. Through these networks, information, technology and natural resources can flow more smoothly within the relevant firms. In the meantime, as the overseas nodes of the networks are attached to business networks in the host countries, the contents of the flows are likely to be better in quality, larger in volume or more secure in a supply-demand relationship. Direct benefits from such investment are transaction cost saving and efficiency improving. Indirect benefits include the improvement of the market power of the investing firm. For these reasons, Chinese enterprises were very active in engaging in such investments in the last two decades.

NOTES

1. China has devaluated its currency many times since the onset of the reform. The exchange rate of RMB to US dollars decreased from 1.7:1 in 1978 to 8.7:1 in 1994. Some economists specialising in comparative international economics believe that the actual size of China's GDP and GNP calculated on the basis of the official exchange rate has been greatly underestimated. Therefore they have attempted new estimates of China's national income, including those obtained by adopting the method of Purchasing Power Parity (PPP) (Lin *et al.*, 1996, p.10). The International Monetary Fund (IMF) and the World Bank supply such figures. Even so, the PPP GNI per capita of China in 2004 was just US$4980, only 13.20 per cent of that of the United States, 17.50 per cent of Japan's, 27.67 per cent of South Korea's and smaller than that of Dominica (US$5020) (World Bank, 2005).
2. Here we quote a few projections:

   • *World Bank's projection*. China's GDP will overtake that of the United States before 2020 on the assumption that the average annual growth rate of China's GDP is 8.4 per cent during 1995-2000 and gradually reduces thereafter to 5 per cent by 2020 (World Bank, 1997a).
   • *Asian Development Bank's three projections*. Optimistically, China's GDP will grow at an average annual rate of 6.6 per cent in the 1995-2025 period if it continues the economic reform and has a relatively high capital formation and productivity increase. Pessimistically, the average annual growth rate of China's GDP will be 4.4 per cent in 1995-2025 if the reform stalls and economic growth is hindered by structural bottlenecks. The basic projection is that China's GDP will grow at an average annual rate of 6.05 per cent from 1995 to 2025 if the natural and political conditions of 1995 remain unchanged over the whole period (Asian Development Bank, 1997).
   • *OECD's projection*. China's PPP GDP will overtake that of the United States in 2015 on the assumption that the average annual growth rate of GDP in the 1995-2010 period is 5.5 per cent (Maddison, 1998).

3. Maddison (1998, p.98) holds that China is likely to be able to grow faster than most other Asian countries in the future for these reasons: (a) its level of real income/productivity is quite low; (b) it has sustained a high growth trajectory for two decades and has proved it is capable of maintaining high rates of investment in physical and human capital; and (c) it has been less exposed to the shocks which other dynamic Asian countries sustained in 1997.
4. Due the unavailability of data on the number of large- and medium-sized industrial enterprises in 1998, there is a one-year difference between the periods for these two growth rates. However, this will not affect the validity of the comparison as the time span is very long (18 years).
5. Full time work equivalent.
6. The World Trade Organisation admitted China as a member in 2001.

APPENDIX

Main Science, Technology, and Innovation Policies and Plans in China

Time	Important events	Essentials and Objectives
1982	Plan for technology improvement	Improve technological equipment in SOEs (with focus on technology import)
1983	National plan for key technological tasks	National technological plan (as a part of the national five-year plan)
Early 1980s	National plan for key technological development projects	Support key products and technologies in SOEs
Early 1980s	Non-state-owned technological enterprises	The emergence of research-development-production business entities, which puts an end to the unitary state-managed R&D system
1984	Plan for building key national laboratories	Reinforce basic research
1984	Plan for key national industrial experiment projects	Linking to plans for key technological tasks and R&D
1984	Technology market	Improve technology exchange environment
1984	State awards for technology changes	Encouraging the application and extension of technology achievements
1985	Patent law and regulations	Introduce patent system into China
1985	Venture investment	Establish venture capital investment institutions
1986	Reform appropriation system of R&D	Reform the unitary state appropriation system, expand sources of funding for R&D, adopt contract system
1986	Establish the National Natural Science Fund	Introduce competition mechanisms, support basic research
1986	Institute engagement system	Adopt the system of engagement for professional positions
1986	National plan for high-tech R&D	Support high-tech R&D in several key areas
1987	High and new technological industry development zones	Create good environment for the development of high and new technological industry
1987	State Spark Award	Reward the development of commercial technology, support the implementation of the plan for spark programme

(Continued)

1987	Law of contract for technology	State policy and regulations for fostering technology market
1988	Plan for experimental manufacturing of national class new products	Support the experimental manufacturing of national class products by tax reduction/exemption and favourable loans
1988	Plan for the Torch Programme	Develop and diffusion of high and new technology, support the development of high and new tech industry
1990	National plan for the extension of key tech achievements	Diffuse key tech achievements
1990	Loan for technological development	Support the extension of technological achievements
1991	Plan for establishing the State Engineering Research Centre	Speed up the application of technological achievements
1991	Centre for Productivity Acceleration	Provide technology and information for medium- and small-sized enterprises
1992	Climbing Programme	Key basic and application research
1992	Plan for joint development projects by firms, universities and research institutes	Support the application and commercialisation of technological achievements
1993	Plan for establishing technology centres within firms	Strengthen the capability of R&D institutes in firms
1993	Law for changes of science and technology	Promote technological changes by legislation
1994	Agenda for China in the 21st century	Strategy, policy and action plan for the sustainable development of China
1995	Decision on accelerating changes in science and technology	Speed up the advancement of science and technology, implement the strategy of strengthening the nation by science and education
1996	Technological innovation programme	Promote technological innovation in large- and medium- sized enterprises and key industries
1997	The Ninth Five-year Plan and the Programme for Long-term Objectives till 2010	Comprehensive arrangements for technological development and reform

Source: IIE (1999), pp.62-3.

9. Geographical Distribution of Outward FDI

Within the network framework, the previous two chapters have analysed the rationale for the growth of China's outward direct investment in the last two decades. The results suggest that the growth of China's outward FDI is most likely to be a consequence of changes in economic organisation during the process of economic reform and development. The transition of the economic system is reflected in the diversification of industrial organisational forms, the enhancement of the market mechanism and the acceleration of the integration of the Chinese economy into the world economy. During the process of these changes, Chinese enterprises sought to establish and expand their networks, including overseas networks. Outward FDI enabled Chinese firms not only to gain access to foreign resources, created assets, markets, as well as international business experience, but also to exploit the domestic two-track system of the economic transition.

This chapter analyses the geographical distribution of China's outward FDI. China's FDI is heavily concentrated in a limited number of destinations, namely, the United States, Canada and Australia. Developing countries are not major destinations. This pattern is in contrast to the pattern suggested by the conventional theory of FDI, which holds that FDI from a developing country would be directed at countries with economic, geographical and cultural proximity. Nevertheless, when China's investment is considered in the framework of networks, the pattern of location choice for China's outward FDI can be viewed as consistent with the aims of seeking various networking benefits.

9.1. NETWORKING AND LOCATION CHOICE FOR FDI

From a network perspective, foreign direct investment is a means of establishing and developing positions for the investing firm in relation to its counterparts in foreign networks. As noted earlier in Chapter 6, FDI achieves this objective in the following manner: an FDI project is a node (in the case of initial investment) or an improvement in an existing node (in the case of subsequent incremental investment) in the investing firm's global business networks and this node connects not only different business activities of the firm but also the firm's business networks to the market networks of the host country. Through the node, intended assets are created, developed or acquired. As FDI can be classified according to motivation as well as to the evolution process of a firm's international networking, the location choice for FDI is essentially a function of the firm's motives and the evolution of the investing firm's international networking. As China's outward direct investment as a whole is basically of the greenfield variety, we focus on the location choice of initial outward direct investment.

The first round of direct investment is aimed at extending a domestic firm's network to a foreign country. The investing firm sets up its first ownership-based node in the host country and this node couples the firm's business network with networks in that country. It is such a coupling that serves the specific motives of the investment. Compared with investment by well-established multinational enterprises, first-round investment is the beginning of going international. Therefore the node which is going to be established has the specific purpose of seeking either a specific type of resource or a market for the firm's products. Therefore the location choice for an FDI project mainly depends on the motive in respect of geography and information airing.

As discussed in Chapter 6, the principal motives of investing firms are resource exchange, enforcing market transactions and improving firms' positions in the networks; the impact of these on the location of FDI is discussed below.

9.1.1. Location choice for resource-seeking FDI

Resource exchange FDI aims at obtaining strategic resources required by the investing firm. The importance of such FDI lies in the heterogeneity of resources in use, value, transaction and mobility.

In this perspective, resources have two dimensions: scarcity and relationship. Conventional economics emphasises the dimension of scarcity and to some extent derives the purpose of the firm from such resource scarcity. Thus, it is argued that the very purpose of the firm is economising on scarce resources and the emphasis must be on the control of resources (Håkansson and Snehota, 1995, p.134). Such a view regards resources as being homogeneous and their value is considered to be independent of other resources they are combined with when used. In the real world, resources are heterogeneous and their value depends crucially on which other resources they are combined with and in what combinations and constellations (Alchian and Demsetz, 1972).

While a firm would have direct control over certain resources, it still needs to acquire some other resources external to itself. In other words, a firm would always have to make some resources available through exchange with others. In most cases outsourced resources cannot be simply transferred, rather they have to be accessed and made available only through relationshipsand the control over these resources is *indirect, joint control* shared with the counterpart.

Generally, tangible resources can be made available mainly through ownershipand access to and control over these resources depends less on relationships. However, the softer resources such as material know-how, knowledge of the market, application know-how or technology are not embedded in physical products and cannot be simply transferred. Therefore, relationships play a much important role in accessing and asserting control over these resources. This implies that networking would be the preferred mode for acquiring such soft resources.

If the spatial distribution of resources is brought into the analysis of economic organisation, the collection and combination of resources must consider mobility of resources within and across nations.

Individual factors of production are also heterogeneous in terms of mobility: the degree of mobility varies among factors and from one nation to another. If it can be said that the dimension configuration of a particular resource mainly determines how to collect that resource and combine it with other resources, then the mobility of that resource mainly determines where to obtain it and where to combine it with other resources.

Natural resources are completely immobile. It is physically impossible to move land area, climate, soil, forests, mines, landforms and other gifts of nature from one place to another. Since the international distribution of natural resources is most haphazard, their immobility assures a permanent dissimilarity in the supplies of natural land factors. A further related issue is that international movement of the products derived from certain scarce natural resources may be hindered by high transaction costs, either due to monopoly or government protection of the related resources. In such cases, the establishment of ownership control over the required resource at the location of the source is most likely to be the choice.

Labour is physically able to move from one country to another. However, potential mobility of labour is severely constrained by legal restrictions, opportunities and information, especially in the case of unskilled workers. Besides attachment to one's place of birth, family, friends, language, customs, the way of life of the native country and of other similar conditions, the uncertainty and limited opportunities to immigrate are major barriers to large-scale international movement of ordinary workers at present. In contrast, the international mobility of professional workers, such as engineers and scientists, is much higher for several reasons. Mainly, these workers possess highly valued skills that meet international standards. In the meantime, they have a superior knowledge of job opportunities in foreign countries because they belong to a profession that is international in scope. Furthermore, due to their higher education, they have a greater capacity to adapt to foreign cultures, such as language. On the other hand, they are likely to be interested in professional advancement whether at home or abroad (Root, 1973, pp.124-5). It should be noted that the international movement of professional workers has a specific spatial trend. Professional workers tend to move from less developed countries to more developed ones and tend to be concentrated in particular areas within a specific country. This trend helps and is a part of the formation of some famous regional agglomerations such as Silicon Valley in California, Route 128 in

Greater Boston, Baden-Württemberg in Southern Germany, and Emilia-Romagna in Northern Italy. Conventional economic theory might say that these regions have benefited from having low transaction costs and high external economies, both of which contribute to what Marshall called the 'industrial atmosphere' of a centre of specialised industry (Cooke and Morgan, 1996, p.26). This feature of the international movement of professional workers constrains firms' efforts to recruit such foreign workers if these firms are located outside such innovation regions, especially those located in less developed countries.

Intangible resources have high international mobility in form, as few of them have any physical constraints on their international movement. It is easy to move a draft, blueprint or a manual about a process of production from one country to another. However, there are severe constraints upon transferring most intangible resources from one agent to another. Intangible resources are essentially information based. The tradability of information depends on the communication costs and contractual problems involved. The more difficult a transfer of the content of information is, the higher the communication costs would be. Communication costs are highest for information of a tacit nature (Polanyi, 1964; Winter, 1988), as such information is shared among a firm's employees and cannot easily be copied or appropriated by other firms without learning on the spot. Contractual problems are greatest for information if it is difficult to patent and if its quality is difficult to assess (Buckley and Casson, 1976), as arm's-length transfers of such information between firms are prone to market failure, including being priced inefficiently, impactedness and opportunism. Of course there is also structural transactional market failure affecting the transfer of intangible resources: owners of intangible resources may set entry barriers by way of monopoly behaviour. When sources of information are localised and costs of communication are high, those who are closest to these sources can obtain information more cheaply than others (Hayek, 1937; Richardson, 1960). This implies that firms which require such resources should go close to the sources of the resources.

Synthesising the results of the above analysis shows that the location choice for resource-acquiring FDI is mainly determined by three features of the required resources, that is, scarcity, relations, mobility (including both natural mobility and transaction-related mobility). Specifically, scarcity and relation to required resource determine the degree of control over the resource, and immobility determines the location for establishing such control. For example, if the required foreign resource is very scarce and its mobility is sufficiently low, the firm should directly control this resource via FDI in the place of source. By doing so, transaction costs can be reduced and security of supply can be improved. If the required resource is very relation-specific, FDI in the place of source is also a preferred choice but the FDI subsidiary would mainly function as a tangent plane to get access to the resource. The impact of resource features on FDI is shown in Figure 9.1.

	Low	High
Scarcity	Wider choice	Direct control
Relation	Wider choice	Indirect control
Immobility	Wider choice	Close to source

Figure 9.1 Features of resource and resource-acquiring FDI

9.1.2. Location choice for transaction-enforcing and position-improving FDI

FDI aimed at enforcing transactions in the market reduces the gap between the minimum enforceable performance and quality performance. The impact of gap on a firm's business depends on the frequency, uncertainty and asset specificity of the transactions involved. High frequency implies that the firm's circulating process is highly attached to its partner's operation and exchange behaviour. Therefore the firm's circulating process will face slowdown or suspension risk when changes occur in its partner's exchange behaviour and operation. Similarly, high asset specificity implies low tradability of the transaction assets. In such a situation, the firm will be exposed to opportunistic behaviour as well as poor management by its partner. In the meantime, uncertainty, which can result from various institutional events and/or competition behaviour, will widen the gap between the minimum enforceable performance and quality performance. Therefore, if any one of the frequency, uncertainty and asset specificity is high, the firm is likely to be at bay if it has not found some means of filling the gap.

FDI can reduce the gap between the minimum enforceable performance and quality performance if it establishes a node in the place closest to the partner in the network or improves the existing node in the network where the partner is located, for such a node will benefit the firm in obtaining information and network positioning. When the firm has established such a node in the market networks, it can obtain more information at a quicker speed and such information will be more accurate in content, for the firm is now able to contact the partner as well as the partner's networks more directly. This is most likely to increase the adaptive and innovative capacity of the firm as well as its partner.

As the information increases in volume, the firm is able to select investment options that are less risky (Gilroy, 1993, p.110). In the meantime, the direct presence of the firm in the network where the partner is situated increases the firm's network position relative to its partner. This reduces the possibility of contract violation by the partner.

Therefore, FDI aimed at enforcing market transactions would be most beneficial when gaps between the minimum enforceable performance and quality performance are relatively large. When transactions for the investing firm are large in volume and important for its business and reducing uncertainty in the transaction is a high priority for its management, the firm can either expand its boundary by FDI to cover the overseas production or distribution of products previously transacted via the market or just set up a 'small' node in the foreign market to tighten its relationships with partners in the transactions. In addition, when external transactions are carried out in economies dominated by networks, transaction-enforcing FDI is also important. These imply that transaction-enforcing FDI is most likely to be located in important export or import markets.

Market-position-improving FDI contains purposes of both resource exchange and transaction-enforcing FDI. It aims to increase the firm's power in the networks to enable the firm to get access to external resources or undertake transactions in foreign countries on more favourable terms. As indicated in Chapter 6, the rationale is that business networks rely on strongly normative social bonds and operate in a hierarchy of some degree in nature. By investing abroad, a firm establishes and develops positions in relation to its counterparts in foreign networks. It would be further beneficial if a firm has improved its position through FDI, as a firm's position in the national network prescribes its process of internationalisation because that position determines its ability to mobilise resources within the network for such an endeavour (Johanson and Mattsson, 1988).

Foreign investment into either vertically controlled networks or horizontally controlled networks has two main meanings for the investing firm in terms of improving its position in the networks. First, the firm becomes an insider in the networks of the host country and will not be treated as an outsider thereafter. Compared with those non-involved firms which can only receive lower priority from firms in the network, an insider will be given a higher priority (Hertz, 1992, p.117). Secondly, when a firm establishes or improves its position in one network, its positions in other networks will be improved for two reasons: (i) it now can get access to more resources; and (ii) it is given more opportunities to disperse risk among the participants of a network value system when using contractual arrangements. This implies that as with transaction-enforcing FDI, position-improving investment should also be located in places where important overseas markets exist.

It is worth noting that in practice a node can serve several purposes and one type of FDI can help achieve another purpose of FDI. For instance, resource exchange FDI can also function as a node for improving market transactions of the required resource or other market transactions. In order to present the issue clearly, the following analysis will be carried out into the main purpose of FDI.

9.2. TARGET COUNTRIES FOR CHINA'S RESOURCE SEEKING FDI

The results of the above analysis about the features of resources imply that there are two types of countries which would be the main target countries for China's resource-seeking direct investment. They are: (1) countries with abundant natural resource endowments and (2) countries with technological leadership. Both these countries are discussed below.

9.2.1. Countries with abundant natural resource endowments

China badly needs some of the major staple minerals consumed in large amounts and on which economic development depends, such as oil, natural gas, uranium, iron, bauxite, copper, lead, zinc, gold, sulphur, phosphorus, sylvite, sodium and cement raw materials. From the perspective of the Chinese economy, the value of these resources is very high as China's country-specific (advantaged) resources need to be combined with these resources. Because most of the above resources involve high transaction costs stemming either from various types of monopoly or government protection, direct control over these resources is the preferred choice. Therefore countries with rich endowments of these resources are the main targets for China's natural-resource-seeking FDI. FDI in this field aims to establish direct control over the required resources at their sources.

9.2.2. Countries with technological leadership

In the era of the knowledge based economy, 'for most developing countries, tapping into the global stock of knowledge is critical' (World Bank, 1999, p.26). In China's case, the most important task is to reduce its gap with developed countries in technology-creating and managerial techniques, rather than in general product and process technology, as in the latter aspect China has already reached a certain level. One of the main aims of China's investment in this field is to establish indirect control over the necessary created assets at places close to their sources.

Table 9.1 lists the Chinese government-approved outward FDI in the 1979-98 period in its main destinations, including numbers of FDI projects, the average size of projects and total flows. Among these countries/regions, the United States, Canada, Australia, Hong Kong, Peru and Russia were the major recipients of FDI flows. They accounted for about 60 per cent of China's government-registered outward FDI flows. They were followed by Thailand,

Macau, South Africa, New Zealand, Papua New Guinea and Zambia. In terms of the number of FDI projects, the United States, Russia, Hong Kong, Thailand, Australia, Japan, Canada, Singapore, Malaysia, South Africa, Macau and Indonesia were the major recipients. They accounted for 60 per cent of China's government registered outward FDI projects. Most of these countries/regions either have rich natural resource endowments or advanced technology stocks or both.

Natural resource FDI normally involves large amounts of capital injections. As China's overseas manufacturing FDI is just emerging with relatively small-scale projects, a large average size of FDI projects implies that there are major natural resource extraction and development investments. For example, up to 1997, the average size of FDI projects in Peru was US$17.9 million, much higher than the average size of FDI projects in most other countries. This is because in 1996 Shougang (The Capital Steel and Iron Co. headquartered in Beijing) took over 98.4 per cent of the equity of an iron mine company in that country with more than US$118 million. This iron mine has about 1.4 billion tonnes of iron ore reserves plus a large amount of copper, cobalt and zinc reserves. This investment entitles the subsidiary to extract the reserves over an indefinite time.

Table 9.1 shows that China also has some large resource development investments in Canada, Australia, New Zealand, South Africa, Papua New Guinea, Zambia, Brazil, Zimbabwe, Mali, Chile, Tanzania, Nigeria and Egypt. The investment fields vary in accordance with each country's natural resource endowments. In some African countries, metal resources are the focus. In oil-rich countries, investment focuses on oil extraction and processing. An example is an oil extraction subsidiary in Sudan set up by a Chinese oil corporation with an investment of US$1.8 billion. This subsidiary produced 2 million tonnes of oil in 2000 (*Zhongguo Gongshang Shibao*, 25 June 2001).

China's investment in natural resources fields in Australia, Canada and New Zealand focuses on metal mines, forestry and fishing. CITIC investment is a typical investor in natural resources fields. In 1986 it established CITIC Canada Inc., a wholly owned subsidiary in Canada. This subsidiary initially invested in pulp mills and later on in lumber mills. CITIC Canada Inc. currently wholly owns Sundance Forest Industries Ltd, a logging and saw mill enterprise located in Edson, Alberta. CITIC first invested in Sundance as a minority partner in June 1989, increased its interests to two-thirds by 1991 and became a full owner in 1999. The annual revenue for Sundance is about US$34.5 million. Also in 1986 CITIC set up a wholly owned overseas subsidiary in Australia: CITIC Australia Pty Ltd. CITIC Australia focuses on investment and trading in resources and primary industries. In 1986 it acquired a 10 per cent interest in the Portland Aluminium Smelter in Victoria and in 1998 it further acquired another 12.5 per cent interest in that company from the Aluminium Smelter of Victoria Pty Ltd (ALUVIC) which was owned by the Victorian government. It is now entitled to 77 000 tonnes of primary aluminium ingots each year. In 1997, CITIC Australia acquired a 10 per cent interest in the Coppabella Coal Mine in Queensland, which has an annual production capacity of over 3 million tonnes of PCI coal (Pulverised Coal Injection) as well as a 50 per cent share in C&S Joint Venture, which is involved in active exploration activities in Queensland.

Table 9.1 China's FDI in selected countries

	Projects (1979-98)	Average size of projects (US$M) (1979-97)	Chinese Investment (US$M) (1979-98)
US	274	2.0	401.0
Canada	82	8.7	356.5
Australia	96	13.4	329.2
Hong Kong	197	2.1	230.5
Peru	9	17.9	120.7
Russia	259	0.6	99.6
Thailand	136	1.5	67.2
Macau	49	2.5	57.4
South Africa	50	2.7	54.2
New Zealand	15	6.7	45.9
Papua New Guinea	16	3.7	43.3
Zambia	10	2.0	43.2
Brazil	23	2.6	42.1
Cambodia	27	1.7	34.7
Malaysia	78	0.9	31.6
Indonesia	42	1.4	30.3
Zimbabwe	6	11.7	29.9
Singapore	79	0.8	28.7
Mali	3	12.6	28.2
Mexico	32	0.7	25.9
Chile	6	3.8	20.9
Tanzania	9	3.0	20.8
Nigeria	22	1.7	20.5

Note: These 23 economies accommodate more than 63 per cent of China's FDI projects and about 84 per cent of China's FDI flows between 1979 and 1998.

Source: MOFTEC, various issues.

Southeast Asian countries are also an important target for China's resource-seeking investment. According to the Malaysian Industrial Development Authority, China's earliest investments in Malaysia were predominantly resource seeking in nature, especially in rubber and metal products. At the end of 1995, China's total investment in the base metals industry accounted for about 82 per cent of its cumulative manufacturing investment in Malaysia between 1985 and 1995 and 4.6 per cent for rubber. In recent years, the paper industry has been a keen interest of Chinese investors too. In January 2001, a US$760 million Sino-Malaysian 64%-36% joint venture was established to produce pulp and paper in Sabah. In Thailand, the agriculture sector has attracted significant resource-seeking investments in areas such as fertilisers, chemicals and rubber production. For example, in June 2001, Sinochem Chemicals made a US$1.5 million investment there in an antioxidants plant with a 1000 tonne capacity. Of the plant's output 30 per cent will be exported. In early 2002, CNOOC agreed to buy the Indonesian assets of Spanish oil major Repsol-YPF for US$585 million. The purchase will bring 360 million barrels of oil equivalent (BOE) in proved networking interest reserves and add 15-20 million BOE to CNOOC's annual output. As CNOOC already had a presence there through a 39.51 per cent interest in the Malacca Strait production-sharing contract (PSC), the acquisition will make CNOOC the largest offshore oil producer in Indonesia (Reuters, 18 January 2002).

FDI as a conduit for technology acquisitions and transfers drives many Chinese investments to be located in developed countries. In this respect, several cases need to be considered. One is to set up overseas trade companies which serve as a channel for exporting domestic goods to host countries and in the meantime also serve as a channel for importing foreign technology for domestic firms. For example, a Sino-Japanese joint venture set up in 1980 in Tokyo by CITIC, a Japanese bank and a Japanese trade company imports advanced technology and equipment for domestic Chinese firms as its main business. In the meantime it also engages in export activities. Similarly, soon after its establishment, Suihua, a joint venture in Hong Kong set up by a domestic firm and overseas Chinese, imported eight production lines on behalf of domestic firms, including a refrigerator production line with a capacity of 100 000 refrigerators a year, the first of its type in China at that time (MOFTEC, 1985, pp.256-7). This type of overseas subsidiary is the driving force for acquisitions and transfers of foreign technology, especially in the early days of economic development. This is one of the main reasons why certain developed countries have been major destinations of China's outward direct investment.

Other firms set up posts for themselves in developed countries by investing there. These posts can serve multiple purposes, including information collection, technology acquisition and transfer, the recruiting of high-level technical professionals, etc. An example is Haier, the world's sixth-largest white goods manufacturer with thirteen overseas factories and twelve overseas sales companies with more than 40 800 sales outlets, which has set up eight design centres and local headquarters outside China, including in midtown Manhattan and the southern United States. Konka, an electronics company and one of the largest colour television producers, has also set up overseas R&D centres in developed countries, including in Silicon Valley in California, the United States.

9.3. TARGET COUNTRIES FOR CHINA'S TRANSACTION-ENFORCING AND POSITION-IMPROVING FDI

According to the analysis in Section 9.2, both transaction enforcing and position improving FDI would be located in places closest to important trading partners, so as to improve the transaction conditions by reducing the distance from partners. To a certain extent the geographical distribution of China's FDI reflects the requirements of networking. The results of the regression show that the geographical distribution of China's investment is positively correlated with the geographical distribution of China's trade, and the correlation between the number of FDI projects and trade is stronger than that between FDI flows and trade (Table 9.2).

Table 9.2 Correlation coefficient between China's FDI and trade

		1978-90		1978-98	
		Number of FDI projects	FDI flows	Number of FDI projects	FDI flows
All destinations	R	0.7850	0.4027	0.6490	0.4983
(152 countries)	t	(15.5200)	(5.3886)	(10.4483)	(7.0382)
23 largest	R	0.7452	0.2964	0.6993	0.6002
destinations*	t	(13.6869)	(3.8006)	(11.9810)	(9.1905)

Note: * The 23 largest destinations for the 1978-98 period were Australia, the US, Hong Kong, Canada, Thailand, Soviet Union, Chile, Macau, Brazil, Malaysia, D. R. Congo, Japan, France, Singapore, Nigeria, Germany, Mauritius, Papua New Guinea, Bermuda, Turkey, the Philippines, Guyana and Bangladesh.

Source: MOFTEC, various issues.

The strong correlation between the number of FDI projects and trade indicates that, overall, China's outward FDI is strongly influenced by the desire to secure overseas markets. There are two reasons for this. The results in Table 9.2 are generated by data on China's FDI and trade for the same period (that is, without time lag). As in most cases, a direct investment project can only function normally after some time has been spent on construction (greenfield project) or adjustment (takeover project). The results in the table are, therefore, more likely to suggest that trade has been leading China's FDI. Here FDI is at first a response to trade conditions, though it can also have an impact on trade afterwards. In addition, trade-served FDI projects are normally small in size of investment, so the correlation coefficient between FDI flows and trade would underestimate the weight of small investment projects, leading to correlation coefficient between FDI flows and trade to be much smaller than the correlation coefficient between the number of FDI projects and trade.

This finding is also supported by the results of two surveys regarding the motives of Chinese enterprises to investing abroad. The first survey was carried out by Zhang and Bulcke in 1993. Its results show that the top motives for investing abroad are overseas market seeking, including expansion into a new market, promoting exports of the parent company, to be near export markets and to obtain access to third country markets. The results of this survey also show that the largest subsidiaries give a slightly lower index to overseas market seeking (Zhang and Bulcke, 1996a). Another survey was carried out by a research group under the MOFTEC and the Ministry of Finance in 1999. Of the 170 effectively responded questionnaires, 47.1 per cent specified exploring overseas markets as the main motive for their outward FDI (Li, 2000, p.21).

As market-seeking investment accounts for a large share in outward FDI projects, countries hosting a large number of investments are most likely to be the main target countries for China's transaction-enforcing and position-improving investment. Therefore, from the geographical distribution of China's outward FDI projects we can see that Chinese firms target the United States, Russia, Japan, Thailand, Australia, Singapore, Germany and Canada as the main destinations for their market-seeking investment (Figure 9.2). While a few of these (for example, Singapore) may serve mainly as a platform for a third country's market, their domestic markets are the attraction for Chinese firms. Some are the world's principal developed countries; products from developing countries have price competition advantages in these markets.

As a form of transaction-enforcing and position-improving investment, market-seeking FDI would also facilitate other types of transactions, including imports, information collection, technology acquiring and transfer, etc. A specific type of market-seeking investment is overseas manufacturing, especially in developing countries. Intensifying domestic competition, immobility of ordinary labour and unfavourable trade conditions in previous exporting markets are the main factors which push Chinese firms to set up overseas production facilities.

Most of China's overseas manufacturing investments are located in developing countries where export markets exist. Manufacturing facilities established afterwards lead investing firms to be closer to their partners and customers through the nodes and these nodes facilitate investing firms in various aspects, including network position improving, and therefore strengthen the bonds and ties of firms' networks. Therefore, transaction costs can be greatly reduced. In the meantime, as labour costs in developing countries are relatively low, overseas manufacturing in developing countries at least would not largely increase production costs. As a consequence, investing firms gain in net cost-saving from overseas manufacturing investment. An example is Gree, one of the major air conditioner producers in China. It set up a wholly owned air conditioner manufacturing subsidiary in Brazil with an investment of US$20 million in 1999. This investment has several benefits. First, tariff and tax savings are considerable. In Brazil, imports of finished goods from China have to pay an import tariff of 20 per cent, an industrial product tax of 20 per cent and a commercial circulation tax of 18 per cent, but imports of production materials only pay a tariff of 5-10 per cent. Secondly, meeting the customers' needs is easier. Air conditioners are semi-finished goods before installation. As large-sized durable goods they also need long-term after sales services. Retailers and customers had misgivings about the products before Gree was present in the market. Thirdly, time and transportation cost saving are also important. It takes more than 50 days to ship products from China to Brazil, and the transportation cost is quite high, as air conditioners are space consuming.

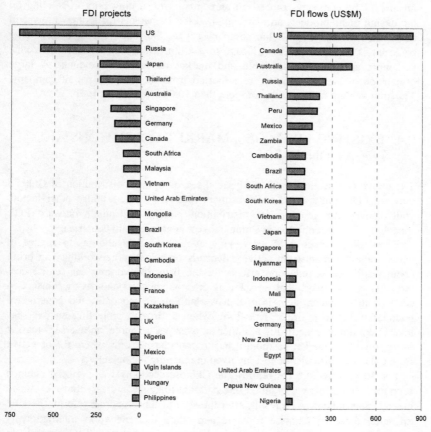

Note: These two figures cover about 42 per cent and 50 per cent of China's government registered FDI outflows and projects respectively.

Source: MOFTEC, various issues.

Figure 9.2 Twenty-five largest destinations of China's outward FDI (1979-2002)

Some overseas manufacturing investments are located in developed countries. Normally, such investments enable firms to respond quickly to changes in local markets as well as to compete effectively with other firms. SUTEC USA Inc. is a Sino-US joint venture by Jiangsu Technology Import and Export Company in a small city near Chicago. The initiative for it came from the company general manager's visit to an annual US mower fair. When he found that the products at the fair were almost exclusively produced by European and US manufacturers and the yearly total sales of mowers in the United States was about US$6.8 billion, he was determined to have his company engaged in that business. The company reached an agreement with a university in Nanjing on the design of its products and later applied for 19 patents for its new mower in the United States. In 1998 the company set up the joint venture with a large bankrupted mower firm near Chicago to use the firm's existing sales networks, personnel and plant to assemble and market its patented products. A large proportion of the components are imported from the Chinese parent company. The joint venture realised sales of more than 10 000 mowers in 1999.

9.4. EXISTING LINKAGES, MARKET CONDITIONS AND LOCATION OF FDI

The above two sections have analysed the geographical distribution of China's outward FDI with a focus on investment motives. There are also other factors which shape the geographical distribution pattern of China's outward FDI, especially the concentration of China's investment in certain countries.

From the perspective of networking, whether a firm chooses to engage in networking to organise an activity depends on whether networking can bring about positive cost reduction effects for the firm. Networking can realise cost reduction in two ways, that is, reducing governance costs and saving transaction costs, both of which stem from the overlapping of economic and governance boundaries between firms. Therefore, when a firm is projecting an overseas investment aimed specifically at either an overseas resource, an overseas market or improving its market position, it has to consider not only where the objective is, but also the difficulty or cost involved in reaching the objective.

For 30 years before the reform, the Chinese economy was a closed planned economy which had very limited international linkages and essentially excluded market mechanisms. As a result, after the start of the economic reform, the vital difficulty faced by Chinese firms in expanding their networks internationally was lack of experience in international business and the market economy. In order to establish and expand networks at the lowest possible cost, Chinese firms were most likely to choose as their main destinations countries with high transaction efficiency as well as possible linkages which could be exploited.

As noted above, the three largest recipients of China's outward FDI are the United States, Canada and Australia, each accounting for about 16 per cent, 14 per cent and 13 per cent of China's government-registered outward FDI for the 1979-98 period. These countries have many common features. They are all developed economies with a stable political environment and well-established market system which provide ideal conditions for market activities, including transactions of both goods and labour. English is the official language and Anglo-Saxon culture is the dominant culture in all these countries. This cultural and linguistic homogeneity has greatly reduced barriers to communication and therefore is very beneficial for business operations, especially in the aspects of internal human resources management and external contract negotiation. As developed countries they provide good education for their nationals and overseas students. Therefore foreign-invested firms face little difficulty recruiting the skilled labour required. All these factors contribute greatly to the efficiency of transactions for goods and labour.

From the perspective of Chinese firms, the transaction conditions for goods and labour in these countries are even more suitable for their FDI when the following factors are taken into consideration. First, compared with other foreign languages, English is by far the most important foreign language by number of learners in China. Most of China's university students take English as their compulsory foreign language subject. There are also many other institutions which provide English learning, including nationwide television and broadcasting programmes as well as local television and broadcasting programmes. Therefore a Chinese firm would find it much easier to recruit expatriates who could use English as the working language if it undertakes FDI in one of these three countries. Second, these three countries have the largest ethnic Chinese communities outside Asia. For example, in the United States, more than a million overseas Chinese live in California alone. Overseas Chinese are exerting overwhelming economic power through the so-called 'China networks' based on a sense of belonging and common experience (Choo, 2000, p.139). Due to a similarity in culture, China's investors can use the overseas Chinese networks as effective platforms to quickly access local markets and business communities, just as Slater indicates:

> The United States, Australia and Canada are relatively homogeneous compared to Europe's cultural and linguistic diversity. The Chinese diaspora is more strongly represented in these countries, providing a progressive airlock for reducing cultural distance. (Slater, 1998, p.271)

While the above factors enable Chinese firms to enjoy high transaction efficiency for goods and labour and high international transfer efficiency for cross-border factor movement, the international transaction conditions for goods between China and these countries to some degree provide an incentive for Chinese firms to undertake investment to bypass the trade barrier. Developed countries often impose technical and other non-tariff barriers to restrict imports from developing countries. For instance, there were often episodes of Sino-US trade conflicts due to United States imposed trade barriers to imports from China before China became a member of the World Trade Organisation (WTO). One of the main reasons that Haier set up a refrigerator factory in South Carolina, United States in the late 1990s was to bypass trade barriers. Previously this company had served the US market by trade for eight years. Through investment this company has maintained its US market and now it holds more than 20 per cent market share of 180 litre and below refrigerators in the United States (Li, 2000, p.190).

It is worth noting that the share of China's outward FDI in these three countries was even larger in the early days. Between 1979 and 1990, more than 63 per cent of China's outward FDI went to Australia, Canada and the United States. In 1991 Canada even attracted 83.7 per cent of China's FDI (Table 9.3). This reflects the more decisive role of the host country's factors in determining China's outward FDI location in the early days of China's outward FDI. As we indicated earlier, there was basically no outward FDI before the economic reform. In the early days of the economic reform, Chinese firms were not only unfamiliar with international business, but also lacked experience of operating in a market economic system. Therefore in making their decisions about where to locate their FDI, investors had to give great weight to host country transaction conditions – they did not have sufficient ability to deal with risks related to unfavourable transaction conditions. Therefore they had to choose countries with the lowest possible transaction barriers as their ideal investment destinations.

When Chinese firms became more experienced in the market economy and international business as the economic reform deepened and international business grew, their ability to deal with market transaction risks improved and they invested in countries where the market system was less favourable compared with developed countries. The improvement in transaction conditions in China further gave investing firms the edge to deal with less favourable conditions in host countries. As a result, Chinese firms have greatly expanded their investment in Southeast Asian countries since the early 1990s. Between 1979 and 1990, China's investment in five ASEAN countries (Indonesia, Malaysia, the Philippines, Singapore and Thailand) accounted for just 5.4 per cent of its total outward FDI, about 8.5 per cent of China's total investment in Australia, Canada and the United States. But during the 1991-8 period, China's investment in the five ASEAN countries increased to 7.5 per cent, nearly 28 per cent of China's FDI in Australia, Canada and the United States in the same period (Table 9.3).

Southeast Asian countries are close to China in geography and culture. China's direct investment in this region benefits from convenient communications and transportation with them. The relative similarity in economic development level between China and these countries to some extent restrains the negative effect of international transaction efficiency for goods on the expansion of FDI. In addition, this region has about 21 million overseas Chinese, the largest overseas Chinese community (Choo, 2000), which exhibits enormous economic power and business networks. The common cultural heritage among the Mainland Chinese and overseas Chinese enables China's investors to settle down to business quickly. All these factors contribute greatly to the growth of China's outward FDI in these countries.

Table 9.3 Trends of China's FDI in select destinations (FDI flows, %)

	Hong Kong	ASEAN-5*	Russia	US	Canada	Peru
1979-90	9.6	5.4	2.6	28.1	5.2	0.1
1991	0	2.5	5.9	1.8	83.7	0
1992	14.9	9.6	20.5	6	2.8	0.2
1993	7.3	19.6	6.7	14.5	2.9	1.5
1994	0.2	24.9	0.8	9	1.4	0
1995	19.5	18.5	0	19.9	0.3	0
1996	19.1	9.1	0	1.4	0.3	40.2
1997	2.9	8	0.6	0	0.5	0
1998	5	15.4	1	9.9	1.9	0.1
1999	4.1	12.2	0.6	13.7	0	12.8
2000	3.2	19.7	2.5	4.2	5.7	0
2001	28.4	26.5	1.8	7.6	0.5	0.4

Note: * Indonesia, Malaysia, the Philippines, Singapore and Thailand.

Source: MOFTEC, various issues.

Similarly, along with the improvement in transaction efficiency at home and the enhancement of international business abilities, the 1990s witnessed the expansion of China's outward FDI in other developing countries (Figure 9.3). Nevertheless, China's outward FDI is still unevenly distributed among individual developing countries. For example, in ASEAN (except for Thailand, Malaysia, Indonesia, Singapore and the Philippines), each country has had only a very small share of China's investment. In Africa, North Africa received only a very small share of China's FDI in that region, with the majority of China's investment going to central and southern African countries. Among them, South Africa, Zambia, Zimbabwe and Mali were the major destinations. The other major recipients in Africa were Tanzania, Nigeria, Egypt, Côte D'Ivoire, Sudan and Gabon. In Latin America, Peru was the biggest recipient of China's outward FDI. On the whole, West Asia, Central Asia and East Europe (except for Russia) were the regions that attracted little interest from Chinese investors. For example, twelve West Asian countries (Cyprus, Iran, Israel, Jordan, Kuwait, Oman, Qatar, Saudi Arabia, Syria, Turkey, United Arab Emirates, Yemen) together received only US$24.95 million of Chinese investment in the 1979-98 period. Similarly, six Central Asian countries, Georgia, Kazakhstan, Kyrgyzstan, Tadzhikistan, Turkmenistan and Uzbekistan, together received only US$25.08 million of Chinese investment until 1998. Until 1998, China invested US$123.55 million in Central Asia and East Europe, of which more than 80 per cent went to Russia. All those countries which have received a small share of China's outward FDI are either experiencing difficulties in transition or do not have good transaction conditions as required by FDI.

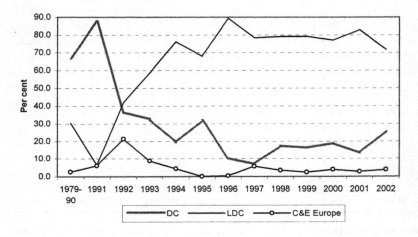

Source: MOFTEC, various issues.

Figure 9.3 Distribution of China's outward FDI among three groups of countries

9.5. CONCLUSION

China's outward FDI has shown specific characteristics in its geographical distribution. While it covers almost all countries in the world, it is highly concentrated in a few developed countries plus a limited number of developing countries. The analysis in this chapter shows that the distribution reflects the motives of Chinese firms in investing abroad and how far conditions in target countries meet the investors' needs. In general, investments in resource seeking are concentrated in some natural-resource-rich countries and technologically advanced countries. Market-transaction-enforcing and position-improving investments are distributed in countries with relatively large markets for the products of the investing firms. In particular, overseas manufacturing investments mainly go to developing countries to serve local markets. Target countries' domestic transaction efficiencies for goods and labour and their existing linkage with China further shape the direction of China's FDI flows.

So far, China's FDI is still in the early stages of growth. Except for a small number of firms which have established overseas affiliates in many countries, most of the investments are initial investments for the firms involved. An initial investment has relatively simple and rather specific functions. For example, it is for a certain type of resource or a particular product market niche in a particular country. Therefore, the location choice involves fewer decision factors. The specific motive for an investment and a foreign country's conditions for meeting the investor's needs would in most cases determine the destination for the investment. As the internationalisation proceeds to the extent that a firm has more overseas affiliates, integrating the geographically scattered affiliates would become especially important in strengthening the international competitiveness of the investing firm. Then the location choice for foreign investment will involve more factors, resulting in changes in the geographical distribution pattern of China's outward investment.

PART IV

Conclusion

INTRODUCTION

In the framework of the network model of FDI, the previous part has analysed in detail the determination of the pattern of China's outward FDI in the three aspects of economic organisation, namely, the governance configuration, technological configuration and spatial distribution. It shows that as the nature and benefit of networking changes along with the process of economic reforms, the locus of the growth of China's outward direct investment is very closely interrelated with firm-related reforms for some time after the start of the economic reform and the interrelationship becomes less strong as the marketisation matures. As the transition of the economic system proceeds towards completion, factors relating to technological configuration in economic organisation are becoming more important to Chinese investors. International networking via FDI is thus a good means for Chinese firms to tackle difficulties related to natural resource shortages, technology gaps and intensified domestic competition as they attempt to capitalise on the huge opportunities for growth which are provided by economic development. And the spatial distribution of China's outward FDI reflects the motives of Chinese firms in investing abroad and how far conditions in target countries meet investors' needs.

The task of this part is to synthesise the findings in the previous parts, so as to provide a whole picture interpreting China's outward direct investment and to conclude this book. A section describing the recent development and prospects of China's investment overseas is also included.

10. Networking and China's Outward FDI

The goal of this concluding chapter is to summarise the material presented in the previous chapters and to present an overall picture of China's outward FDI. The documentation is carried out in terms of the network model developed in Chapter 6 and the information presented in the subsequent chapters.

10.1. PATTERN OF CHINA'S OUTWARD FDI AND THEORETICAL ISSUES

10.1.1. Features of China's outward FDI

China's outward FDI emerged in the early phase of the economic reforms. In its very short history, it shows some distinct features.

First, in contrast to the widely acknowledged pattern that firms become international in a slow and incremental manner (Andersen *et al.*, 1993) and therefore that the development of FDI of a country is a gradual process (Dunning and Narula, 1997), China's outward FDI has grown very rapidly. According to the Ministry of Commerce of China, by the end of 2003, the number of foreign affiliates approved by the Chinese government was over 7470, covering almost all countries in the world (MOFCOM, 2004, p.760). Average annual FDI outflows increased substantially from US$150 million in 1980-85 to US$711 million in 1986-90. This figure increased further to more than US$2.66 billion during the next five-year interval (1991-5), nearly quadrupling the FDI outflow of the 1986-90 period. Average annual FDI outflows kept at a level above US$2.65 billion in the following eight years (1996-2003) (UNCTAD, 1994-2004).

The rapid expansion of FDI outflows soon made China one of the main FDI source countries within the developing country group. During 1985-98, it was among the top five of those countries in terms of annual FDI outflows. Its outward FDI stock climbed to US$27.6 billion in 2001, close to that of South Africa (US$29 billion) (Table 10.1). Six of the top 50 multinational enterprises based in developing economies, ranked by foreign assets in 1997, were from China (UNCTAD 1999, pp.86-7).

Secondly, far from the generally acknowledged pattern that FDI from a developing country would initially be directed at neighbouring developing countries, China's outward FDI is highly concentrated in a small number of countries, particularly three developed countries, namely, the United States, Canada and Australia. As noted in Chapter 2, up to 2001, 30 per cent of Chinese FDI outflows went to these three countries, each accounting for 13, 9 and 8 per cent, respectively. These three countries, plus Hong Kong, Peru, Thailand, Mexico, Zambia, Russia, Cambodia, South Africa and Brazil, accounted for about 67 per cent of China's FDI outflows, leaving the remaining 143 countries accounting for only 33 per cent of China's outward FDI. European countries as a whole only received 6 per cent, the lowest share among all regions.

Table 10.1 Seven largest FDI source economies of the developing country group (stock, US$ million)

	1980	1985	1990	1995	2000	2001
Singapore	3718	4387	7808	35050	53009	63225
Taiwan	97	204	12888	25144	49187	54667
South Korea	127	461	2301	7787	50552	40825
South Africa	5722	8963	15027	23305	32333	28999
China	..	131	2489	15802	25804	27579
Chile	42	102	178	2809	18293	22084
Argentina	5997	5945	6106	10696	20859	20736

Source: UNCTAD (2002), pp.307-17.

Thirdly, the earlier the period, the more skewed towards a few developed countries was the geographical distribution of China's outward FDI. During the 1979-90 period, the United States, Canada and Australia attracted 63.3 per cent of China's FDI outflows. Their share fell to 47 per cent in 1991-5 and further to 9.8 per cent in the next five-year interval (Figure 10.1). This was mainly due to the reduction in the distributional share of China's investment in Canada and Australia. Given the fact that European countries and Japan have received relatively limited FDI from China, the reduction in the share of China's FDI in these three countries implies that, as China's outward FDI develops, developing countries have a growing attraction for Chinese investors. During the periods 1979-90 and 1991-95, only 30 and 35 per cent respectively of China's FDI outflows went to developing countries. However, this figure rose to 80 per cent in 1996-2000 (Table 2.1).

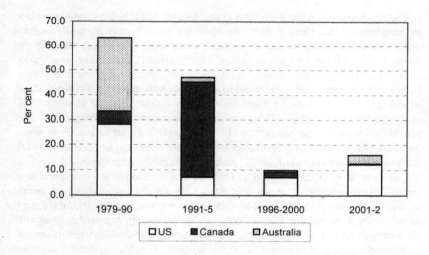

Source: MOFTEC, various issues.

Figure 10.1 China's FDI to US, Canada and Australia (% of China's total FDI outflows)

10.1.2. Theoretical issues raised by China's outward FDI

It has been argued in Chapter 4 that the pattern of China's outward FDI cannot be satisfactorily explained in terms of mainstream theories of FDI. This argument is based on the following reasons.

According to mainstream theories, the possession of some kind of proprietary advantage is a critical factor underlying a firm's FDI. This holds regardless of whether the investment is claimed to be motivated by the firm's desire to exploit these advantages overseas to avoid transaction costs (the internalisation model) or as a part of the firm's strategy within imperfect international competition (the market power model). These proprietary advantages are derived from the ownership of some intangible resources, such as production process, managerial skills, marketing techniques or organisational capabilities. They can be easily transferred from one country to another within a firm, but are difficult to transfer between firms. So they are termed firm-specific ownership advantage.

However, this pattern of proprietary advantage is hardly reflected in China's outward FDI, especially when considering the fact that China's outward FDI has been directed at developed countries as its major destinations. The discussion in Chapter 4 shows that, compared with their counterparts from developed and newly industrialised countries, Chinese firms do not possess clear competitive advantages. Rather, they are typically smaller in average size, and weaker in R&D activities and management.

The timing of the rapid growth of China's outward FDI also raises questions for mainstream theories of FDI. As discussed in Chapter 4, according to Dunning's *investment-development path* (Dunning, 1988), the growth of outward FDI is related to the economic development of the source country, or more specifically, to the source country's inward direct investment position. Before the emergence of its outward FDI, a country is expected to pass a stage in which even inward direct investment does not exist. Even if it has started outward FDI, the country will still have to experience another stage in which inward FDI starts to rise but outward FDI remains low or negligible. Only when the country has entered the third stage can the rate of growth of its outward FDI increase while that of inward direct investment gradually decreases.

However, in China's case, the emergence and development of outward and inward direct investment flows coincided with each other, instead of being sequential. The period 1979-2001 witnessed a steady growth of inward and outward FDI. It seems that China's outward FDI in its development has skipped the first and part of the second stage of the investment-development path, and has now entered the early period of the third stage.

In addition, mainstream theories of FDI hold that national firms enjoy the general advantage of better information about their country's economy, language, law, politics and so forth. As foreign firms do not possess that knowledge, they will incur additional transaction costs in operations conducted within that country. Accordingly, a foreign firm must have sufficient firm-specific advantages (ownership advantages) to offset the comparative disadvantage of being foreign if it is to compete successfully in the host country. On the other hand, if a firm chooses to invest in countries with less cultural, economic or physical distance from the home country, it will need fewer ownership advantages to tackle the barriers to international operation, as a 'short' distance in this sense implies fewer barriers. It follows that FDI from a developing country is likely to be directed at other developing countries, especially neighbouring ones, at lower stages of economic development. Only after having gained international experience through overseas operations and consolidated their firm-specific advantages can firms invest on a relatively large scale in more developed countries that are distant geographically (Dunning and Narula, 1996; Riemens, 1989; Tolentino, 1993). In contrast to this view, as noted above, China's outward FDI is heavily concentrated in a few developed countries and the share of investment in these developed countries was even higher in the early period. Developing countries have not been a major destination for China's FDI in the early period. This fact seems to deny the decisive role of proximity between home and host countries for the choice of destination of FDI, as suggested by mainstream theories of FDI.

10.2. NETWORKING AND FDI

The difficulties in providing a convincing explanation of the pattern of China's outward FDI by using mainstream theories call for a different approach. For this purpose a network model of FDI was developed in Chapter 6.

10.2.1. Methods and institutions for economic organisation

According to the network model, economic activity in the market economy involves two methods of organisation (price and hierarchy) and three possible institutions (the market, network and firm) which use these methods in organisation. While the market uses the price system to organise transactions between firms and the firm organises internal activities via hierarchy, the network organises activity across the market and the firm by using a mixture of price and hierarchy. For a transaction via the market, firms are faceless, sharp in and sharp out; and the boundaries between in and out at the beginning and in and out at the end, are clear (MacNeil, 1974, p.750). In contrast, for organising economic activity via the network, a certain kind of interlocked relationship between the firms involved is formed due to the overlapping of economic and governance boundaries between these firms. This interlocked relationship leads to the formation of external networks around the hub firm, and the boundaries of the firm are reshaped according to the organisation of networking activities.

The network would become the preferred choice for economic organisation if networking could bring about positive cost reduction effects for the firm. Networking can raise net benefit by a reduction in costs in two ways: reducing governance costs and saving transaction costs. As discussed at length in Chapter 6, a firm can move its economic boundary outwards to overlap with its partner's governance boundary while keeping its own governance boundary unchanged or changed less in scale than its economic boundary. The expansion of the economic boundary implies that the firm directly or indirectly has some claim over the usage of some of the required resources owned by the partner. This would be beneficial for the firm if the required strategic resources such as crucial know-how, for one reason or another, are difficult to acquire in the market and their transaction involves high transaction costs (Teece, 1985). In the meantime, as the firm's governance boundary has hardly changed, the firm does not have to increase governance cost. Even if there were an increase in governance cost, the firm would still benefit if the resulting reduction in transaction cost were larger than the increase in governance cost. This can be seen as an indirect saving of governance costs.

One of the most noticeable benefits of networking is that the overlapping of the economic and governance boundaries of the firms involved forms a good environment for more effective transaction and transfer of information between networked firms. The interlocked relationship between two firms helps to bring transaction costs down, because information flows between the people rather than the plants (Casson and Cox, 1997). Therefore, while the social bonds sustained by networks reduce the cost of both communicating information and assuring its quality, the consequent reduction in information costs encourages greater sharing of information.

In addition, networking can also help the realisation of economies of scale and/or scope, such as joint research, marketing or production (Contractor and Lorange, 1988; Håkansson and Snehota, 1989). In the era of globalisation and the knowledge-based economy, the accelerating increase of R&D expenditure and the shortening of the technology life span have greatly increased the importance of R&D cost sharing as well as R&D benefit exploitation among the relevant firms.

10.2.2. Location of economic activity and FDI

Economic organisation involves not only the issue of how to organise economic activity, but also decisions regarding the geographical location of economic activity. For various reasons, the market place is not universal and homogeneous, but consists of many markets at different locations for different factors and products, and economic activity can take place in different locations, including at home and abroad. In addition, a firm is not deemed to be a single-plant production unit with all its activities based in a single location. In principle it is natural that, in a market economy, entrepreneurs are free to displace market transactions by increasing the scope of allocations made administratively within their firms, and the most profitable pattern of enterprise organisation should ultimately prevail. Where more profitable results can be obtained from placing plants under wholly or partly common administrative control, multi-plant enterprises will predominate and single-plant firms will merge or go out of business.

As discussed in Chapter 6, the fact that the organisation of economic activity has three institutional choices (that is, via market, through networking or within the firm) means that a firm that is prepared to consider locating its activity has six possible choices, namely, to organise the activity via one of these institutions at home or abroad.

A multinational enterprise (MNE), the main subject of FDI and a consequence of such investment, is a firm which controls and manages production establishments – plants – located in at least two countries (Caves, 1996, p.1). It involves not only the question of the boundary between the administrative allocation of resources within the firm and the market allocation of resources between firms, but also the question of the international setting of the boundary between the firm and the market as well as the question of the form of hierarchy. In the perspective of economic organisation, wholly owned overseas subsidiaries are the international expansion of the parent firm's boundary by using hierarchy, while joint ventures are the international expansion of the parent firm's boundary through networking by using a mixture of price and hierarchy. Overall, a firm and its overseas subsidiaries form an international network (Ghoshal and Bartlett, 1993, pp.77-104). Accordingly, FDI can be defined as a process in which resources are committed to creating, building or acquiring assets in foreign countries so as to establish and develop positions for the investing firm in relation to its counterparts in foreign networks (Johanson and Mattsson, 1988). An FDI project is a node (in the case of initial investment) or an improvement at an existing node (in the case of subsequent incremental investment) in the network of the investing firm's global business and this node not only connects different business activities of the firm but also connects the firm's business network to the market networks of the host country.

10.3. NETWORKING AND CHINA'S OUTWARD FDI

Based on the results of the analysis in Chapters 7 and 9, the rationale underlying China's outward FDI can be presented within the framework of the network model of FDI as follows.

10.3.1. No outward FDI before the reforms

As shown in Chapter 7, the market, network and firm are institutional forms for organising economic activity in a market economy. While the market uses price and the firm uses hierarchy to organise economic activity, networks use a hybrid of price and hierarchy. FDI is a form of international economic organisation using methods ranging from partly to wholly-owned involvement of hierarchy based on ownership. It leads to the expansion of the investing firm's boundary into the host country and forms a node there, and this node can be used for further networking. It therefore relies on the functioning of these market elements. When an economic system essentially rules out these market elements, it is beyond the scope of an enterprise to use these institutional forms and measures to organise economic activity. Under such conditions, the possible occurrence of outward FDI would entirely depend upon the government planning and arrangement. FDI will not occur if the economy concurrently adopts the principle of autarky in its foreign economic relations. This is exactly the case of China before the reforms.

Under the Maoist economic system, the Chinese government ran the country as a planned economy, similar to the Soviet Union. The state-owned sector was dominant in the economy. Non-state-owned enterprises were very small in size and volume, and they were controlled by the state through indirect planning and other administrative arrangements. So the state was essentially the owner, operator and employer. Each enterprise specialised in particular activities. The government set output quotas for each production enterprise and similar tasks for commercial enterprises. The sources and quantities of supply of input for production were arranged by government planning, as were the procurement and supply in commercial enterprises. Prices and markets in the sense of a market economy were basically excluded from the economy. Though there were 'prices', these were mainly set by the state. They neither revealed information about the relationship between demand and supply, nor reflected the quality of products. In addition, firms operated within the peculiar system of dual financial flows with the government acting like a financial straitjacket. They turned over their revenues (profit) to the state and the state in turn allocated funds to cover the expenditures of enterprises. Fixed capital investment and investment for technological improvement in enterprises were also allocated by the state.

In this system, enterprises did not have the autonomy to expand their boundaries of business, nor did there exist a market mechanism for the external transaction of factors and goods that would be associated with expansion. As a consequence, there was no possibility of enterprises undertaking FDI autonomously.

If it can be said that the planned economic system ruled out enterprises' automatic engagement in FDI activity, the principle of self-reliance in foreign economic relations adopted by the state before the reforms further blocked FDI. For three decades before the reforms, China's economy was basically an autarky economy, de-linked from the rest of the world economy. Foreign economic relations were generally restricted to foreign trade, and higher-level international economic activities, such as FDI, were basically rejected.

Due to the country's de-linking from the world market and the enterprises' de-linking from outsiders, there was basically no FDI activity for the three decades before the reforms.

The above argument would not arise in the mainstream theory of FDI which is based principally on the experience of developed countries and assumes as a precondition the existence of the market and the autonomous firm. This argument only arises in a country such as China, where neither the market nor the autonomous firm existed before the 1980s.

10.3.2. Emergence of outward FDI

Changes to China's closed planned economic system have taken place since the late 1970s when China began to reform its economic system. It had adopted two main policy measures to move the economic system towards the Western model: dismantling state administered economic activity and integrating the economy with the world economy.

The focus of the reform of corporate governance was to decentralise economic power from the state to economic agents, including state-owned enterprises and collective enterprises. Various approaches were adopted for this purpose. These included a profit-retention system adopted in 1979, a tax-for-profit system instituted in two successive steps in 1983 and 1984, a contractual management system introduced in 1987 and the corporationisation of state-owned enterprises in the 1990s. These changes increased progressively the autonomy enjoyed by enterprises in business operations.

Along with the expansion of the autonomy of enterprises, markets developed for goods and factors. By 1988, the market economy had expanded, and factor markets started to emerge. Significant changes have taken place since then, especially after 1992. Stock markets, real estate markets, foreign exchange markets, and futures markets began to open to the public. Other factor markets spread all over the country. By 1998, the market mechanism covered the prices of more than 85 per cent of factors, 90 per cent of manufacturing products and 95 per cent of commercial goods (IIE, 1998). The emergence of factor and product markets has paved the way for enterprises to operate according to the rules of market economies.

The increasing introduction of the elements of a market economy into China's economy implies that enterprises gained increasing freedom in organising economic activity by using different measures (that is, price and hierarchy) and through alternative institutions (namely, market, network and the firm). Accordingly, enterprises were able to decide on the boundary between the administrative allocation of resources within the firm and the market allocation of resources between firms. As a consequence, entrepreneurs were to a growing extent able to displace market transactions by increasing the scope of resource allocations made administratively within their firms. An enterprise may expand its scope of governance by complete or partial replacement of market transactions for a growing range of economic activities. Roughly, complete replacement is using hierarchy and partial displacement is using networks to organise that activity.

For a firm which is deciding to expand its geographical boundary in relation to the market as well as the form of hierarchy, the formation of industrial conglomerates is one type of displacement of market transactions, undertaking overseas direct investment is another.

The development of industrial conglomerates in China formally started in 1987 when economic reforms gradually cut off the supply-demand arrangements between enterprises that had existed under central planning. But price reforms had not yet kept pace reflecting the supply-demand relationship. In particular, raw materials and intermediate products were under-priced and final products were over-priced. These had given under-paid firms upstream incentives to evade the supply quotas assigned by central planning in one way or another. The evasion affected, in many cases seriously, the production of downstream firms or firms over-paid. In order to secure supply and smooth business, many large manufacturers downstream sought to establish conglomerates of reverse integration with former suppliers, or some firms established conglomerates with other related firms to compete with larger ones. Therefore, there was a boom in the establishment of conglomerates in China in the 1980s. In 1988 there were 1630 self-styled conglomerates of different types (La Croix *et al.*, 1995, p.37). The trend to set up conglomerates had later moved to developing 'pillar' industries, pushing forward technological advancement, expanding exports and competing with foreign-based multinational enterprises. The main approaches to forming conglomerates were merging with or taking over other companies, buying shares of other companies, establishing financial companies, and assets licensed operation. The institutional forms involved range from the firm which uses hierarchy to networking which uses a mixture of price and hierarchy.

Like the formation of industrial conglomerates, the emergence and development of China's outward FDI are attributed to market-oriented reform, which expanded the autonomy of the firm and put an end to the de-linking of China's economy from the world economy. Before the economic reforms, China's domestic industrial enterprises were cut off from international markets. Twelve state-owned foreign trade companies, each with responsibilities for a specific category or specific categories of commodities, were the only intermediaries between domestic firms and the international markets. However, the monopoly status of these trade companies made them 'poor conductors' between domestic firms and overseas markets, especially in respect of market information supply and response. In the meantime, local governments had no autonomy in foreign trade.

Since 1979, several measures have been adopted in reforming the system of foreign economic relations. One of these was to decentralise the right to conduct foreign trade, permitting local governments, some industrial sectors, many large- and medium-sized enterprises and business conglomerates to engage in foreign trade. Another measure was to reduce the extent of command planning. Foreign trade was gradually regulated through adjustments to exchanges rates, tariffs, credits, licences and quotas. While the emergence of factor and product markets gave firms the opportunity to obtain factors and sell products in the market, the opening up of the economy provided firms with the possibility of engaging in international business. As a consequence, Chinese firms which had a 'licence' for FDI began to invest abroad.

Investors in the early period were basically trade enterprises, which may be grouped into two types: specialised foreign trade corporations with import and export licences and technological cooperation firms under the administration of provincial governments. Encouraged by the open-door policy, these firms tried to enter into overseas business arrangements by taking advantage of their existing international business links and their higher autonomy in operation that had been granted by central and local governments.

10.3.3. Growth rate of outward FDI

As FDI is a networking behaviour of the firm and networking activities rely on the functioning of market elements, the development of China's outward FDI, like its emergence, would depend on the character and progress of marketisation reforms in the country.

Economic reforms in China have adopted a dual track approach, moving the economic system towards the Western model by gradually shortening the 'non-market track' while gradually lengthening the 'market track'. During the transition, the two tracks exist in every aspect of Chinese economy, and the relative 'length' of the two tracks (measured in marketisation) at a particular time differs among different aspects of the economy. This implies that at any particular time and in a particular area, a firm could benefit from exploiting the two tracks by networking activities.

Motivated to search for more network benefits, Chinese firms began to undertake outward direct investment almost at the same time as foreign investors began to invest in China. The locus of the development of China's outward direct investment coincides with the evolutionary process of firm-related reforms in China.

Before 1984, the urban and industrial reform measures introduced basically focused on the reform of the industrial management system and the expansion of enterprise power. As reforms during this period were partial, and only covered some experiments in state-owned enterprises, neither did the enterprises have enough authority to engage in international business, nor were there relevant market mechanisms for such activity. Only a very limited number of enterprises invested abroad during this period and the investment was small in both volume and number of projects. Investors were mainly large companies which enjoyed the status of ministries plus a few enterprises directly under the provinces (Li, 2000, p.15).

Two big steps in firm-related reforms occurred the 1980s. A tax-for-profit system was instituted in 1984 and a contractual management system was applied to the Chinese enterprises in 1987. These reforms significantly increased the autonomy and internal incentives of enterprises. Correspondingly, there were big jumps in overseas investment in the two years. China's FDI outflows in the two years increased about 669 per cent and 1142 per cent respectively on the previous year's base.

Economic reforms slowed down in 1989 and 1990 due to a combination of factors, including the internal debates on economic reforms between the conservatives and the reformers in the Party leadership, problems associated with economic growth and modernisation, and especially, the incident in Tian'anmen Square. As a result, the Chinese government backtracked towards re-tightening central control and suspended the approval of trade-type overseas enterprises in 1989. Correspondingly, outward direct investment in 1990 fell to the level of 1988. It should be pointed out that there was an increase in FDI outflows in 1989. Also it is certain that a part of the increase was due to the lag between the approval and undertaking of outward investment projects that has been approved in previous years but carried out in 1989,[1] some of the increase was most likely to involve capital flight behaviour of investors out of concern over political uncertainty.

Economic reform was regenerated in mid 1991 and accelerated in 1992 after Deng Xiaoping's trip to South China. In the 1990s, various general measures were adopted to reform China's macroeconomic structures. While improving the efficiency of state-owned enterprises was still a focus, these measures included deregulating the governance of the exchange rate and taxation, opening capital markets, commercialising the state banks, reforming the systems of social security, circulation and housing, and improving property rights and patent protection. As a result, China's economic system moved a large step towards that of a market economy. Firms had not only gained greater autonomy in operations, but also had a more suitable environment in which to assume their autonomy.

These reforms had two opposite effects on the development of China's outward FDI. While firms gained more freedom to engage in overseas direct investment, the maturing of the market economic mechanism meant that the benefit from international networking was to some extent reduced due to decreasing benefits from exploiting the two-track system. As marketisation in nearly all aspects of the economy proceeded, more and more enterprises were able to carry out FDI with fewer difficulties. It was easier to obtain government approval and more firms were capable of engaging in outward direct investment. Being able to invest abroad was becoming less 'privileged' in taking advantage of the segment (or barriers) between domestic and international markets and between those with and those without overseas investment. For example, when it was very difficult to obtain a 'licence' to invest abroad and only a very limited number of enterprises had such a 'licence', those enterprises which had overseas subsidiaries could relatively easily undertake roundabout investment in the home market in the name of their overseas subsidiaries. They could therefore enjoy the preferential treatment specifically for foreign investors as well as establish internal international commodity chains with one end in China and the other in overseas markets, through which badly needed foreign goods could be supplied to China and overseas markets could be supplied with the products of the parent companies using very low wage labour. The reduction of both international and internal barriers due to marketisation as well as the entry of a large number of competitors inevitably reduced the profit margin of such activities. Of course, the normal benefit of international networking still remained. As a result of the interaction of the two forces, the growth of China's outward direct investment in the 1990s was rapid at first and relatively smooth afterwards, with obvious increases in a few years when major measures were adopted in the reform.

10.3.4. Focus of FDI activity

As highlighted in Chapter 8, while rapid economic development in China has provided firms with opportunities to grow, it has also exposed constraints on Chinese firms' ability to capitalise on their opportunities. These constraints include a shortage of natural resources, gap in technology and a saturated domestic market.

It is generally acknowledged that markets for both natural resources and created assets are very imperfect. Therefore networks could play an important role in obtaining them. For natural resources, networks based on ownership can reduce uncertainty in supply. For created assets, networks can provide an ideal environment for transactions and transfers.

Resource-seeking direct investment is aimed at obtaining important strategic foreign resources, including natural resources and created assets. The importance of such investment is attributable to resource heterogeneity. For economic organisation, resources are not homogeneous, rather they are heterogeneous: business firms have to collect and combine a set of different resources in their operations. The importance of a resource element depends not only on its scarcity, but also on other resources with which it is combined. Therefore the value of a resource must be evaluated in different combinations and constellations. This is the reason why Penrose claims that individual firms are collections of heterogeneous resources (Penrose, 1995), and Alchian and Demsetz claim that the very existence of firms can be explained by resource heterogeneity (Alchian and Demsetz, 1972).

It is obvious that the lack of certain resources and the gap in technologies in China have to a large extent reduced the relative values of other resources. Also the huge growth potential of the national economy and the perceived barriers to economic development, namely, shortages of natural resources and the technological gap, have increased pressures on firms in their operation and development as well as opportunities to explore. With the former, firms are facing uncertainty in and scarcity of resource sourcing, including natural resources and technologies. With the latter, while China is one of the world's most dynamic economies providing firms with huge opportunities for growth, those firms that have possessed scarce resources and much-needed technologies, due to demand and supply relationships, would gain much more in market power and competitiveness. Under such circumstances, firms would be motivated to engage in FDI associated with exploiting opportunities as well as tackling pressures.

As a result, resource-seeking FDI has been a focus ever since China's outward FDI emerged. MOFTEC data show that natural resource exploiting FDI accounted for about 30 per cent of China's total outward direct investment between 1979 and 1998. For investment in natural resources, FDI affiliates, in most cases joint ventures, are established to extract and process the required natural resources. For investment in obtaining technology, research centres and other types of window entity are set up in advanced countries to carry out transaction and transfer activities, such as information collection, training and R&D.

Up to 1998, trade investment flows and manufacturing investment flows accounted for 60.1 and 11.4 per cent, respectively, of China's outward FDI flows (MOFTEC, quoted from Li, 2000). As expansion of China's exports is an important business for trade investment affiliates and overseas manufacturing also aims mainly at host countries' markets, these figures show that exploiting overseas markets is another focus of China's outward FDI. As indicated in previous chapters, foreign direct investment can establish a node in the place closest to the firm's partners and customers and such a node can benefit the firm in obtaining information and improving network position. Here the firm's market transactions are improved. For example, by establishing overseas manufacturing and marketing facilities, firms can provide better after-sales services and effectively penetrate growing markets. It is worth noting that the share of overseas manufacturing investment in China's total outward FDI is expanding, and more industrial firms have set up manufacturing plants, established sales networks and marketed their brands abroad (Zhang, 1999).

10.3.5. Geographical distribution of outward FDI

From the above analysis, the geographical distribution of China's outward FDI will be concentrated in countries with suitable environments for FDI activities of Chinese investors.

One such suitable environment is the relatively rich endowment of natural resources required by Chinese firms. This is one of the main reasons that countries such as Australia, Canada, Peru, South Africa and New Zealand have attracted a large portion of China's outward FDI, especially in the earlier period. CITIC investment is an example. It invested heavily in natural resource projects, including investments in pulp and lumber mills in Canada and in aluminium smelting in Australia in the mid 1980s. Other examples include Shougang's investment of US$312 million in Herroperu SA in Peru and a Chinese oil company's investment of US$1.8 billion in oil extraction in Sudan. This type of investment is concentrated in Oceania, North and Latin America and some African countries.

Countries with technological leadership are another attraction for Chinese investors. The United States is an example in this respect. It has received the largest share of China's FDI outflows. Besides its huge market and rich natural resources endowment, its technological leadership is an important factor underlying China's investment in that country. For example, Haier and Konka, two of China's largest electronic and white goods producers, have R&D centres in the United States. In addition, investment in the United States can also serve the purpose of building up knowledge of advanced business practices corresponding to its highly developed market economic system. Such knowledge is badly needed by Chinese firms which are embracing and internalising economic institutions and practices appropriate for a market economy.

The reason why some other developed countries have not received as much attention from Chinese investors may be their lack of market conditions enjoyed by countries such as the United States. The three largest recipients of China's outward FDI, the United States, Canada and Australia, share many common features. They are all developed economies with a stable political environment and a well-established market system, which provide ideal conditions for market activities, including transactions of both goods and labour. English is the official language and Anglo-Saxon culture is the dominant culture in all these countries.

This cultural and linguistic homogeneity has greatly reduced barriers to communication and therefore is very beneficial for business operations, especially in the aspects of internal human resources management and external contract negotiation. As developed countries they provide good education for their nationals and overseas students. Therefore foreign-invested firms face little difficulty in recruiting workforce with the required skills.

For China's firms, the transaction conditions in these countries are even more suitable for their FDI when the following factors are taken into consideration. Compared with other foreign languages, English is by far the largest foreign language by the number of learners in China. A Chinese firm would therefore find it easier to recruit expatriates who can use English as working language if it undertakes FDI in one of these three countries. In addition, these three countries have the largest ethnic Chinese communities outside Asia. Due to the similarity in culture, China's investors can use the overseas Chinese networks as effective platforms to access local markets and business communities.

Another focus of Chinese outward FDI is transaction enforcing and position improving. Destinations of this type of investment are mainly countries where export markets exist. Table 9.2 shows the positive correlations between the geographical distribution of China's trade and the outflows and number of projects of China's outward FDI. While investment of this type in developed countries is mainly export oriented, investment of this type in developing countries is mainly overseas manufacturing, including Russia, Thailand, Malaysia, Singapore, South Africa, Indonesia, Cambodia, Brazil, Mexico, Zimbabwe and Bangladesh.

10.4. PROSPECTS OF CHINA'S OUTWARD FDI

10.4.1. Recent development of China's outward FDI

The last few years have witnessed a more rapid expansion of FDI from China. From 2001 to 2004, Chinese firms undertook US$13.87 billion outbound direct investment into non-financial areas. This amount is more than one-third of the nation's accumulated net FDI outflows in the previous two decades (SAFE, various issues).

China's outward FDI during this period went mainly into areas of information technology, resources, and commercial services. Up to 2003, about 33 per cent of China's outward FDI stock was concentrated in information, computer, and software business. Some large Chinese firms were actively engaged in undertaking FDI of this type. In 2004, Lenovo, China's leading PC maker, bought the PC business of IMB for US$1.75 billion. Under the terms of the deal, Lenovo acquired the right to use the IBM name on its computers for five years.

Resource exploration and related activities have been yet another focus in the last few years. As a result, investment in the mining industry accounted for 18 per cent of China's outward FDI stock in 2003. In January 2002, CNOOC (China National Offshore Oil Corporation) paid Spanish oil company Repsol-YPF US$585 million for its Indonesian oil and gas assets, which made it the biggest offshore oil producer in the country. CNOOC also signed a US$12 billion, 25-year supply contract with Australia's Northwest Shelf project for liquefied natural gas and a $7 billion supply contract for liquefied natural gas from Indonesia's Tangguh field. In June 2003, CNPC (China National Petroleum Corporation) increased its stake in Kazakh oil producer Aktobemunaigaz from 60 per cent to more than 80 per cent. In 2004, mining investment even amounted to 52.8 per cent of China's total FDI.

Commercial services attracted about 20 per cent of China's outward FDI by 2003. This type of investment mainly went to developed countries, with Europe as one of its major destinations in the last few years. According to MOFCOM, in 2003 about 70 per cent of China's direct investment in Europe was put into commercial services. In 2004, China's FDI in commercial services increased further to 26.5 per cent of its total outward FDI.

While China's FDI in the last few years continued to bear its earlier characteristics, it also exhibited some noteworthy new features. First, the operating body is growing stronger rapidly and large companies play a significant role. Correspondingly, the average size of FDI projects is increasing. For example, the average Chinese investment in FDI projects increased from US$3.05 million in 2001 to US$4.09 million in 2003, and further to US$4.48 million in 2004 (MOFCOM, various issues). This has shown the distinct improvement in the investment ability of Chinese firms.

Secondly, investment means are becoming increasingly diverse and modes other than greenfield investment, such as overseas merger and acquisition (M&A) and equity swap, are becoming popular for China's investors. In 2003 Chinese firms made an overseas investment of US$834 million in the form of transnational merger and acquisition, which accounted for about 40 per cent of the contracted Chinese investment that year. Many Chinese firms have been engaged actively in acquiring foreign assets whose prices may have been depressed by the current international economic downturn. For example, TCL bought the bankrupt Schneider Electronics (Germany) in 2002 for US$8 million; Huayi Group of Shanghai bought the bankrupt Moltech Power Systems (United States) for an estimated US$20 million; BOE Technology acquired Hynix Semiconductor's flat panel display unit (South Korea) for US$380 million in February 2003; Shanghai Haixing Group bought Glenoit Corp-Speciality Fabrics in the United States for US$14 million; Shanghai Electric Group bought the financially troubled Akiyama Publishing Machinery Company (Japan); and D'long Group acquired Fairchild Dornier 728 passenger jet programme (Germany).

Thirdly, while those large state-owned enterprises designated by the government as 'national champions' are still the dominant force in outbound FDI, a growing number of new globalisers are joining the ranks of overseas investment. Among the newcomers some have made much headway. For example, consumer electronics manufacturer TCL is now the global giant of television production, holding a 67 per cent stake in a manufacturing joint venture formed with France's Thomson in November 2003. That followed its takeover of Germany's Schneider Electronics AG for US$10.6 million in 2002. TCL also fused its mobile-phone division with Alcatel's handset operations in 2004, gaining know-how, brand and a big foothold in Europe. It is worth noting that more and more new globalisers are non-state-owned enterprises. The private enterprise Huawei, a producer of telecommunications equipment, is an example. It is one of China's most dynamic and ambitious companies and one of a handful, alongside Haier in white goods, Lenovo in personal computers, TCL in televisions and steel maker Baosteel, whose names are starting to be heard around the world. Over 3300 of Huawei's 24 000 employees are overseas nationals, deployed in research labs in the US, India, Russia and Sweden, and in marketing offices in 90 countries. And two-fifths of its more than US$5 billion revenues in 2004 were made outside China.

The rapid growth of China's outward FDI in the last few years was attributable to a series of factors. A notable factor was China's accession to the WTO in December 2001, which bought about both pressure and impetus for the internationalisation of Chinese firms. Becoming a WTO member has three consequences: marketisation, internationalisation and improvement of legislation. 2005 is the fourth year of China's accession to the WTO. It also marks the end of the transition period of protection for most of the industries in China as agreed during the accession negotiations. With foreign firms flocking to China and the trend of globalisation continuing unabated, internationalisation is an inevitable development direction for Chinese enterprises, which have to face the challenges of marketisation and internationalisation whether they like them or not. While facing these challenges, Chinese firms have been given opportunities to take advantage of China's entry into the WTO, for entry will act as a shift parameter for both foreign MNEs in China and Chinese MNEs abroad, because it reduces transaction costs for both sets of economic actors (Rugman and Verbeke, 2004). As the Chinese market is more and more internationalised, the competition in it is actually increasingly equal to that in the international market. As a result, the international competitiveness of Chinese firms has gradually strengthened. This has given them an edge in competition when they invest abroad in pursuit of various networking benefits.

For a long period since China's reform and opening up, the Chinese government adopted a discrimination policy which favoured foreign-capital-invested firms but put the private sector in the most unfavourable condition. The result of the implementation of this policy is a corporate landscape of a few big private companies, a mass of lumbering state-owned firms and increasingly powerful foreign multinationals. The approach of the end of the transition period of protection granted by the WTO challenged such a policy: if national treatment was to be granted to foreign companies there was no excuse not to grant national treatment to domestic private enterprises. So through WTO accession, domestic private sectors, despite their weak political voice, were able to wrench away the monopoly rights of the SOEs and become a growing part of the Chinese economy. So when WTO liberalisations eliminate the remaining investment restrictions and the discrimination against the private sector is steadily reduced, the size and pace of overseas direct investment by private firms will almost certainly rise.

The experience and lessons of previous Chinese investors have also encouraged their fellows. 'We're seeing a new breed of global aspirants that have learned a lot from past failures,' indicates Frank-Jurgen Richter, president of Swiss-based strategy advisory firm Horasis. 'They benefit from an important advantage: talented and successful Chinese have preceded them abroad. Those who stay overseas form a potential network of allies; the returnees bring home a vast wealth of know-how about foreign markets and cultures.' With this network of allies and knowledge, the new globalisers can relatively easily establish nodes in foreign markets by expanding their boundaries geographically.

The developments in China's outward FDI in the last few years have demonstrated the efforts of Chinese globalisers in the direction of creating Chinese multinationals as well as their strength in doing so. Correspondingly, China's ranking in the Outward FDI Performance Index moved from 69th in 1998-2000 up to 58th in 2001-2003, higher than India (61), Brazil (91) and Argentina (83), almost in the middle of the 128 country list (UNCTAD, 2004, p.291).

10.4.2. Prospects of China's outward FDI in the near future

China's outward FDI has a very short history. In spite of a quarter century of rapid growth in volume, it is still very small in relative terms. For example, China's outward FDI in 2003 was US$2.9 billion, which was less than 6 per cent of China's inward FDI and 0.5 per cent of world total FDI in the same year (MOFCOM, 2004). And China's outward FDI stock in 2003 accounted for just 2.6 per cent of the country's GDP, much lower than Brazil (11 per cent) and South Africa (14.8 per cent) (UNCTAD, 2004, pp.403-7). As far as the trends of its rapid economic development, inward FDI and foreign trade are concerned, China's outward FDI has therefore had a huge potential. Hence it can be reasonably predicted that there will be new booms in FDI from China sometime in the near future, as happened in FDI from Japan and South Korea in the 1970-1980s and 1990s, respectively.

Given its unique combination of first world infrastructure and third world labour costs as well as its comprehensive national economic system, China's outward FDI will be a more complex picture, with resource seeking and trade promoting as the focus. While the impressive overseas M&A actions in the last few years by the three big oil companies, PetroChina, Sinopec and CNOOC, are most likely to be a prelude to larger-scale FDI in natural resource seeking, outbound investment by firms like Haier and TCL in developed countries to a large extent preludes larger-scale created-resource-seeking FDI. As Chinese firms move up the 'value chain', they will be keen to obtain created resources from abroad to consolidate or complement their advantages. The growth of trade-promoting FDI may be a different story. Given the huge size of China's economy, trade and cheap labour forces, in the coming decades trade conflicts between China and many developed countries, due to social and political concerns from the relevant countries, are likely to occur more often and be more serious. Therefore more and more Chinese firms will use FDI as a means to protect their overseas markets in these countries. In the meantime, some Chinese firms will also transfer their production to less developed countries to avoid the erosion of cost advantages due to rising wage rates in China. Correspondingly, China's outward FDI in the future will penetrate further into all regions and countries. Nevertheless, if China's catch-up can be very successful, leading to an ever narrowing gap in technology and management between China and developed countries, a growing share of China's FDI will go to developing countries during a relatively long period before China becomes a relatively developed country, for catching up will reduce the attraction of developed countries for China's created-resource-seeking investment.

In the future China's investors will be more diverse and private firms will play an increasing role. The dominant contributing factor for this trend is marketisation process at home. Though China's economy so far is still in the throes of a gradual transition from state control to the free market, with the entry into the WTO, this transition is nearing completion. As the privatisation of some enterprises is a major priority of the government at the last stage of economic reform, more and more former SOEs will be restructured into private firms. In the meantime, the establishment of a level playing field for all types of firms will certainly facilitate the growth, both in terms of number and average individual size, of the firms which are private in origin. Therefore a growing number of private firms will join the ranks of outward FDI.

The diversification of investors will to some extent reshape the international networking pattern of China's outward FDI. While SOEs are the dominant forces of FDI, the international pattern of FDI is more or less politically coloured. The will of the government would be exercised directly via the government approval procedure for overseas investment projects and indirectly via the governance structure of the firms and access to government-related sources. So the success or failure of an SOE's FDI is more dependent on the investing firm's relationships with government bodies and correspondingly less on its relationships with market agents. On the contrary, when private firms undertake outward FDI, networks among market agents will play a much more important role. Given the fact that Chinese private firms are relatively small in size due to their short history compared with SOEs and most foreign counterparts, their overseas investment will rely heavily on networks, for networking is more important for small firms than for large ones when operating in a different environment about which they have relatively limited knowledge.

10.5. CONCLUDING REMARKS

This book set out to find a plausible explanation of China's outward FDI. In reviewing the existing literature, it became obvious that the traditional theories of foreign direct investment were unable to offer such an explanation. It then became necessary to develop an alternative explanation, which has been done using the networking model. This model was developed by applying economic norms to capturing the ideas of networks in business analysis. As it takes into consideration networking effects on both governance cost and transaction cost and as networks are spatially disposed in nature, the model can capture the underlying rationale for determining the organisational form of economic activity and its location. In contrast to paradigms in mainstream theory of FDI, the forte of this model lies in its quantitative specification of the cost structure in FDI and other organisations of economic activity. As such specification is based on acknowledging, in addition to the market and the firm, network effects which exist extensively in business practices but are ignored in mainstream economic theory, this model has made a contribution to the knowledge of economic organisation in general and FDI in particular. Also, the explicit specification of the cost structure for economic organisation in this model makes it relatively easy to build econometric models based on it. The absence of firm-level data in China's case made it impossible to test the propositions of the networking model at the firm level. Instead, the explanation provided in this book runs in terms of the overall size of FDI, the timing of its growth and the pattern of its destinations. These patterns seem to coincide remarkably with the progress of economic reforms in China, which provided greater decision-making autonomy to business units. As the reforms progressed, firm-level motives of outward investment started to play an important role in determining the flows and their directions. It is hoped that, within the limitations imposed by the available data and information, the book has offered a plausible set of explanations that are new and may be testable subsequently when more information becomes available.

Based on this research, future efforts can be made in the following directions. First, one improvement would be to make this model a general equilibrium model, so as to reduce its looseness. One outstanding feature of the network is its blurring boundary. This makes it difficult to formalise the network phenomenon in the economic literature. And it is expected that topological knowledge will also be required in such a formalisation.

Secondly, empirical study based on the network model of FDI should carefully choose variables to capture the network effects. Due to the complex structure and blurring boundary of the network, this would require a large amount of data. If the sample is very large, the analysis would be a time-consuming task. Therefore, it would be worthwhile if some simplified econometric models are developed specifically for the purpose of a country case study.

China's outward FDI has so far entered a stage in which a growing proportion of FDI will be subsequent incremental investment by existing globalisers in pursuing network expansion and integration. Such FDI will lead to an increase in the transnationality of the investing firms and to the formation of a web of Chinese international business. The nature and structure of the inter-organisational network of a Chinese MNE and the relationships between this network and that of the firm's allies and counterparts will to a large extent define the essentials of China's outward FDI. Investigation into the nature and structure of Chinese MNEs should therefore be another direction of study. In addition, the differences in networking behaviour between different types of investors and the changes in the networking pattern of Chinese investors would bear much information about the development of China's outward FDI, so efforts should also be made in this respect.

NOTE

1. MOFTEC data on FDI, which is allowed to be carried out in a particular year after government approval. There is a lag between the approval and undertaking of outward investment.

Bibliography

Abolafia, M. Y. (1984), 'Structured Anarchy: Formal Organization in the Commodity Futures Markets', in Adler, P. and P. Adler (eds), *The Social Dynamics of Financial Markets*, Greenwich, Conn.: JAI Press, pp.129-50.

Agarwal, J. P. (1985), 'Intra-LDCs Foreign Direct Investment: A Comparative Analysis of Third World Multinationals', *Developing Economics*, **23** (3), 236-53.

Alchian, A. A. and H. Demsetz (1972), 'Production, Information Costs, and Economic Organisation', *American Economic Review*, **62** (5), 777-95.

Aliber, R. Z. (1970), 'The Theory of Direct Foreign Investment', in Kindleberger, C. P. (ed.), *The International Corporation*, Cambridge, Mass.: MIT Press, pp.17-34.

Amin, S. (1992), *Empire of Chaos*, New York: Monthly Review Press.

Andersen, O. and L. S. Kheam (1998), 'Resource-Based Theory and International Growth Strategies: An Exploratory Study', *International Business Review*, **7** (2), 163-84.

Andersen, P. H., P. Blenker and P. R. Christensen (1993), 'Generic Routes to Subcontractors' Internationalisation', Paper presented at the Rent IX Conference on Entrepreneurship and SMEs in Milan, Italy, November.

Anderson, E. and H. Gatignon (1998), 'Modes of Foreign Entry: A Transaction Cost Analysis and Propositions', in Beamish, P. W. (ed.), *Strategic Alliances*, Cheltenham, UK and Northampton, Mass.: Elgar, pp.1-26.

Aoki, M. (1988), *Information, Incentive, and Bargaining in the Japanese Economy*, Cambridge: Cambridge University Press.

Aoki, M. (1990), 'Toward an Economic Model of the Japanese Firm', *Journal of Economic Literature*, **28** (1), 1-27.

Asian Development Bank (1997), *Emerging Asia: Changes and Challenges*, Malina: Asian Development Bank.

Axelsson, B. and G. Easton (eds) (1992), *Industrial Networks: A New View of Reality*, London: Routledge.

Balassa, B. (1982), *Development Strategies in Semi-Industrialized Economies*, Baltimore: Johns Hopkins University Press.

Bartlett, C. A., Y. Doz and C. Hedlund (1990), *Managing the Global Firm*, New York: Routledge & Kegan Paul.

Barnet, R. J. and R. E. Muller (1974), *Global Reach: The Power of the International Corporations*, New York: Simon & Schuster.

Barro, R. and X. Sala-i-Martin (1995), *Economic Growth*, New York: McGraw-Hill.

Bellak, C. and J. Cantwell (1996), 'Foreign Direct Investment: How Much Is It Worth? Comments on S. J. Gray and A. M. Rugman', *Transnational Corporations*, **5** (1), 85-97.

Benito, G. R. G. and G. Gripsrud (1995), 'The Internationalisation Process Approach to
the Location of Foreign Direct Investments: An Empirical Analysis', in Green, M. B.
and R. B. McNaughton (eds), *The Location of Foreign Direct Investment: Geographic
and Business Approaches*, Hampshire: Avebury, pp.43-58.

Bernard, A. B. and S. N. Durlauf (1995), 'Convergence in International Output', *Journal
of Applied Econometrics'*, **10** (2), 97-108.

BIE (1991), *Networks: A Third Form of Organisation*, Discussion paper 14, Canberra:
Australian Government Publishing Services.

Biggart, N. W. and G. G. Hamilton (1997), 'On the Limits of a Firm-Based Theory to
Explain Business Networks: The Western Bias of Neoclassical Economics', in Orrù,
M., N. W. Biggart and G. G. Hamilton (eds), *The Economic Organization of East
Asian Capitalism*, London: Sage Publications, pp.33-54.

Blois, K. J. (1972), 'Vertical Quasi-Integration', *Journal of Industrial Economics*, **20** (3),
253-72.

Blomström, M. (1991), 'Host Country Benefits of Foreign Investment', in McFetridge,
D. G. (ed.), *Foreign Investment, Technology and Economic Growth*, Toronto: Toronto
University Press.

Blomström, M. and A. Kokko (1997), 'How Foreign Investment Affects Host Countries',
Policy Research Paper 1745, Washington, DC: World Bank.

Boisot, M. and J. Child (1996), 'The Institutional Nature of China's Emerging Economic
Order', in Brown, D. and R. Porter (eds), *Management Issues in China: Volume II
Domestic Enterprises*, London: Routledge.

Bowen, S. (1993), 'A Mutually Beneficial Link with China', *Financial Times*, 21
September, p.7.

Boyd, G. and A. M. Rugman (1997), *Euro-Pacific Investment and Trade: Strategies and
Structural Interdependencies*, Cheltenham, UK and Lyme, US: Edward Elgar.

Brush, C. G. (1992), *Factors Motivating Small Companies to Internationalise: The Effect
of Firm Age*, Boston: Boston University.

Buckley, P. J. (1985), 'New Forms of International Industrial Co-operation', in Buckley,
P. J. and M. Casson (eds), *The Economic Theory of the Multinational Enterprise*,
London: Macmillan, pp.39-59.

Buckley, P. J. (1997), 'Trends in International Business Research: The Next 25 Years', in
Islam, I. and W. Shepherd (eds), *Current Issues in International Business*,
Cheltenham, UK and Lyme, US: Edward Elgar, pp.218-28.

Buckley, P. J. and M. Casson (1976), *The Future of the Multinational Enterprise*,
London: Macmillan.

Buckley, P. J. and M. Casson (1988), 'A Theory of Cooperation in International
Business', in Contractor, F. and P. Lorange (eds), *Cooperative Strategies in
International Business*, Lexington, Mass.: Lexington Books.

Buckley, P. J. and J. Clegg (1991), *Multinational Enterprises in Less Developed
Countries*, Basingstoke: Macmillan.

Burt, R. S. (1992), 'The Social Structure of Competition', in Nohria, N. and R. G. Eccles
(eds), *Networks and Organizations: Structure, Form, and Action*, Boston, Mass.:
Harvard Business School Press, pp.57-91.

Carr, D. L., J. R. Markusen and K. E Maskus (1998), 'Estimating the Knowledge-Capital Model of the Multinational Enterprise', *NBER Working Paper,* No. 6773, Cambridge, Mass.: National Bureau of Economic Research.

Casson, M. (1979), *Alternatives to the Multinational Enterprises,* London: Macmillan.

Casson, M. (1997), *Information and Organization,* Oxford: Oxford University Press.

Casson, M. and H. Cox (1997), 'An Economic Model of Inter-Firm Networks', in Ebers, M. (ed.), *The Formation of Inter-Organizational Networks,* Oxford: Oxford University Press, pp.174-96.

Caves, R. E. (1971), 'International Corporations: The Industrial Economics of Foreign Investment', *Economica,* **38** (149), 1-27.

Caves, R. E. (1996), *Multinational Enterprise and Economic Analysis,* Cambridge: Cambridge University Press.

Caves, R. E. (1998), 'Research in International Business: Problems and Prospects', *Journal of International Business Studies,* **29** (1), 5-20.

Chamberlin, E. H. (1938), *The Theory of Monopolistic Competition,* 3rd ed, Cambridge, Mass.: Harvard University Press.

Chen, E. K. Y. (1983), 'Multinationals from Hong Kong', in Lall, S. (ed.), *The New Multinationals: The Spread of Third World Enterprises,* Brisbane: John Wiley & Sons, pp.88-136.

Chen, E. K. Y. (1997), 'The Total Factor Productivity Debate: Determinants of Economic Growth in East Asia', *Asian-Pacific Economic Literature,* **11** (1), 18-38.

Chen, E. K. Y. and P. Drysdale (1995), *Corporate Links and Foreign Direct Investment in Asia and the Pacific,* Pymble: Harper Educational.

Chen, H. and T.-J. Chen (1998), 'Network Linkages and Location Choice in Foreign Direct Investment', *Journal of International Business Studies,* **29** (3), 445-68.

Chen, Y. (1986), *Selected Essays of Chen Yun 1956-1985* (Chen Yun Wenxuan 1956-1985) (in Chinese), Beijing: People's Press.

Chen, Z. and B. Zhou.(1998), 'Research on the Marketisation Process of China's Economic System', *China Social Sciences Quarterly* (in Chinese), summer, pp.110-22.

Cheng, W., J. Sachs and X. Yang (1999), 'An Inframarginal Analysis of the Heckscher-Ohlin Model with Transaction Costs and Technological Comparative Advantage', Harvard Centre for International Development, *Working Paper,* No. 9.

Chesnais, F. (1992), 'National Systems of Innovation, Foreign Direct Investment and the Operations of Multinational Enterprises', in Lundvall, B.-A. (ed.), *National Systems of Innovation: Towards a Theory of Innovation and Interactive Learning,* London: Pinter, pp.265-95.

Cheung, S. N. S. (1983), 'The Contractual Nature of the Firm', *Journal of Law and Economics,* **26** (1), 1-21.

Choo, M.-G. (2000), *The New Asia in Global Perspective,* London: MacMillan Press.

Ciborra, C. (1991), 'Alliances as Learning Experiments: Cooperation, Competition and Change in Hightech Industries', in Mytelka, L. K. (eds), *Strategic Partnerships: States, Firms and International Competition,* London: Pinter, pp.51-77.

Coase, R. H. (1937), 'The Nature of the Firm', *Economica*, **4** (November), 386-405. Reprinted in Stigler, G. J. and K. Boulding (eds) (1953), *Readings in Price Theory*, London: Allen and Unwin, pp.331-51.

Contractor, F. J. (1990), 'Contractual and Cooperative Forms of International Business: Towards a Unified Theory of Modal Choice', *Management International Review*, **30** (1), 31-54.

Contractor, F. J. and P. Lorange (eds) (1988), *Cooperative Strategies in International Business*, Lexington, Mass.: Lexington Books.

Cooke, P. and K. Morgan (1996), 'The Creative Milieu: A Regional Perspective on Innovation', in Dodgson, M. and R. Rothwell (eds), *The Handbook of Industrial Innovation*, Cheltenham, UK and Brookfield, US: Edward Elgar.

CSIESR *et al.* (China State Institute of Economic System Reform, Renmin University of China, and the Institute of Research on Comprehensive Development) (1999), *Report on the Development of China's International Competitiveness 1999* (in Chinese), Beijing: Renmin University Press.

CSPC (China State Planning Committee) (1996), *A Guide to the Ninth Five Year Plan for the National Economic and Social Development and the Programme for the Long Range Goal by 2010*, (in Chinese), Beijing: China Economic Publishing House.

Culpan, R. (ed.) (1993), *Multinational Strategic Alliance*, New York: International Business Press.

Dahl, R. A. (1957), 'The Concept of Power', *Behavioral Science*, **2** (1), 201-15.

Dobson, W. and C. S. Yue (1997), *Multinationals and East Asian Integration*, Ottawa: International Development Research Centre and Singapore: Institute of Southeast Asian Studies.

Drysdale, P. and Y. Huang (1995), 'Technological Catch-Up and Economic Growth in East Asia', *The Economic Record*, **733** (222), 201-11.

Dunning, J. H. (1958), *American Investment in British Manufacturing Industry*, London: George Allen & Unwin.

Dunning, J. H. (1977), 'Trade, Location of Economic Activity and the MNE: A Search for an Eclectic Approach', in Ohlin, B., P.-O. Hesselborn and P. M. Wijkman (eds), *The International Allocation of Economic Activity: Proceedings of a Nobel Symposium Held at Stockholm*, London: Macmillan, pp.395-418.

Dunning, J. H. (1979), 'Explaining Changing Patterns of International Production: In Defence of the Eclectic Theory', *Oxford Bulletin of Economics and Statistics*, **41** (4), 269-95.

Dunning, J. H. (1981), 'Explaining the International Direct Investment Position of Countries: Towards a Dynamic or Development Approach', *Weltwirtschaftliches Archiv*, **117** (1), 30-64.

Dunning, J. H. (1986), 'The Investment Development Cycle and Third World Multinationals', in Khan, K. M. (ed.), *Multinationals of the South: New Actors in the International Economy*, New York: St. Martin's Press, pp.15-47.

Dunning, J. H. (1988), *Explaining International Production*, London: Unwin Hyman.

Dunning, J. H. (1990), 'Changes in the Level and Structure of International Production: The Last One Hundred Years', in Buckley, P. J. (ed.), *International Investment*, Aldershot, UK and Brookfield, US: Edward Elgar, pp.3-24.

Dunning, J. H. (1992), 'The Competitive Advantage of Countries and the Activities of Transnational Corporations', *Transnational Corporations*, **1** (1), 135-68.

Dunning, J. H. (1993a), 'Government and Multinational Enterprises: From Confrontation to Co-operation', in Eden, L. and E. H. Porter (eds), *Multinationals in the Global Political Economy*, New York: St. Martin's Press; London: Macmillan Press, pp.59-83.

Dunning, J. H. (1993b), *Multinational Enterprises and the Global Economy*, Wokingham: Addison-Wesley.

Dunning, J. H. (1994a), 'Explaining Foreign Direct Investment in Japan: Some Theoretical Insights', Paper presented at the Wharton School, University of Pennsylvania, October 7.

Dunning, J. H. (1994b), 'Reevaluating the Benefits of Foreign Direct Investment', *Transnational Corporations*, **3** (1), 23-52.

Dunning, J. H. and R. Narula (1996), 'The Investment Development Path Revisited: Some Emerging Issues', in Dunning, J. H. and R. Narula (eds), *Foreign Direct Investment and Governments: Catalysts for Economic Restructuring*, London: Routledge, pp.1-41.

Dunning, J. H. and P. Robson (1987), 'Multinational Corporate Integration and Regional Economic Integration', *Journal of Common Market Studies*, **26** (2), 103-25.

Dunning, J. H., R. van Hoesel and R. Narula (1997), 'Third World Multinationals Revisited: New Development and Theoretical Implications', *Discussion Papers in International Investment and Management*, Series B, **9** (227), Reading: University of Reading.

Easton, G. (1992), 'Industrial Networks: A Review', in Axelsson, B. and G. Easton (eds), *Industrial Networks: A New View of Reality*, London: Routledge, pp.1-27.

Easton, G. and L. Araujo (1994), 'Market Exchange, Social Structures and Time', *European Journal of Marketing*, **28** (3), 72-84.

Emmanuel, A. (1972), *Unequal Exchange: A Study of the Imperialism of Trade*, New York: Monthly Review Press.

Encarnation, D. J. and L. T. Wells (1986), 'Evaluating Foreign Investment', in Moran, T. H. and J. M. Grieco (eds), *Investing in Development: New Roles for Private Capital*, New Brunswick, NJ: Transaction Books, pp.61-86.

Erramilli, M. K. and C. P. Rao (1993), 'Service Firms' International Entry Mode Choice: A Modified Transaction-cost Analysis Approach', *Journal of Marketing*, **57** (3), 19-38.

Ernst, D., T. Ganiatsos and L. Mytelka (1998), 'Technological Capacities in the Context of Export-led Growth: A Conceptual Framework', in Ernst, D., T. Ganiatsos and L. Mytelka (eds), *Technological Capacities and Export Success in Asia*, London: Routledge, pp.5-45.

Ethier, W. J. (1994), 'Conceptual Foundations from Trade, Multinational Firms, and Foreign Direct Investment Theory', in Bredahl, M. E., P. C. Abbott and M. R. Reed (eds), *Competitiveness in International Food Markets*, Colorado: Westview Press, pp.105-28.

Ethier, W. J. and J. R. Markusen (1996), 'Multinational Firms, Technology Diffusion and Trade', *Journal of International Business*, **41** (1-2), 1-28.

Ferrantino, M. J. (1992), 'Transaction Costs and the Expansion of Third-World Multinationals', *Economics Letters*, **38** (4), 451-56.

Florida, R. and M. Kenney (1991), The New Age of Capitalism, *Futures*, **25** (6), 637-51.

Ford, J. D. (1978), 'Stability Factors in Industrial Marketing Channels', *Industrial Marketing Management*, **7** (6), 410-22.

Franko, L. G. (1976), *The European Multinationals: A Renewed Challenge to American and British Business*, Stamford, CT: Greylock.

Gao, Zhihua (1988), 'What Is the Best Economic System for China' (in Chinese), *China Social Sciences* (Zhongguo Shehui Kexue), **1**, 7-17.

Garnaut, R. (1996), 'Sino-Australian Economic Relations, 1983-95', in Mackerras, C. (ed.), *Australia and China: Partners in Asia*, Melbourne: Macmillan Education Australia Pty Ltd, pp.68-89.

Gereffi, G. (1994a), 'The Role of Big Buyers in Global Commodity Chains: How U.S. Retail Networks Affect Overseas Production Patterns', in Gereffi, G. and M. Korzeniewicz (eds), *Commodity Chains and Global Capitalism*, Westport, CT: Greenwood Press, pp.95-122.

Gereffi, G. (1994b), 'Capitalism, Development and Global Commodity Chains', in Sklair, L. (1994) (eds), *Capitalism and Development*, London: Routledge, pp.211-31.

Gereffi, G. (1998), 'More than the Market, More than the State: Global Commodity Chains and Industrial Upgrading in East Asia', in Chan, S. and D. Lam (eds), *Beyond the Development State: East Asia's Political Economies Reconsidered*, Houndmills: Macmillan Press, pp.38-59.

Ghoshal, S. and C. A. Bartlett (1993), 'The Multinational Corporation as an Interorganizational Network', in Ghoshal, S. and D. E. Westney (eds), *Organization Theory and the Multinational Corporation*, Basingstoke: St. Martin's Press, pp.77-104.

Gilroy, B. M. (1993), *Networking in Multinational Enterprises: The Importance of Strategic Alliance*, Columbia: University of South Carolina.

Gomes-Casseres, B. (1989), 'Ownership Structures of Foreign Subsidiaries: Theory and Evidence', *Journal of Economic Behavior and Organization*, **11** (1), 1-25.

Gordon, W. (1961), 'The Contribution of Foreign Investment: A Case Study of United States Foreign Investment History', *Inter-American Economic Affairs*, **14** (spring).

Graham, E. M. (1978), 'Transatlantic Investment by Multinational Firms: A Rivalistic Phenomenon?' *Journal of Post-Keynesian Economics*, **1** (1), 82-99.

Graham, E. M. (1997), 'The (Not Wholly Satisfactory) State of the Theory of Foreign Direct Investment and the Multinational Enterprise', in Stein, J. L. (ed.), *The Globalization of Markets: Capital Flows, Exchange Rates and Trade Regimes*, Heidelberg: Physica-Verlag, pp.99-122.

Graham, E. M. and P. R. Krugman (1991), *Foreign Direct Investment in the United States*, Washington, DC: The Institute for International Economics.

Granovetter, M. (1985), 'Economic Action and Social Structure: The Problem of Embeddedness', *American Journal of Sociology*, **91**, 481-510.

Grant, R. M. (1991), 'The Resource-based Theory of Competitive Advantage: Implications for Strategic Formulation', *California Management Review*, **33** (3), 114-35.

Grewal, B., X. Lan, P. Sheehan and F. Sun (2002), *China's Future in the Knowledge Economy:Engaging the New World*, Melbourne: CSES Victoria University and Beijing: Tsinghua University Press.

Guillet de Monthoux, P. (1975), 'Organizational Mating and Industrial Marketing Conservatism: Some Reasons Why Industrial Marketing Managers Resist Marketing Theory', *Industrial Marketing Management*, **4** (1), 25-36.

Gunter, F. R. (1996), 'Capital Flight from the People's Republic of China: 1984-1994', *China Economic Review*, **7** (1), 77-96.

Guo, Ju'e (1996), 'Natural Resources and Economic Development in China', *Chinese Economic Studies*, **29** (1), 5-21.

Hagg, I. and J. Johanson (1983), *Firms in Networks*, Stockholm, Sweden: Business and Social Institute.

Håkansson, H. (1982), *International Marketing and Purchasing of Industrial Goods: An Interaction Approach*, Chichester: Wiley.

Håkansson, H. and J. Johanson (1992), 'A Model of Industrial Networks', in Axelsson, B. and G. Easton (eds), *Industrial Networks: A New View of Reality*, London: Routledge, pp.28-34.

Håkansson, H. and C. Östberg (1975), 'Industrial Marketing: An Organizational Problem?' *Industrial Marketing Management*, **4** (2-3), 113-23.

Håkansson, H. and I. Snehota (eds) (1995), *Developing Relationships in Business Networks*, London: Routledge.

Håkansson, H. and I. Snehota (1989), 'No Business is an Island', *Scandinavian Journal of Management*, **5** (3), 187-200.

Hall, R. (1993), 'A Framework Linking Intangible Resources and Capabilities to Sustainable Competitive Advantage', *Strategic Management Journal*, **14** (8), 607-18.

Hallen, L., J. Johanson and N. Seyed-Mohamed (1991), 'Interfirm Adaptation in Business Relationships', *Journal of Marketing*, **55** (2), 29-37.

Hamilton, G. G. and R. C. Feenstra (1997), 'Varieties of Hierarchies and Markets', in Orrù, M., N. W. Biggart and G. G. Hamilton (eds), *The Economic Organization of East Asian Capitalism*, London: Sage Publications, pp.55-94.

Hamilton, G. G. and T. Waters (1995), 'Chinese Capitalism in Thailand: Embedded Networks and Industrial Structure', in Chen, E. K. Y. and P. Drysdale (eds), *Corporate Links and Foreign Direct Investment in Asia and the Pacific*, Pymble: Harper Educational Publishers, pp.81-111.

Hannan, K. (1998), *Industrial Change in China: Economic Restructuring and Conflicting Interests*, London: Routledge.

Hayek, F. A. von (1937), 'Economics and Knowledge', *Economia* (new series), **4**, 33-54, reprinted in F. A. von Hayek (1959), *Individualism and Economic Order*, London: Routledge and Kegan Paul, pp.33-56.

Hennart, J.-F. (1991), 'The Transaction Cost Theory of Joint Ventures: An Empirical Study of Japanese Subsidiaries in the United States', *Management Science*, **37** (4), 483-97.

Hennart, J.-F. (1993a), 'Control in Multinational Firms: The Role of Price and Hierarchy', in Ghoshal, S. and D. E. Westney (eds), *Organisation Theory and the Multinational Corporation*, New York: St. Martin's Press, pp.157-81.

Hennart, J.-F. (1993b), 'Explaining the Swollen Middle: Why Most Transactions Are a Mix of "Market" and "Hierarchy"', *Organization Science*, **4** (4), 529-47.

Hertz S. (1992), 'Towards More Integrated Industrial Systems', in Axelsson, B. and G. Easton (eds), *Industrial Networks: A New View of Reality*, London and New York: Routledge, pp.105-28.

Hirsch, S. (1976), 'An International Trade and Investment Theory of the Firm', *Oxford Economic Papers*, **28** (2), 258-69.

Horst, T. (1973), 'The Simple Analytics of Multinational Firm Behaviour', in Connolly, M. B. and A. K. Swoboda (eds), *International Trade and Money*, London: Allen & Unwin, pp.72-84.

Horstmann, I. and J. R. Markusen (1987a), 'Licensing versus Direct Investment: A Model of Internationalisation by the Multinational Enterprise', *Canadian Journal of Economics*, **20** (3), 464-81.

Horstmann, I. and J. R. Markusen (1987b), 'Strategic Investments and the Development of Multinationals', *International Economic Review*, **28** (1), 109-21.

Horstmann, I. and J. R. Markusen (1992), 'Endogenous Market Structures in International Trade', *Journal of International Economics*, **32** (1-2), 109-29.

Hu, Yaobang (1986), 'On Issues of Foreign Economic Relations', in the Institute of Industrial Economy (ed.), *Selected Documents of Economic Policies since the Third Plenum of the Eleventh Central Committee* (in Chinese), Beijing: China Economic Press, pp.95-112.

Hymer, S. H. (1960), *The International Operations of National Firms: A Study of Direct Foreign Investment*, PhD Dissertation, MIT (published: Cambridge, Mass.: MIT Press, 1976).

IIE (Institute of Industrial Economics under the Chinese Academy of Social Sciences) (1996), *China's Industrial Development Report (1996)* (in Chinese), Beijing: Economic Management Publishing House.

IIE (1998), *China's Industrial Development Report (1998)* (in Chinese), Beijing: Economic Management Publishing House.

IIE (1999), *China's Industrial Development Report (1999)* (in Chinese), Beijing: Economic Management Publishing House.

IMF (1993), *Balance of Payments Manual*, 5th edition, Washington: IMF.

IMD (International Institute for Management Development) (1998), *The World Competitiveness Yearbook 1998*, Lausanne: IMD.

ITD (Industrial and Transportation Department of National Bureau of Statistics) (1998), *China Industrial Economic Statistical Yearbook 1998*, Beijing: China Statistics Press.

Jansson, H., M. Saqib and D. D. Sharma (1995), *The State and Transnational Corporations: A Network Approach to International Policy in India*, Aldershot: Edward Elgar.

Jefferson, G. H. and T. G. Rawski (1993), 'A Theory of Economic Reform', *Working Paper*, No.273, Pittsburg: Department of Economics, University of Pittsburg.

Jefferson, G. H. and I. Singh (eds) (1999), *Enterprise Reform in China: Ownership, Transition, and Performance*, Oxford: Oxford University Press.

Johanson, J. and L.-G. Mattsson (1985), 'Marketing and Market Investments in Industrial Networks', *International Journal of Research in Marketing*, **2** (3), 185-95.

Johanson, J. and L.-G. Mattsson (1988), 'Internationalisation in Industrial Systems: A Network Approach', in Hood, M. and J. E. Vahlne (eds), *Strategies in Global Competition*, New York: Croom Helm, pp.287-314.

Johanson, J. and L.-G. Mattsson (1992), 'Network Positions and Strategic Action: An Analytical Framework', in Axelsson, B. and G.F. Easton (eds), *Industrial Networks: A New View of Reality*, London: Routledge, pp.205-17.

Johanson, J. and J.-E. Vahlne (1992), 'Management of Foreign Market Entry', *Scandinavian International Business Review*, **1** (3), 9-27.

Jones G. and C. Hill (1988), 'Transaction Cost Analysis of Strategy-Structure Choice', *Strategic Management Journal*, **9** (2), 159-72.

Jorgensen, D. W. and Z. Griliches (1967), 'The Explanation of Productivity Change', *Review of Economic Studies*, **34** (99), 249-83.

Katz, J. and B. Kosacoff (1983), 'Multinationals from Argentina', in Lall, S. (ed.), *The New Multinationals: The Spread of Third World Enterprises*, Brisbane: John Wiley & Sons.

Keohane, R. O. and V. D. Ooms (1975), 'The Multinational Firm and International Regulation', in Bersten, C. F. and L. B. Krause (eds), *World Politics and International Economics*, Washington: Brookings Institute, pp.169-209.

Kidd, J. and J. Lu (1999), 'Networks as Comparative Advantage: The Role of Chinese Sogo Shosha in Managing Paradox', in Richter, F.-J. (eds), *Business Networks in Asia: Promises, Doubts and Perspectives*, Westport, Conn.: Quorum Books.

Kim, W. C. and P. Hwang (1992), 'Global Strategy and Multinationals' Entry Mode Choice', *Journal of International Business Studies*, **23** (1), 29-53.

Kindleberger, C. P. (1973), *International Economics*, 5th edition, Homewood, Ill.: Richard D. Irwin.

Klepper, S. and E. Graddy (1990), 'The Evolution of New Industries and the Determinants of Market Structure', *Rand Journal of Economics*, **21** (1), 27-45.

Kogut, B. (1983), 'Foreign Direct Investment as a Sequential Process', in Kindleberger, C. P. and D. B. Audretsch (eds), *The Multinational Corporation in the 1980s*, Cambridge, Mass.: MIT Press, pp.38-56.

Kogut, B. (1988), 'Joint Ventures, Theoretical and Empirical Perspectives', *Strategic Management Journal*, **9** (4), 319-33.

Kogut, B. (1993), 'Foreign Direct Investment as a Sequential Process', in Gomes-Casseres, B. and D. B. Yoffice (eds), *The International Political Economy of Direct Foreign Investment*, Camberley, UK and Brookfield, US: Edward Elgar, pp.273-291.

Originally in Kindleberger, C. P. and D. B. Audretsch (eds), *The Multinational Corporation in the 1980s*, Cambridge, Mass.: MIT Press, pp.38-56.

Kojima, K. (1978), *Direct Foreign Investment: A Japanese Model of Multinational Business Operations*, London: Croom Helm.

Krugman, P. (1989), 'Industrial Organization and International Trade', in Schmalensee, R. and R. D. Willing (eds), *Handbook of Industrial Organization*, Vol.2, Amsterdam: North-Holland, pp.1179-223.

Krugman, P. (1991), 'Increasing Returns and Economic Geography', *Journal of Political Economy*, **99** (3), 483-500.

Krugman, P. (1995), *Development, Geography and Economic Theory*, Cambridge, Mass.: MIT Press.

Krugman, P. and B. Venables (1995), 'Globalisation and the Inequality of Nations', *Quarterly Journal of Economics*, **110** (4), 857-81.

Kumar, K. and M. McLeod (eds) (1981), *Multinationals from Developing Countries*, Lexington, Mass.: D. C. Heath.

Kutschker, M. (1982), 'Power and Dependence in Industrial Marketing', in Håkansson, H. (ed.), *International Marketing and Publishing of Industrial Goods: An Interaction Approach*, New York: Wiley.

La Croix, S. J., M. Plummer and K. Lee (eds) (1995), *Emerging Patterns of East Asian Investment in China from Korea, Taiwan and Hong Kong*, New York: M. E. Sharpe.

Lall, S. (ed.) (1983a), *The New Multinationals: The Spread of Third World Enterprises*, Brisbane: John Wiley & Sons.

Lall, S. (1983b), 'The Rise of Multinationals from the Third World', *Third World Quarterly*, **5** (3), 618-26.

Lall, S. (1998), 'Changing Perceptions of Foreign Direct Investment in Development', in Tharkan, P. K. M. and D. V. D. Bulcke (eds), *International Trade, Foreign Direct Investment and the Economic Environment*, New York: St. Martin's Press.

Lan, P. (1996), *Technology Transfer to China through Foreign Direct Investment*, Brookfield and Sydney: Avebury.

Laumman, E. O., L. Galskeiwicz and P. V. Marden (1978), 'Community Structure as Interorganizational Linkages', *Annual Review of Sociology*, **4** (1), 455-84.

Lawrence, R. Z. (1997), 'The World Trade and Investment System and Developing Countries', in Dunning, J. H. and K. A. Hamdani (eds), *The New Globalism and Developing Countries*, New York: United Nations University Press, pp.51-77.

Lecraw, D. J. (1977), 'Direct Investment by Firms from Less Developed Countries', *Oxford Economic Papers*, **29** (3), 442-57.

Lecraw, D. J. (1989), *Third World Multinationals in the Service Industries*, London: Routledge.

Lee-in Chen Chiu (1995), 'The Pattern and Impact of Taiwan's Investment in Mainland China', in La Croix, S. J., M. Plummer and K. Lee (eds), *Emerging Patterns of East Asian Investment in China from Korea, Taiwan and Hong Kong*, New York: M. E. Sharpe, pp.143-65.

Levitt, T. (1983), *The Marketing Imagination*, New York: The Free Press.

Levy, M. J., Jr. (1966), *Modernisation and the Structure of Societies*, Princeton: Princeton University Press.

Li, Gang (2000), 'Go *Abroad*': *Opening-Up Strategy and Case Study* (in Chinese), Beijing: China Foreign Economic and Trade Press.

Liew, Leong (1997), *The Chinese Economy in Transition: From Plan to Market*, Cheltenham, UK and Lyme, US: Edward Elgar.

Lin, J. Y., C. Fang and L. Zou (1996), *The China Miracle: Development Strategy and Economic Reform*, Hong Kong: The Chinese University of Hong Kong.

Liou, K. T. (1998), *Managing Economic Reforms in Post-Mao China*, Westport, Conn.: Praeger Publishers.

Lipsey, R. E. (2001), 'Foreign Direct Investment and the Operations of Multinational Firms: Concepts, History, and Data', *NBER Working Paper*, No. 8665, Cambridge, Mass.: National Bureau of Economic Research.

Little, I. M. (1970), *Industry and Trade in Some Developing Countries: A Comparative Study*, London: Oxford University Press.

Liu, Guoguang and Renwei Zhao (1979), 'The Relationship between the Plan and the Market in Socialism' (in Chinese), *Economic Research* (Jingji Yanjiu), **5**, 46-55.

Liu, S. X. (1997), *Foreign Direct Investment and the Multinational Enterprise: A Re-examination Using Signalling Theory*, London: Praeger Publishers.

Lo, D. (1997), *Market and Institutional Regulation in Chinese Industrialization, 1978-94*, Houndmills: Macmillan Press.

MacNeil, I. R. (1974), 'The Many Futures of Contracts', *Southern California Law Review*, **47** (3), 691-816.

Maddison, A. (1998), *Chinese Economic Performance in the Long Run*, Paris: OECD.

Madhok, A. (1996), 'Know-how-, Experience- and Competition-Related Considerations in Foreign Market Entry: An Exploratory Investigation', *International Business Review*, **5** (4), 339-67.

Mansfield, E. (1985), 'How Rapidly Does New Technology Leak Out?' *Journal of Industrial Economics*, **34** (2), 217-23.

Mao, Zedong. (1968), *Selected Works of Mao Zedong*, Vol. 4, Beijing: Foreign Language Press.

Markusen, J. R. (1995), 'The Boundaries of Multinational Enterprises and the Theory of International Trade', *Journal of Economic Perspectives*, **9** (2), 169-89.

Markusen, J. R. (1997), 'Foreign Direct Investment, Country Characteristics and Lessons for Policy', in OECD, *Industrial Competitiveness in the Knowledge-Based Economy: The New Role of Governments*, Paris: OECD.

Markusen, J. R., A. J. Venables, D. E. Konan and K. Zhang (1996), 'A United Treatment of Horizontal Direct Investment, Vertical Direct Investment, and the Pattern of Trade in Goods and Services', *NBER Working Paper*, No. 5696, Cambridge, Mass.: National Bureau of Economic Research.

Masen, T. K. and P. Servais (1997), 'The Internationalization of Born Globals: An Evolutionary Process?' *International Business Review*, **6** (6), 561-84.

Mattsson, L.-G. (1988), *Interaction Strategy: A Network Approach*, AMA Marketing Educator's Conference, summer, San Francisco, California.

Michalet, C.-A. (1991), 'Strategic Partnerships and the Changing Internationalisation Process', in Mytelka, L. K. (ed.), *Strategic Partnership: States, Firms and International Competition*, London: Pinter Publishers.

MOFCOM (Ministry of Commerce of the People's Republic of China) (2003–2004), *China Commerce Yearbook*, Beijing: China Commerce and Trade Press.

MOFTEC (Ministry of Foreign Trade and Economic Cooperation), *Almanac of China's Foreign Economic Relations and Trade*, 1993/94; 1994/95; 1995/96; 1996/97; 1997/98; 1998/99; 1999/2000; 2000/01; 2001/02; 2002/03, Beijing: China Prospects Publishing House.

Mundell, R. A. (1957), 'International Trade and Factor Mobility', *American Economic Review*, **47** (3), 321-35.

Mytelka, L. K. (1999), 'Competition, Innovation and Competitiveness: A Framework for Analysis', in Mytelka, L. K. (ed.), *Competition, Innovation and Competitiveness in Developing Countries*, Paris: OECD.

Nachum, L. (1999), *The Origins of the International Competitiveness of Firms*, Cheltenham, UK and Northampton, MA, USA: Edward Elgar.

Narula, R. (1996), *Multinational Investment and Economic Structure*, London: Routledge.

NBS (China National Bureau of Statistics) (1990–2000) *China Statistical Yearbook*, Beijing: China Statistics Press.

Ohlin, B. (1933), *Interregional and International Trade*, Cambridge, Mass.: Harvard University Press.

O'Brien, P. (1980), 'The New Multinationals: Developing Country Firms in International Markets', *Futures*, August.

OECD (1992), *Detailed Benchmark Definition of Foreign Direct Investment*, 2nd edition, Paris: OECD.

Oman, C. (1989), *New Forms of Investment in Developing Country Industries: Mining, Petrochemicals, Automobiles, Textiles, Food*, Paris: OECD.

Orrù, M. (1993), 'Institutional Cooperation in Japanese and Germany Capitalism', in Sjöstrand, S.-E. (ed.), *Institutional Change: Theory and Empirical Findings*, Armonk, NY: M. E. Sharpe, pp.171-98.

Orrù, M., N. W. Biggart and G. G. Hamilton (1997), *The Economic Organization of East Asian Capitalism*, London: Sage Publications.

Ozawa, T. (1992), 'Foreign Direct Investment and Economic Development', *Transnational Corporations*, **1** (1), 27-54.

Pananond, P. (1998/9), 'The International Expansion Process of MNEs from Developing Countries: A Case Study of Thailand's CP Group', *Discussion Papers in International Investment and Management*, No. 258, Reading: University of Reading.

Peng, M. W. (1995), 'Foreign Direct Investment in the Innovation Driven Stage: Toward a Learning Option Perspective', in Green, M. B. and R. B. McNaughton (eds), *The Location of Foreign Direct Investment: Geographical and Business Approaches*, UK: Avebury, pp.29-42.

Penrose, E. (1995), *The Theory of the Growth of the Firm*, Oxford: Oxford University Press.

Perez, C. and L. Soete (1988), 'Catching Up in Technology: Entry Barriers and Windows of Opportunity', in Dosi, G., C. Freeman, R. Nelson, G. Silverberg and L. Soete. (eds), *Technical Change and Economic Theory*, London: Pinter Publishers, pp.458-79.

Polanyi, M. (1964), *Science, Faith and Society*, Chicago: University of Chicago Press.

Porter, M. E. (1986a), *Competition in Global Strategies*, Boston, Mass: Harvard Business School Press.

Porter, M. E. (1986), 'Changing Pattern of International Competition', *California Management Review*, **28** (2), 9-40.

Porter, M. E. (1990), *The Competitive Advantage of Nations*, New York: Free Press.

Porter, M. E. and M. B. Fuller (1986), 'Coalitions and Global Strategy', in Porter, M. E. (ed.), *Competition in Global Industries*, Boston: Harvard Business School Press, pp.315-43.

Prebisch, R. (1950), *The Economic Development of Latin America and its Principal Problems*, New York: ECLA, United Nations.

Qu, Tao and M. B. Green (1997), *Chinese Foreign Direct Investment: A Subnational Perspective on Location*, Sydney: Ashgate.

Ravenhill, J. (1998), 'Australia and APEC', in Aggarwal, V. K. and C. E. Morrison (eds), *Asia-Pacific Crossroads: Regime Creation and the Future of APEC*, London: Macmillan, pp.143-64.

Redding, S. G. (1991), 'Weak Organizations and Strong Linkages: Managerial Ideology and Chinese Family Business Networks', in Hamilton, G. (ed.), *Business Networks and Economic Development in East and Southeast Asia,* Hong Kong: Centre of Asian Studies, University of Hong Kong, pp.30-47.

Ren, R. (1998), 'A Further Examination of the International Competitiveness of China's Manufacturing' (in Chinese), *Economic Research*, **2,** 1-7.

Richardson, G. B. (1960), *Information and Investment*, Oxford: Oxford University Press.

Richardson, G. B. (1972), 'The Organisation of Industry', *Economic Journal*, **82** (327), 883-96.

Richter, F.-J. (1999), 'Industrial Restructuring in Post-Deng China: Toward a Network Economy', in Richter, F.-J. (ed.), *Business Networks in Asia: Promises, Doubts and Perspectives*, Westport, Conn.: Quorum Books, pp.237-49.

Riedel, J. (1988), 'Economic Development in East Asia: Doing What Comes Naturally?', in Hughes, H. (ed.), *Achieving Industrialisation in East Asia*, Cambridge: Cambridge University Press, pp.1-38.

Riemens, P. J. H. (1989), *On the Foreign Operations of Third World Firms*, Amsterdam: Koninklijk Nederlands Aardrijkskundig Genootschap, Insituut voor Sociale Geografie, Faculteit Ruimtelijke Wetenschappen, Universiteit van Amsterdam.

Robertson, P. L. and R. N. Langlois (1995), 'Innovation, Networks, and Vertical Integration', *Research Policy*, **24** (4), 543-62.

Romer, P. M. (1990), 'Endogenous Technical Change', *Journal of Political Economy*, **98** (5, II), 71-102.

Root, F. R. (1973*), International Trade and Investment: Theory, Policy, Enterprise*, Cincinnati: South-Western Publishing.

Root, F. R. (1987), *Entry Strategies for International Markets*, Lexington, Mass.: Lexington Books.

Ross, M. C. (1994), 'China's International Economic Behaviour', in Robinson, T. W. and D. Shambaugh (eds), *Chinese Foreign Policy: Theory and Practice*, New York: Oxford University Press.

Roy, D. (1998), *China's Foreign Relations*, Houndmills: Macmillan Press.

Ruffin, R. J. (1984), 'International Factor Movements', in Jones, R. W. and P. B. Kenen (eds), *Handbook of International Economics*, Vol. 1, Amsterdam: Elsevier Science Publishers, pp.237-88.

Rugman, A. M. (1985), 'Internalization is Still a General Theory of Foreign Direct Investment', *Weltwirtschaftliches Archiv*, **121** (3), 570-75.

Rugman, A. M., D. J. Lecraw and L. D. Booth. (1985), *International Business: Firm and Environment*, New York: McGraw-Hill.

Rugman, A. and A. Verbeke (2004), 'Towards a Theory of Regional Multinationals: A Transaction Cost Economics Approach', *British Academy of Management Annual Conference*.

SAFE (1999), *China International Balance of Payments*, Beijing: SAFE.

Slater, J. (1998), 'Outward Investment from China', in Strange, R. (ed.), *Management in China: The Experience of Foreign Business*, London: Frank Cass Publishers.

Stalk, G., Jr. (1988), 'Time: The Next Source of Competitive Advantage', *Harvard Business Review*, 66 (4), 41-51.

Sun, H. (1996), 'Direct Foreign Investment and Linkage Effects: The Experience of China', *Asian Economics*, **25** (1), 5-28.

Taussig, F. W. (1927), *International Trade*, New York: Macmillan.

Teece, D. (1981), 'The Multinational Enterprise, Market Failure and Market Power Consideration', *Sloan Management Review*, **22** (3), 3-17.

Teece, D. (1985), 'Multinational Enterprise, Internal Governance, and Industrial Organization', *American Economic Review*, **75** (2), 233-37.

Teng, W. (1982), 'Socialist Modernization and the Pattern of Foreign Trade', in Xu, Dixin *et al.* (eds), *China's Search for Economic Growth: The Chinese Economy since 1949* (A. Watson trans.), Beijing: New World Press.

Thorelli, H. B. (1986), 'Networks: Between Markets and Hierarchies', *Strategic Management Journal*, **7** (1), 37-51.

Tolentino, P. E. (1993), *Technological Innovation and Third World Multinationals*, London: Routledge.

Tseng, C.-S. (1994), 'The Process of Internationalisation of PRC Multinationals', in Schütte, H. (ed.), *The Global Competitiveness of the Asian Firm*, Houndmills: Macmillan Press, pp.121-8.

Tseng, C.-S. and S. K. M. Mak (1996), 'Strategy and Motivation for PRC Outward Direct Investments with Particular Reference to Enterprises from the Pear River Delta', in MacPherson, S. and J. Y. S. Cheng (eds), *Economic and Social Development in South China*, Cheltenham, UK and Brookfield, US: Edward Elgar, pp.140-61.

Turpin, T. and X. Liu (2000), 'Balanced Development: The Challenge for Science, Technology and Innovation Policy', in Harvie, C. (ed.), *Contemporary Developments and Issues in China's Economic Transition*, Houndmills: Macmillan Press, pp.191-211.

UNCTAD (1994–2004), *World Investment Report*, New York and Geneva: United Nations.

UNCTAD (1997), *Sharing Asia's Dynamism: Asian Direct Investment in the European Union*, New York and Geneva: United Nations.

UNCTC (1983), *Salient Features and Trends in Foreign Direct Investment*, New York: United Nations.

UNCTC (1993), *Transnational Corporations from Developing Countries: Impact on Home Countries*, New York: United Nations.

Urata, S. (1998), 'Foreign Direct Investment and APEC', in Aggarwal, V. K. and C. E. Morrison (eds), *Asia-Pacific Crossroads: Regime Creation and the Future of APEC*, London: Macmillan, pp.87-117.

Van Den Bulcke, D. and H. Zhang (1998), 'Foreign Equity Joint Venture in China: Interactions between Government Policies and Multinational Investment Strategies', in Tharkan, P. K. M. and D. V. D. Bulcke (eds), *International Trade, Foreign Direct Investment and the Economic Environment*, Basingstoke, UK: Macmillan, pp.135-59.

Vernon, R. (1966), 'International Investment and International Trade in the Product Cycle', *Quarterly Journal of Economics*, **80** (2), 190-207.

Vernon, R. (1971), *Sovereignty at Bay: The Multinational Spread of U.S. Enterprises*, New York: Basic Books.

Wang, L. (1997), *Report on Foreign Direct Investment in China: Industrial Distribution of Foreign Direct Investment*, Beijing: Economic Management Publishing House.

Wang, S., S. Wang and Y. Xu (1992), (eds), *An Introduction to China's Foreign Trade*, (in Chinese), Beijing: Foreign Trade Education Press.

Webster, F. E., Jr. (1979), *Industrial Marketing Strategy*, New York: Wiley.

Welch, L. S. and R. Luostrarinen (1988), 'Internationalisation: Evolution of a Concept', *Management Papers*, No. 14, Melbourne: Graduate School of Management, Monash University.

Wells, L., Jr. (1983), *Third World Multinationals: The Rise of Foreign Investment from Developing Countries*, Cambridge, Mass.: MIT Press.

Wells, L., Jr. (1998), 'Multinationals and the Developing Countries', *Journal of International Business Studies*, **29** (1), 101-13.

Wesson, T. (1999), 'A Model of Asset-Seeking Foreign Direct Investment Driven by Demand Conditions', *Canadian Journal of Administrative Sciences*, **16** (1), 1-10.

Wilkins, M. (1970), *The Emergence of Multinational Enterprise: America Business Abroad from the Colonial Era to 1914*, Cambridge, M.A.: Harvard University Press.

Williamson, O. E. (1975), *Markets and Hierarchies: Analysis and Anti-trust Implications*, New York: Free Press.

Williamson, O. E. (1985), *The Economic Institutions of Capitalism*, New York: Free Press.

Williamson, O. E. (1991), 'Comparative Economic Organizations: The Analysis of Discrete Structural Alternatives', *Administrative Science Quarterly*, **36** (2), 269-96.

Wind, Y. (1970), 'Industrial Source Loyalty', *Journal of Marketing Research*, **7** (4), 450-7.

Winter, S. G. (1988), 'On Coase, Competence and the Corporation', *Journal of Law, Economics and Organisation*, **4** (1),163-80.

World Bank (1992), *Enterprise Survey*, China and Mongolia Department and the Socialist Economies Unit.

World Bank (1997a), *China 2020: Development Challenges in the New Century*, Washington, DC: The World Bank.

World Bank (1997b), *Clear Water, Blue Skies: China's Environment in the New Century*, Washington, DC: The World Bank.

World Bank (1999), *World Development Report 1998/99: Knowledge for Development*, Washington, DC: The World Bank.

World Bank (2000), *World Development Indicators 2000*, Washington, DC: The World Bank.

World Bank (2003), *World Development Indicators 2003*, Washington, DC: The World Bank.

World Bank (2005), *World Development Report 2006: Equity and Development*, Washington, DC: The World Bank.

World Economic Forum (1998), *Global Competitiveness Report 1998*, Geneva: World Economic Forum.

Yang, D. (1997), 'China's Direct Investment in Australia: Trends and Prospects', Seminar Paper, Canberra: Australia-Japan Research Centre, Australian National University.

Yang, X. and Y.-K. Ng (1995), 'Theory of the Firm and Structure of Residual Rights', *Journal of Economic Behavior and Organization*, **26** (1), 107-28.

Yeung, H. W.-C. (1997), 'Business Networks and Transnational Corporations: A Study of Hong Kong Firms in the ASEAN Region', *Economic Geography*, **73** (1), 1-25.

Yeung, H. W.-C. (1998), *Transnational Corporations and Business Networks: Hong Kong Firms in the Asean Region*, London: Routledge.

Zhan, J. (1995), 'Transnationalisation and Outward Investment: The Case of Chinese Firms', *Transnational Corporations*, **4** (3), 67-100.

Zhang, H. and D. van D. Bulcke (1996a), 'China: Rapid Changes in the Development Path', in Dunning, J. H. and R. Narula (eds), *Foreign Direct Investment and Government: Catalysts for Economic Restructuring*, London: Routledge, pp.380-422.

Zhang, H. and D. van D. Bulcke (1996b), 'International Management Strategies of Chinese Multinational Firms', in Child, J. and Y. Liu (eds), *Management Issues in China* (II), *International Enterprises*, London: Routledge, pp.149-64.

Zhang, Y. (1998), 'China and APEC', in Aggarwal, V. K. and C. E. Morrison (eds), *Asia-Pacific Crossroads: Regime Creation and the Future of APEC*, London: Macmillan, pp.213-32.

Zhang, Y. (1999), Seminar to Spur Investing Abroad, *China Daily*, 12 May.

Index